Life Before Heaven

A Pilgrim's Progress in a New World

The Story of the Dutch-American Artist Harry M. Veenstra

as told to Scott Van Genderen

Copyright © 2014 Scott VanGenderen
All rights reserved.
ISBN: 1502765543
ISBN-13:978-1502765543

Additional print and Kindle copies of *Life Before Heaven* are available from Amazon.com

For Hattie, Alta, and Heidi,
without whom there would be no story

Chapter 1

It is still dark when the guide and I step outside on to the narrow boardwalk in front of the hotel. The tread of our feet across the wood is the only sound on the dark street. To the east, just a glimmer of dawn can be detected along a ridge of the Rocky Mountains. We are up early to climb to the Mount of the Holy Cross, a fabled hidden mountain of the Rockies reputed to bear an immense cross. Not able to imagine such a thing, I scarcely believe that it exists. I am commissioned to find the mystical peak and hopefully capture it on a canvas. By leaving this small hotel in the mining camp of Redstone, Colorado at the hour of four in the morning, my guide promises that we will catch the best of the morning light, a prospect that delights me as an artist.

He mumbles something about how he could not round up the horses we would need for our trip. That is fine by me. I don't like horses, and the thin mountain air is bracing to my diminished lungs. How he thought he could catch horses in the dark is beyond me. I did not relish bashing into low hanging pine branches in the inky woods. My guide grabs my easel and paint box, securing them to a wooden frame which he hoists on to his back with rawhide straps.

We set out though the quiet streets of the town before we were soon making our way through the woods. I can barely make out my equipment lashed to the pack frame bobbing ahead from side to side. The trail we follow soon steepens and my breath becomes more labored under the steady pace set by my guide who, though twenty years my senior, has no problem with the trail he had climbed many times. Breathing heavily in the enveloping silence, I have ample opportunity to reflect on the many steps I had taken before these labored ones through this Colorado forest. If I had not lived this life, I certainly could not have imagined it, since I am now a world away and many years departed from the land of my birth. Where I came from there were few forests and no mystical mountains. With each step I rejoice in the gift of life and the gift of our Savior to make the living of it worth the while.

When and where I was born, I could scarcely imagine the travels or adventures that befell me. My grandfather never traveled more than 50 kilometers from his village in the northern reaches of the Netherlands. He thought it was crazy when his son, my father, traveled to Amsterdam to learn advanced house painting and decorating techniques. Now I live an ocean and a continent away from the village in the Netherlands where I was born. None of my forbearers could have predicted this life. I could not imagine any of it myself, but always tried, to the best of my ability, to be ready for what came next.

It is my destiny to be born at the time of the greatest transformation to human life that ever occurred in history. During my lifetime, mankind harnessed the power of coal, oil, and electricity to create a world anew. We now take for granted the telephone, the automobile, the electric light, and the airplane. None of these existed when I was born. In Holland, kerosene lit our dim houses where we huddled around a smoldering peat grate for heat. Outside, plodding mules hauled the barges towards similar villages whose steeples we could make out on the horizon.

Now I call on a telephone, and trains and automobiles carry me across this new continent, America, including high into the Rocky Mountains. With the commission from this oil painting, I hope to buy a radio, which are now becoming widely available. I am so used to these modern conveniences that I can scarcely recall the world without them.

Laboring up this grade, however, it is not the constant change wrought by technology that amazes me, but the ever present power of God's grace in my life. I would have been overwhelmed by the many changes that occurred if not for the steady guidance of our Lord and Savior and the road map laid out for us in the Bible. Indeed, it seems that the more strange and difficult life became, the more steadfast His guidance proved to be. I came to appreciate that no burden or trial was so great that it could not be overcome with His support. Life is no different than the struggle up this steep trail. I knew I could make it and that the reward at the end would be worth it.

With Christ's steadfast guidance, you realize that only your trust in him is all that matters. I made a small fortune, only to lose it. I was an athlete who nearly died. I have experienced the joy of love and that of birth and the turmoil of death of many near and dear to me. Only through the perspective that God's grace gives me can I take all of this in stride, knowing that they are all gifts from Him. Life is nothing more than a chance to learn more about God and your relationship with Him. If you focus solely on yourself, and not Him, you will become lost and confused. The turbulence of life is too powerful to confront on your own.

We plod ever upward before taking a short break, when I lean on my staff.

"We are almost there, Mr. Veenstra."

"I hope so," I gasp in reply, vainly trying to gulp in the thin air.

...

I took my first breath in a small house warmed by peat and lit by kerosene into a family who rarely left their small village near the *Noorden See* of Holland. My first home was Surhuisterveen, in Friesland, a province reluctantly attached to the country of the Netherlands. Few would consider my place of birth as the new Eden, but the few who found ourselves there (certainly by fate and not by choice, since to my knowledge, no one ever freely moved to Friesland) did not object to our circumstance. Indeed, most Friesians, if not proud of their homeland, were proud of themselves, primarily for being tough enough to occupy a part of Europe that no one else could. Living on a sandy spit hard by the "Noord Zie", my ancestors were left alone by the Vikings and other marauders who made Europe their sport. Our locale was too poor, too isolated, and too wet to be worth the effort. The Vikings quickly realized that we were worse off than they, and opted for the comforts of rich English monasteries or the pleasures to be found in sacking Paris. The isolation of Friesland bred in us a hard-headed independence borne from the daily struggle of eking out a meager life from the damp sands and clays of our humble home.

Living in this backwater, we were neither inclined nor motivated to explore much of the world beyond our villages. Likewise, we were happy that the outer world did not pursue us. The sturdy boats plying the network of canals that lace Holland sailed to other villages no different from the one in which we lived. There was no reason to ever leave. Amsterdam was far enough away to be as exotic as another planet. Even though occupying a very small country, we Fries stubbornly clung to our own language, as incomprehensible to the adjacent Dutch as to the neighboring Germans.

If we were self-contained and contented, we were certainly not rich. We made an accommodation with the clays to supply an adequate supply of potatoes and swine, so that one generation might survive long enough to give issue to the next. Life was an endless succession of days merging into months, blending into the endless years. Change was imperceptible. Little distinguished the past from the future. What was to come mirrored what had already passed. Time had little meaning. Each day was the same as the last. Life was simple, organic, and direct. We lived in direct relation to the land and to God. If this was paradise, however, we were too hungry to think so. Life could be quickly extinguished by a bad harvest or any of the numerous diseases which struck young and old indiscriminately. The sole marker of time was the extent of a previous famine or flood.

But those struggles are now not my struggles. Now, constant change replaces the endless string to identical days that made up life in an old country. Privation is replaced by bounty. My children and I will never starve, a very real prospect after a bad harvest in Holland. My ancestors may have helplessly watched as their children withered and died, but they knew that those who survived would be married and buried in the bosom of our Reformed Faith, immune from the temptations of city life. Satan has far more tools at his disposal in America. Here, Satan tempts us from above with the apples of riches, envy, and flesh. In Friesland, he prodded us from below with a fork whose tines were privation, hunger, and fear. However, the God of our fathers did not abandon us in the new land, any more than he abandoned Abraham when he sought better pastures for his flocks.

This is not to say that Friesland was a paradise of god-fearing Christians whose wooden shoes protected us from Satan and the ever-present muck. Some of our fellow poor souls were addled, lazy, or drunk. Our congregations confronted jealousy and covetousness the same as in any church. The Apostle Paul could have easily admonished our churches as the ones in Galatia, Corinth, or America. But in Friesland, it was easier to raise children, sure that they would find good mates faithful to each other and the church. If you avoided gin, there were few other temptations strewn across your path, other than coveting your neighbor's cow. Friesian cows, fat and productive, are easy to covet.

The Fries think of themselves as better than even their neighbors 25 meters across the "kanaal". My older brother Klaas challenged our mother for not being Friesian. Her family was from Groningen, to the north of Friesland, almost in Germany, and of a higher social class than father's. Holland may be egalitarian, but as in any old country, everyone knew where he stood in the social hierarchy. Her family wore leather shoes; father's wore wood.

"Well, Klaas," she sniffed, "The Fries were the biggest deadbeats in my father's store. They never paid their bills until you harangued them."

To which Klaas replied, "Well, you have to admit, mother, in that, they are not mediocre." Klaas had learned the wonderfully stubborn pride of a true Friesian at an early age.

The composition of Friesian society was as simple as the sandy soil from which it sprang. Immediately above the muck on which they toiled were the farm laborers, year after year coaxing the potatoes out of the ground. This was a contest of wills, since the tubers were as stubborn as the men who tilled them. A thaw in the standoff meant we ate for another year. During the short growing season, the laborers worked from sunup to sundown, which in the northern latitudes meant sixteen-hour days punctuated by skimpy meals and little sleep. The long winter exhausted their meager savings, dooming them to an endless treadmill of servitude. Their sisters and daughters were condemned to service, never with the opportunity to scrape together enough money to pursue any other option. Amsterdam was too far way to try prostitution or a trade. A girl could not go bad in the confines of a village.

This neglect was often a complete waste of talent. I later met a man who escaped to America who was highly intelligent, but had never been taught to read or write in Friesland. Though Friesland never bore a strong feudal culture, these farm laborers lived a life no better than that of the serfs of medieval times. They were not attached to the land, but their inability to save their meager wages prevented any fate other than constant labor. At the end of the workday, they laid their weary bones in the barns, huddled with the livestock. Light was discouraged, since an open flame could burn a structure to the ground long before the village bucket brigade could douse the fire. Few learned to read, so perhaps the light was not sorely missed. I often wonder on the murmured conversations in those musty cold dark barns. They rarely bathed. Their thick woolen underwear was a second skin, the texture and odor of the fur of their animal companions in the barn.

Fortunately, my family was not condemned to such a fate. We were of the next caste above: the skilled artisans, thanks to my father's skills, taught to him by his father, as a painter and paperhanger. He was hired by the merchants and the few rich farmers comprising the "gentry" in our little world. Though the social stratification of Friesland was about as flat as the land on which we lived, it was difficult to climb above your station. For what success America afforded me, I will be forever grateful. I leveraged my father's legacy as a house painter to become a commercial, and later, a fine artist, opportunities that would have not been available to me in the land of my birth, and certainly not in our village.

As a tyke, I saw father infrequently since he was away from our house decorating someone else's. Father came from a long line of painters and decorators and was a master painter in his own right, having served a long apprenticeship under his father and uncles before I was born. I knew little of his work, since it was unheard of a child to attend the adult world of trade. I know he was respected and worked hard. He left the house before the sun came up, returning after it had gone down.

Father decorated wooden shoes as a sideline. For this he had cans of black "Japan" lacquer, made from the shells of beetles which emitted a most wonderful smell. Two of the greatest delights of my young life were the smell of the lacquer and the taste of black licorice. Maybe I associated the two because both were bitter and black but sweet at the same time. Even as a youngster, the more bitter and chewy the licorice; the better I liked it. I wisely never sampled the lacquer. The wooden shoes blackened by father were for the customer's Sunday dress; daily shoes were the natural color of the unadorned poplar from which they were carved. The glossy black color mimicked the shiny leather shoes of their social betters. Nothing was too good to wear to the Lord's House. I wore wooden shoes or "klompen" (an appropriate onomatopoeia if there ever was one) most of the time when outside, preferring them to my Sunday leather shoes which were too cold. Besides, "klompen" were indestructible; my mother cared not a whit what we did to them in contrast to our expensive leather shoes that had to survive passing down from brother to brother. As the youngest of four brothers, I never owned a new pair of shoes until long after we moved to America. Father wore "klompen" to his jobs, changing there into cloth booties to protect his socks from the paint and glue. It would never do for father to enter the houses of his clientele and stomp around in shoes intended to ward off the damp and muck of a Friesian polder. No one wore "klompen" inside, but instead we padded around in the multiple layers of socks that made wearing shoes made from wood bearable.

Those in the social class above us never wore "klompen" except on ceremonial occasions. It was then that they donned the classic peasant costume of our region of Friesland. I found it ironic that those who were furthest removed from the poverty of our ancestors wore costumes pretending to be peasants. Real peasants still lived just outside the village. For the rest of us, wooden shoes were not a fashion statement or some ethnic affectation, but sensible footwear for where we lived. No one wore valuable leather shoes into the nearby muddy farmland. I laughed when I saw later "klompen" dancing in America, because we never danced in our strictly Dutch Reformed village of Stroobos. You certainly did not want to call attention to your "klompen" by making noise with them. However, I still love to hear the clatter of wooden shoes on pavement.

Yes, it is true, I lived in "Stroobos - Straw Bunch", a small community presided over by a few tradesmen, merchants, and the "dominie" of our Reformed Church. Not that the lives of these few elites were much better than that of the rest of us, but they did enjoy marginally better clothes, homes, and diet (chocolate in addition to licorice, beef in addition to our pork and salted fish). We all attended the same school and worshipped in the same church.

Our life was simple, but I did not go hungry as long as I had a good appetite for potatoes. The same is true of the sole pig we raised to butcher every year. He, too, subsisted on a steady diet of potatoes. The entire economy of the village rested on a mountain of potatoes. Like most people in our village, we supplemented our diet with a pig that we fed potatoes and scraps for the year before slaughtering. I loved one of these pigs as a pet. It was easier to communicate with him than any of my four older siblings, or my baby sister, who were strangely more concerned with their own lives than mine. The pig always listened, never disputing what I said.

"Piggy, I am now going to name you 'Giele – yellow', because that's your color. You look like 'giele' to me."

(Happy assent from Giele.)

I then informed my brother, so that he could properly address the pig. "Gerke, the pig is now to be called Giele, because that's his color and now his name."

He replied, "You cannot name the pig Giele; you might as well name him "Tsliis" – cheese, because in "Slacht Maand – Slaughter Month" (November), father will butcher him and we will eat him. If not, you will have nothing to eat."

"But if I hid him during "Slacht Maand", he could live for another year."

"Not to worry, dolt, father can just as easily slaughter him at Christmas. Besides, if he lives, you might starve."

I needed a different line of logic, since Giele's fate rested in my hands. "Klaas says that there are Israelites, like in the Bible, living in Amsterdam who do not eat pigs, because the Bible forbids it."

"That is from the Old Testament, and Christ Jesus came into this world to save us from such superstition."

Any childhood attachment to the family's swine and the bad feelings resulting from his untimely demise were dispelled by the glorious taste of a chop or bacon that punctuated the endless meals of boiled potatoes. Even so, the dispatch of the pig was a big event in my young life. However, a new friend soon displaced the last, and a young pig is more charming than an old one. This logic became obvious even to my young mind as I quickly adopted a new porcine friend.

Father hung the previous year's poor beast by his rear quarters, splitting it open from top to bottom to thoroughly bleed. Not a part was wasted. I have never eaten as many pork cuts in America as I did as a boy. Even the inedible tallow was saved as lubrication and rust preventive for father's saw. We smoked our own hams and bacon, just how and where, I am not sure, but I believe it was in the chimney of the fireplace. I saw similar ways of curing meats later in the American South. Mother tried out the fat to make lard, delicious when spread on bread with sugar; when we had sugar. We did not use butter very often, if at all. Friesians have an amazing constitution to metabolize fat from generations of eating such a diet. Heart disease claimed a fair number of my relatives, but not until past their seventieth birthdays. Maybe all of that fat lubricated their joints for a spry old age. I think they forgot to die, too busy working. Maybe the "dominie's" sermons frightened them in postponing God's inevitable judgment.

From the pig's unpalatable head, mother made headcheese, which even I resisted. The thoroughly cleaned intestines were stuffed with diced and seasoned meat to become sausage, which I adored. Some of our neighbors made blood sausage, although we did not because of the biblical injunction forbidding the use of blood as food. I have since come to have a more nuanced view of the strictures in Leviticus than brother Gerke's young interpretation. I eat pork, but still foreswear blood sausage and head cheese, for aesthetic, not biblical reasons. I think that God, in his infinite wisdom, may be telling us something in how different foods taste. Unpalatable foods taste bad for a reason. Maybe we should not eat them.

Friesland is renowned for its dairy cattle, but we had little dairy or beef in the house. Beef was a mostly unknown quantity in Friesland, unless it came from Germany. Cows were too valuable for their milk. No one in his right mind would destroy such a valuable producer. Cheese was a rarity, since we had no way to store it for long once the wax coating was cut on the two kilo wheel. Mother ate cheese as a girl since her family could afford the ice that was cut in the winter and stored in the Groningen ice house for use over the summer. Smoked fish were and are a constant in the Dutch diet, which we boys supplemented with the fresh eels caught in the ditches around Stroobos. I was always amazed how a long-dead eel continued wiggling in the skillet as it fried.

The women of Stroobos did little baking. I knew nothing of pie until coming to America. Fruit was a rarity except for apples, so I guess it is little wonder. Sugar was too valuable to pour the cup after cup needed for pie making. After coming to America, mother learned to bake from scratch; considering it a great privilege when it became economically possible. Sophisticated friends mock the diet I adopted in Middle America, but after the Netherlands, it was a cornucopia. Ironically, it was not until America that I discovered many of the delicacies of my native land like "banket", a delicious flaky pastry coating almond paste. In America, beef was freely available and not a rarity. This alone probably made our move worthwhile.

I spent my early days with mother, but even this was limited. Mother ran our small store, or rather she came into the room when the bell above the front door tinkled when someone entered to survey our meager inventory of decorating supplies. By the time I was of memory, she had plenty to do without attending to the wants and wishes of a four-year old. She had to mind the store and our home. Every chore in the home that we now do with an electric device was then done laboriously by hand. Tasks that are now fairly easy such as ironing, washing, or cooking required building and maintaining a fire. Coal was available from the barges that crisscrossed Holland, but it was messy and filthy. We used cheaper peat to heat the house. Our surname of Veenstra meant that some ancestor had been a peat cutter and his adopted name served as an early form of branding. Coal was dirty, but its higher heat was preferred for cooking and heating household utensils.

Mother's family owned a mill, so that she grew up with servants assisting with the household chores. A small household staff did not mean that she led a life of leisure, but that servants performed the most onerous tasks such as fire tending, toting, and cleaning. To my knowledge, mother never complained about her reduced station. I believe she was very happy to be married to such a steady and devout man. My parents were not outwardly affectionate, but that was the norm in our country. Similarly, I recall no fiery arguments, only the occasional brooding silence. Mother's family was well respected. My future brother-in-law, who married my sister Hendrijke, told me that at one time he worked for one of mother's brothers. My uncle was highly regarded because he took trips to neighboring towns buying and selling flour. On those occasions, he wore an overcoat, something the rest of us could not afford. Apparently, mother's family loaned mother and father the money to buy the Stroobos house. There certainly was no bank in our village. Jews in Groningen lent money, but no one in Stoobos took advantage of their offers. Most financial transactions remained confined to within families.

As soon as I was potty trained, I was put out the door in the charge of my older brother, Gerke. New sisters came into the family, replacing me inside the small house. As long as Gerke kept me out of the "kanaal", what trouble could I get into? Everybody knew us; reporting any indiscretion to mother, or worse, father. Discipline, like life, was simple and direct. We took our job of exploring Stroobos seriously. We knew every bridge, canal, and sluice gate that divided up our kingdom. The first thing any youngster in the Netherlands must learn is how not to drown. I gave the water grave respect until I knew how not to fall in. Calling what we did swimming would be an exaggeration, but we could keep our heads above the surface. There were always scares. Every village related a story of a young person (or more likely, a drunkard) who had drowned. Water was everywhere, and it was incumbent on any youngster to learn this quickly and to know how to navigate it.

Brother Gerke, compelled to teach me my lessons, one day asked, "Do you want to see the moon?"

I could have looked up into the sky on my own, but as a gullible four-year old, I replied "Ja."

"Take off your coat, lie on the grass, and look up the sleeve," which he obligingly held above me. Meanwhile, older brother

Klaas ran to the nearby "sloot", filed up his "klompen" with water, pouring it down the sleeve onto the face of his poor unsuspecting brother. I cried of course, but they told me not to be a baby and definitely, "Do not tell mother." I had to wait until I arrived in America until I could share this valuable lesson with my chums.

My older brothers, when they were not imparting important life lessons, were also my protectors and confidantes. As young boys, we explored every nook and cranny of our village, imitating the affairs of the adults at the small market, post office, and pub. I laughed uproariously when Gerke staggered like the town drunk, or nodded his head like the knowing "dominie" while sucking his teeth. We did not play any games except tag and hide and seek. We did share a ball, but that was a toy for a baby. The soccer craze did not sweep Europe until much later. As young boys, we patrolled the village, staying out the sight of the adults. We knew well the margin of the village, the land between the houses and the farms. The canal itself was among our greatest joys. The adults did not mind if we hung out at the drawbridge where we could serve the barge captains when it needed raising or lowering. As an adult, I realized that our parents tolerated our hanging out at the drawbridge because they had done the same when they were young. Opening the bridge was a real service. Even at a young age, we played our role in the life of the village.

We actually lived in the province of Groningen, separated from Friesland by the "kanaal" on which our house was located. My first school was located in Friesland. I clearly remember the first day. Mother attached a pretzel to my arm with a red ribbon; a long-standing custom. I enjoyed the chance to have a bite by just twisting my head and lifting my arm. School did not improve much after that. On the following morning there were no pretzels on ribbons.

Our parents thought that Christian education was essential, so they scrimped that we could attend a church-run school across the canal. After crossing the drawbridge near home, we balanced on a narrow plank across one of the many drainage ditches. Below this rude bridge swam "snoek - eels", barely moving in the water. In addition to good sport, they were good eating. Klaas fashioned a noose out of thin pliable wire. Lying on his stomach on the bridge, he slowly lowered it before a quick jerk brought his prey flapping skyward. The other "snoek" scattered before forgetfully returning to the shade of the bridge a few minutes later. Fortunately, the fish were slightly less intelligent than those who fished for them.

I became bilingual from the lessons in our church school. At home, we spoke our native tongue, Friesian, but the government in den Hague mandated that all schools teach in Dutch. My classmates were in the same strait, so we first learned the language of the nation before proceeding to the Testaments, Old and New, and our sums. In school, I also learned that the world extended far beyond the church spires on the horizon. Until then, I thought that the world was one big Friesland; endless farms interspersed with a network of canals, villages, and churches.

I was a pliable, if not a perfect child, perhaps too curious for my own good. Every man in our village smoked, so the strike of a match was a grown-up activity that a five-year old might emulate. One day, father hired a carpenter. After working together for a while, they adjourned to the next room to their pipes. The wood shavings left behind looked to me like the tobacco the men were enjoying, but certainly did not burn like it.

The explosion startled me before I ran after them, "De spanen zijn in de brand! -The shavings are on fire!"

Fortunately, they quickly rectified my crime with the always-full bucket of water by the pump.

"There. It is out, thanks to the warning of our brave fire warden."

I scarcely believed my ears, expecting to be severely spanked. Perhaps father believed that he had started the blaze himself. Although my fanny was cool, I burned with guilt. I had lied, but not been caught. Why did I feel so bad? Later, I reflected that father probably knew that I was guilty, but wanted me to internalize my regret. He knew that the strongest Christians were those whose faith was fired from within, not dependent on the opinions of others. Since that I day, I tried to live by that principal, asking the Lord as to what I should do; with better success some days than on others. I have not burned down any houses since then, so part of my prayer was answered.

If summer in my memory blends into an endless string of hazy overcast days, winter stands out in sharp contrast. Maybe it was because winter was the time of what little leisure was enjoyed in our country village. As labor slowed on the farms, the workers entertained themselves with games. This was also when the canals froze into an endless ribbon for the skaters. To a strong skater, no town was too far. In the coldest of winters, the entirety of Friesland became a race course for the "Elfstedentoch - the Race of the Eleven Towns", a grueling 120-mile tour around the entire province. It takes an extraordinarily cold winter for the entire course to solidly freeze. When temperatures plummet, the frenzy grows. Friesians, never the most demonstrative in the best of times are said to thaw as the temperature drops, until the cry of "It giet on! - It's on!" is heard.

My family took to the ice to watch the parade speed by. I was totally shocked by what I witnessed. Skaters with skins as white as the surrounding snow raced by.

"Mother, who are those people?"

"Oh, they're just skaters, Cookie," she blithely replied, knowing why I was shocked.

I had never seen a grown man with his shirt off and here complete strangers were flying by in complete dishabille. Friesians, bundled against the inhospitable climate most of the year, stripped off layers of sweat-encrusted wool for an unencumbered aerodynamic shape. It was Mardi Gras on two steel blades, a chance for release in the middle of the dreary winter. Translated to Grand Rapids in Michigan, the races were forbidden as the custom of disrobing was deemed too licentious.

Bodies that defied imagination were exposed to the low sun and biting wind swirling off the "Noord Zie". Likewise, couples glided across the ice linked together arm-in-arm, with an affection that would be unacceptable on a chilly street. We wore not the boot skates that we are familiar with today, but light strips of wood with steel runners. As a youngster, I skated not to the next town, but was content to hold on to a straight-backed chair my folks placed on the ice for balance. I soon made my way to the booth selling "olie koeken - oil cakes", yummy dough fried in hot oil. Hot chocolate or sage flavored milk also warmed my tummy and heart. This was one of the few times, other than at church, that I remember the entire family being together. It may have been when I heard mother laugh.

The only other events that brought the whole community together were house fires and church. Maybe we gathered on these occasions for the same reason: to prevent a conflagration from engulfing the community. In the case of our church, there was little risk of that literally occurring, since the building was unheated. Thrifty Friesians were not about to waste precious coal or peat on the path to salvation. On the coldest days, our warm breath condensed on the frigid ceiling above. The practical women of Friesland then unfurled their umbrellas, preventing the incessant dripping from adding to the frigid misery. The preachers tried to warm the house by turning up the rhetoric. Life in Friesland was so relentlessly hard that the "dominie" had to make hell seem pretty grisly to sufficiently contrast between the drudgery here on earth with the perils of sharing a nice fire somewhere warm with the devil.

Little accommodations helped a soul bear the physical indignity of three hours in the pew. Our "kloster", the church custodian, provided, for a fee, a small metal box with smoldering peat, over which a women might drape her long skirt. Men and women sat on opposite sides of the center aisle of church, not so much for reasons of Christian chastity, but for the women to separate themselves from the tobacco addicts, who, forbidden their pipes, insisted on chewing during the long service. Since cuspidors in the Lord's House would be unseemly, holes had been cut in the floor in the rear of the sanctuary, accommodating the most recalcitrant of the addicts. I wonder what an archaeologist stumbling across the future ruin of this church and its brown stain will think.

With this behavior across the aisle, is it little wonder that my mother carried a small silver box containing a sponge with a splash of eau de cologne. Other than a chance to exhibit her station with the possession of the precious box given to her by her mother, she passed it down the aisle to the benefit of her seatmates, hopefully overcoming the whiff of the Theodorus Niemeijer snuff from across the aisle. This habit continued to the new world when peppermints were passed down the pew. Before church, mother asked, "Heb je centen en pepermetten? - Do you have your pennies and peppermints?" The pennies were for the offering and the peppermints to keep us quiet. One of us children stacked the neat little individual piles on the kitchen table ready for pick up as we rushed out the door for the hurried walk to church.

The "dominies" had an important job. Not only did they steer their flocks away from eternal perdition, but they provided the only entertainment that many in the congregation had for the entire week. In reality, sin was a fairly remote concept, since there was little to steal and less to covet. Sloth and drink were about the extent of the devil's tools, so the preachers amplified Satan's guile, harping on the depravity of man. The Dutch think that they have the patent on Calvinism, so, out of national pride, we embrace these concepts readily. Being so young at the time, I remember little about the sermons except that they covered a lot of ground, tying Old Testament themes and prophecies to New Testament fulfillment. Fire and brimstone were fairly minimal, running counter to the Dutch desire for a thoughtful, unemotional sermon. Besides, it was assumed that the congregants were among God's elect and threatening them with damnation offended their sensibilities. Instead, the letters of the Apostle Paul were parsed continually for the nuances of life in the Christian community.

With a priesthood of so many believers, every congregant was a critic, so the "dominie" had to get out bed pretty early to stay ahead of his flock. One way to do this was to preach for over an hour-and-a-half so that anyone not taking notes could not remember what was said in the first place. The other was to fashion a persona biblical in nature. I have never seen such facial hair as I have on the preachers of my native land; whole clippers in full-sail sprouted from their cheeks, jaws, throats, and chins in chops, eyebrows, and whiskers that would shame Michelangelo in their sculptural inventiveness. No one dared challenge one of these Moseses returning from the top of Mount Sinai with his head whirled about by God's own comb.

This was a world as ancient as the endless string of centuries. Our simple life was marked not by change, but by endless winters, long dark nights, and days of incessant labor. This routine, if not shadowed by the specter of possible starvation, was oddly comforting. Surprises were few, and we knew the demons, such as a bad harvest, which beset us. We were alone and self-reliant in our little corner of the world. Our only contact with outside was the barge supplying our coal and a few out-of-date newspapers. The long blades of the windmills creaking above our heads marked the progress of time, barely keeping ahead of the floods constantly threatening the fields. However, I have never felt as secure as when sitting in the kerosene light after supper, huddled around the peat grate, listening to my father read a Chapter from our precious family Bible. When I think of this time from my youth, it will be in school-house Dutch, but even so, I can recite from memory entire Bible passages in my fathers' sonorous, melodic Friesian drone.

We would again gather around father to read scripture in America, but never would it be as serene or secure as in our cramped cabinet in Stroobos. As a boy, I was ready for new adventures, but I loved the simple life left behind. Like Adam, I would see a new world, but these things were of this world, not God's Kingdom. The older I become, the more I appreciate that Friesland was perhaps a lost paradise. Sure, life was harder and death more certain, but it was lived with more grace. There are more temptations in the America, in spite of more churches. In Friesland, we belonged to our "conventicle" splinter of the Reformed Church. To a little boy, this was the Church Universal. I knew that we had some suspicion of our cousins on my Mother's side in Groningen who supported the official national Reformed Church of the Netherlands, but the doctrinal differences were slight. I was now about to enter a world where the "dominie" was not the final arbiter of all things, nights were not always safely dark, and there was plenty to read other than the Holy Bible. Little did I know that the angel with the flaming sword guarding Eden was now behind me. I would never again see my native Friesland. The lessons I learned in that cold church and cramped house would need to hold me in good stead in an entirely new circumstance. Since those days, I reflect that the more we have here on earth, the harder it is to get off the ground toward our final destination. Those hard headed Friesians were some of the most stubborn people I have ever met. They had to be to endure, but many lived their lives as simple saints, asking not much from God and giving in return pure devotion.

Chapter 2

If I was comfortable and secure in this self-contained world, my father had greater concerns in keeping a roof over our head and potatoes on the table with his limited income. By 1887, the limited distractions available in our village, in conjunction with the long nights after the kerosene lamps were extinguished, blessed our family with four boys and three girls, all under the age of seventeen. A desperate man will consider desperate measures. Since crime was not an option, my father grasped at the most extreme of all gambles: moving to America. To depart our known privation, he and mother gambled all that they owned or ever knew on the chance of finding something better. He knew that our little corner of Holland would not support four more house painters (his sons). As Friesians, we would be little welcome in Amsterdam. So, maybe America was the only option. Why not move to a place where hardworking folk were needed and growth was a real possibility?

In April of the Year of our Lord, 1887, we gathered the belongings we could carry to the New World. Working in teams of two, we ferried our possessions from our house to the quay that was the center of our village. Soon our entire life was on display for the whole village's inspection. None of this was news since the village knew everything we owned from the sale we had conducted during the prior weeks. Mother supervised the older boys while father completed the sale of the house. We stuffed our few clothes into flour sacks given to us by mother's family. The one suitcase held mother's best dress and the other suit that father was not wearing. The only furniture we brought were three mattresses, leaving the one behind that even my thrifty parents thought too worn to make the trip. New furniture we could buy or make, but a mattress was too precious to leave behind. My oldest brothers Sjierd and Klaas wrangled the two large trunks containing all of the valuables: the family Bible, a wind-up mantle clock packed in quilts (a wedding present to my parents from mother's parents), the crockery, and our cooking pots.

We lived alongside of the Colonel Deep, a major shipping channel. Judging by the steady traffic and the frequent boats berthing along the quay in Stroobos, I knew it as the central artery of Friesland, connecting the inland sea of the IJsselmeer with the important town of Groningen, near where mother came from. Before our barge arrived, mother's parents arrived by ferry from Groningen. I had never seen my grandparents hug mother (and certainly not father) before, but they did so before taking their leave to return home. They also gave each of us a hug and a guilder to spend in Amsterdam. So, a few weeks after Easter in 1887, we waited on the quay, saying goodbye to everyone and everything we knew. The barge came and we piled on, nine strong arranging our possessions with as much order and dignity as possible. Stroobos disappeared behind as the plodding mule pulled us west. After an overnight stop, we arrived at the town of Lemmer on the edge of the Netherlands' inland sea, the IJisselmeer. I was excited because now I was in Flevoland, a province of the Netherlands that I had never visited. Already, I was seeing more of the world than in all of my seven years. What else was to come?

I was farther from home than ever before. I had seen a small side-wheel paddleboat make its way along the canal by our house, but had no idea that there could be a craft large enough to carry us over the ocean. What was an ocean? I was amazed, after the trip down the canal, to see the expanse of water beyond Lemmer. There were no farms, only water. We had arrived well before our steamship, so I had ample time to survey the surroundings. There was a long quay, along which were moored a variety of boats including low-slung "skutsjes" with their distinctive lee boards pulled up along their gunwales. Few craft ever appeared as ungainly but were so well suited for the shallow waters of the inland sea. Looking out beyond where we stood, I was confused; certainly something this big must be the ocean, but brother Gerke called me a dummy saying that the ferry we boarded would take us to where we would board an even bigger ship to cross the Atlantic, not this mere inland sea, which looked impossibly big to me.

My brothers, sisters, and I killed time exploring ever further from the watchful eye of mother. I would look around, before warily stopping to regard the endless water. I was not sure what we would find on the other side and I was not sure if I wanted to find out. If my father had second thoughts, he never shared them while he and mother took turns preventing seven children from disturbing the other waiting passengers. However, we were all a little apprehensive to give free reign to our hi-jinx. As a seven-year old, I was probably the most worried of all. I was of an age where I understood the danger of the undertaking, but with little in the way to evaluate the risk. The water was so wide that even the largest boat looked small. Contemplating our imminent doom, I saw the smudge of the steamboat on the horizon. My father, like any Friesian with a weather eye, watched the sky darkening beyond the boat.

The arriving ferry was the largest craft I had ever seen - larger than the big barges that plied the Colonel Deep behind our house. I felt a little more confident as we scrambled to carry our belongings on board as the bewhiskered first mate hollered for us to "make haste." The wind picked up as a few ominous drops splashed on my cap. The securing lines were tossed from the wharf, and the crew on the quay ran back into the shelter of the terminal. My family gathered our belongings into the smallest pile we could manage, huddling in the modest cabin with the other passengers. We sat on the cabin's deck away from the wall where the wind lashed the portholes. The ship strained against the stiffening breeze as the captain signaled to the engineer to open the throttle valve. A huge black puff blew from of the stack, showering the outside deck with cinders. We made way, the boat rocking against the wind that picked up as we made our way from shore. Clearing the jetty, waves splashed over the bow. The first mate entered the main cabin where we and other passengers were leaning up against the bulkheads. He muttered an apology before extinguishing the oil lamps swinging erratically in their gimbals. The small room darkened, except for faint glow of late afternoon visible through the portholes, down which water now ran continuously. Our fellow passengers huddled together with their families, speaking quietly among themselves, glancing nervously at each other for some better understanding of the risk or assurance that our plight might not be as dire as it seemed. The deck of the cabin pitched erratically. I felt queasy, but held on to my scrap of rye bread and butter; a treat too good to lose.

"Gerke, I thought you said that this was a small sea. Will the ocean be worse than this?" I asked my brother in a voice that was smaller than I intended between burps.

He replied without much conviction, "The ocean ship will be larger, but this is a fine craft crewed and captained by good Friesian men." Little did he know that the north wind gathers the shallow waters of the IJsselmeer into a crazy quilt of waves through which our ferry corkscrewed its way south.

Soon it was dark. The first mate entered, acknowledging that the weather was more intense than what was forecast, directing everyone toward the windward side of the boat. Now with no bulkhead on which to lean, we braced ourselves linking our arms together. If the first mate did not sound panicked, he was not very reassuring, quickly returning to the pilot house.

We thought it could not get any worse. It did. We were now being tossed around. My flying elbow hit my baby sister, Hendrijke, so that her sobs became wails. Other youngsters joined in the lament.

In this ruckus, father's voice boomed out in the dark, "Brothers and sisters, boys and girls: be not afraid. Did not our Savior look after his disciples when they were at the mercy of the winds on the Sea of Galilee? And what is it He told the disciples then and us now, in times like these? 'Be not afraid, it is I.' Surely, our Lord is with us in our time of need, now more than ever."

The room quieted back to sobs and murmurs. The sea did not, but we now knew that we would survive. After what seemed to be half the night, but I am sure was closer to an hour, our ferry entered den Briten IJ , the outer harbor of Amsterdam. The crashing of the waves ceased as we made way along the *kanaal*. In the lee of the land, the gale calmed to a stiff breeze. Our ferry that had been but a speck on the sea an hour ago now steamed in quiet dignity towards her berth. After docking, we spent the rest of the evening in damp repose, resting as well as we could, saving the cost of a night's lodging for our family of nine.

The April morning dawned clear with scudding clouds, as if the storm had cleansed the sky of the last of winter's fury. The first mate greeted us in a chipper tone as we departed, as if none of the night's travails had occurred, but our fellow passengers quietly thanked my father for his testimony and courage. As for himself, he was even more quiet than usual. The night's storm had passed. He had more on his mind, ferrying seven children and our possessions through the streets of the great city of Amsterdam. In less than a half-hour we were at the door of "Den Hoop - The Hope Guest House" where we would stay the night before embarking the following evening. The older boys and girls commented that the name was appropriate for our family's venture. It was fortunate that we had brought our own bedding as we piled into one small room with our mattresses filling every inch of floor space.

That morning was the Lord's Day, so we proceeded to a church far larger than any I had ever seen, even than my grandparent's church in Groningen. Not only was it huge, but it was made out of brick and stone, unusual materials in Friesland. How could anything so heavy stand so tall? This was a congregation of the "Nederlandse Hervormde Kerk", the official state church of the Netherlands, the same denomination as our small church in Stroobos. Our small congregation had not left the NHV, I think primarily for financial reasons, but we considered ourselves among the "Doleantie – the Grieving Ones" led by Abraham Kuyper who sought to return the church to more conservative, purer Calvinist roots. So, though thrilled to see such magnificent structure and hear the mighty organ, I noticed Father was subdued and suspicious as he entered. He refused to sing hymns not based on the Psalms, putting far less in the offering plate than normal. He made sure that our own prayers and scripture reading continued when we returned to our room, while my own ears still echoed from the deep swells of the church organ.

If I thought the mighty organ and the bright Sunday morning greeting us was a harbinger of a now smooth trip, I was mistaken. Monday was "Koninginnedag - the King's Day", and the entire city had been converted into a "vrijmarkt - freemarket", celebrating the ascension of Willem III onto the throne of our country. Though Willem was not particularly popular, the people of Amsterdam were more than willing to spend the day celebrating the end of winter. Taking our new guilders, we rushed onto the street. Orange and green banners hung everywhere and I had as much fun as when the "kermis" - the carnival came to Stroobos many years ago. Never had I seen so many large buildings, nor so many people. It dawned on me that I knew not a soul, unlike in our village, where I knew everyone. I nervously looked to Gerke, but his eyes, too, were wide, scanning this entirely new landscape. In Stroobos, the land and farms were never out of sight. Here, in Amsterdam, everything was man-made, whether the buildings or the streets. Here and there I saw a tree or a flower but they were out place, struggling to survive.

I was not the only one in my family who had never been to a big city. Only father had come to Amsterdam previously, learning to apply faux marble and wood grain to walls. Mother took us to Groningen occasionally, but it was nothing like this. The traffic on the canals never stopped. Small steamboats carried loads, belching endless clouds of steam and black coal smoke. The acrid smell of coal was everywhere, as strong outdoors here in the "fresh" air as it had been inside our small house by the canal in the middle of winter. In front of us, the street was as fragrant as a farm, as the multitude of dray horses relieved themselves in the midst of their toil. However, here in the city a man in an official looking uniform picked up the horse droppings. I thought that he must very rich, because he would quickly fill up his fertilizer barge to sell to the surrounding farms. And the noise! After the quiet of Stroobos, I thought my ears would burst from the shouting and the numerous whistles demanding right of way. City life was certainly more exciting than our village in the country, but I am not sure I liked it very much.

Late in the afternoon, it was time to move the family to the docks of the "De Nederlandsch-Amerikakaansche Stoomvaart Maatscappij". Things went smoothly after we found a carter to carry our goods to the steamship docks. I noticed that our high-topped shoes and wide-legged pants were not in the style favored by the Amsterdamers. However, in this we were not alone, for many other rural families lugged mounds of luggage looking for their steamships. Was half of Holland moving to America? Along the quay of the River Amstel, the city's namesake, it appeared that way. I took some comfort in that we were not the only people silly enough to leave a perfectly good village. We found our steamship by early evening, consigning our luggage to the freight agent. The North American Steamship Line had many ships ready to carry passengers to different ports. I was not surprised that ours was the oldest and smallest. Nonetheless, it was the largest ship I had ever seen, dwarfing our ill-fated ferry. I was excited that this magnificent craft would be my home for the next two weeks.

Father went to see the agent managing our visas for entry into America as mother looked after the children. Hoping to give Sjierd some experience in city life that he would need to find work in Amerika, she sent him back to the bakery near the guest house to buy three loaves of rye bread in case of irregular feedings on the ship. As it was about six in the afternoon and the ship was to sail with the tide at one in the morning, there was plenty of time. Or so we thought. Around seven o'clock, father returned, so we were all ready to board the Zaandam, resting slack on her hawsers. It became dark. At eight, mother and father, with great reluctance, dispatched Klaas, in hopes of finding Sjierd. No sooner was Klaas out of sight, Sjierd returned after getting hopelessly lost; too embarrassed by his Friesian accent to ask for directions. As the ship's final boarding whistles screamed in the background, Klaas ran up, out of breath, anxiously declaring he could not find Sjierd, before seeing him at the same moment. We all boarded as father muttered to mother that he did not feel comfortable praying as insistently as he had over the past few days.

"Vader's" prayer life would be one of thanksgiving while we were at sea. He knew that this passage would be the lull before the storm when he would need to live by his wits supporting his family in a new country, no matter how rich the opportunities may be. If life were easy, it would be a gift from the devil. Grace grows from struggle. He looked at the seven of us wearily, amazed that not one of us fell overboard. He knew that it would be easier keeping his family together while on board than in the wilds of Amsterdam or "Amerika". I, too, boarded with greater confidence after our harrowing trip across the IJsselmeer. The Zaandam was certainly larger than the ferry, reminding me of the prints of clipper ships on the wall of my school. It was long and lean, as if built for speed. However, the four masts gracing the hull were not for propulsion, but suspended the antenna for the wireless radio, a new addition. Later in our trip, two square sails might be unfurled from the foremasts in a favorable wind. The Zaandam might not be the pride of the "Nederlandsch-Amerikakaansche Stoomvaart Maatscappij", but had been in service for five years, carrying countless immigrant families to America. She (I had learned the proper gender of ships) looked serviceable, if a bit rusty, as we boarded. We found our area below decks in a "hok" with 26 bunks that we shared with other families. They, too, were Friesian, so communication was not a problem. Sharing the physical reticence natural to all Friesians, we would all wear the same clothes for the next two weeks, including to bed. As children, we were thrilled, because, for the first time since out of the cradle, we each had our own bed; not having to share with a sibling. What luxury in such a cramped space! As one of the younger children, mine was close to the deck. Sjierd, Klaas, and Gerke climbed to bunks in the third tier above. This was our home for the next two weeks, but by the end, the easy bonhomie shared at the outset evaporated from living in such close quarters.

The whole trip was a vacation for mother and father, if they knew what a vacation was. In those days, time off from labor was an unknown concept in Friesland except to maybe visit family or attend a funeral. For once in their lives, they were not shackled to their work. They spent the days in sort of a dumb-founded stupor, wondering what they should be doing that they were not. They lived by the saying "rust roest - rest corrodes". We had no books, magazines, or other amusement. In our Bible-reading village, anything other than scripture and Christian allegories were regarded as "sputen", not to mention a wasteful extravagance. The siblings explored the few parts of the ship open to us. But even this was amusing to a young boy for about a week. I was given a pencil, to make little drawings on scraps of paper with the initials *N.A.S.M.* printed on the top. As steerage passengers, we were limited to a brief time to breathe fresh air on our class' small deck overlooking the stern. A deck above us, the first and second-class passengers enjoyed their promenade at any time, looking down on us with little derision or condescension, if they bothered to look at all. Fortunately, as Netherlanders on "Netherlandische" ship, we were granted optimal times for going up on deck, such as during the mornings. I was stupefied by the vast extent of what, I learned, was merely the English Channel. This was certainly bigger water than even the IJsselmeer, but the Vaandam cut along the shore with easy grace when I came on deck the morning after we departed.

Below our "Netherlandisch" deck were people who I learned were from other parts of Europe, which I understood only as a vague concept; these were places you could get to from Friesland by canal, not by the ocean. They looked somewhat like us, but I noticed that their worsted jackets were cut in different styles than ours as I watched them trudge up the stairs from the decks below to their precious time on the deck. They made a remarkable din on the metal treads. I regarded them with feelings of pity and contempt, no doubt imitating the attitude of my elders. Our passage of two weeks provided no opportunity to break through these mutual prejudices that would carry forward once we set foot on land. We would all be competing for jobs. Each immigrant group inevitably gathered with folk from their home country. We were no different. Speaking only our own language, we had no choice.

As part of a good Dutch steamship line, the Vaandam carried a "Nederlandse Hervormde Kerk" chaplain on board who led services on Sundays. Father, keeping his doctrinal prejudices confined to land, enjoyed these services immensely. Perhaps he wanted to show the nationalities and churches represented by the other passengers that the Dutch took a backseat to no one when it came to the Christianity. He met with chaplain throughout the week, appreciating the depth of his scholarship and breadth of his experience. This minister certainly had seen more of the world than our old village "dominie".

Mother's concern regarding on-board food was unfounded, and I ate better than at home. Stringy meat was now part of every supper until near the end of the voyage. I also ate more bread than in Stroobos. By now, I believed that ships never had tables, as once again, we ate in our "hok" after the berths had been swung up out of the way. The dining crew served their soups and potatoes from impossibly large cauldrons wheeled about on specially made carts. The luxury of a dining cabin in steerage would have prevented the steamship line from selling more berths to passengers.

After a day at sea, we cleared the English Channel. We enjoyed seeing the famous Kurhaus on the beach at Scheveningen and the Chalk Cliffs of Dover in the hazy distance. The long swells of the Atlantic now took their toll, dashing the anticipation of a calm trip. The long and narrow Zaandam, three hundred feet long by fifty feet wide, rocked unencumbered from side to side. The crew made their way with steady grace, but the passengers were tossed from bulkhead to bulkhead in search of a place to rest a queasy stomach. After a while they just gave up, remaining in their bunks. With the demand for meals cut by at least half, the pursers of the N.A.S.M. must have loved this. A thrifty steamship line reflected a thrifty country.

Long after my trip, I learned that America's insatiable appetite for labor drove the construction of a whole new type of ship like ours which were essentially floating dormitories, designed to carry as many steerage passengers as possible. The hulls were topped by a small two-deck superstructure for the first and second class passengers so that they appeared the proper steamship. Our large family was proof that infant mortality in Europe had decreased to the point where even our part of Holland was now full. The reclamation of land as polder did not keep pace with the mushrooming families, which in our case had reached seven children. The marine clay soils of Friesland, while fertile, were susceptible to potato blight. Poor harvests were not unknown. European farming could not feed the growing population.

In addition to economic opportunity, a quest for religious freedom motivated my parents. While the heads of the "Nederlandse Hervormde Kerk" left our small country church alone, you never knew when they would demand stricter obedience to doctrine as they saw it, not as we did in Friesland. There was a constant tension between the national church and the outlying congregations. Sometimes this erupted into divisive disputes. More conservative branches of the Dutch Reformed Church had taken root in the New World. There, without state interference, congregations worshiped as they saw fit. When steamships and railroads made travel easier, millions of Europeans looked west for a new start, especially farmers who did not have access to land. The Zaandam carried over 400 passengers in steerage. In Amsterdam alone, we saw four other ships boarding on the same mission when we were there. The scene was repeated in Hamburg, Southampton and Rotterdam.

These ships returned to Europe virtually empty. Anyone wishing to return to Europe certainly could get a good deal. When Sjierd, my oldest brother, booked a passage to visit the Netherlands twelve years later, not only did he travel in the relative luxury of second class, but paid only twenty-one dollars for the privilege. These were not cruise ships, but the competition to fill the rows of bunks was keen, so the companies made the trip as comfortable as possible for the passengers, even those of us crammed in below decks. The crew was quite professional in their nautical uniforms; even the cabin boys who were not much older than me. My wide country pants were not quite as smart as their bell-bottoms. The ship was presided over by a captain who we never saw once during the passage. I trust that he was there, since we made steady, if slow progress, to arrive eventually at our destination of New York.

We looked forward to our allotted time on deck. One morning during our "airing" I watched a large brown fish swim along with us. I learned that these were porpoises. The sailors thought of them as "good luck", a concept we, as Calvinists, were supposed to shun, but it made me feel better.

Klaas came along side me, pointing to the smokestack initials of "NASM", "Do know what that stands for?"

I mumbled something about "Nederlandsch-Amerikakaansche Stoomvaart..," now feeling quite confident in the ways of the sea.

"Not at all, it means Neemt Alle Skurken Mee - Transports All Scoundrels."

To a seven-year old, this was terribly clever. Klaas protected me from the ravages of Gerke, and was a source of endless jokes and puns. What I remember best from our time on deck was not the sun, the sky, or the jokes, but the smell of freshly baked bread emanating from the bakery's ventilator. In Stroobos, we ate white wheat bread (not the usual Friesian rye) only on Sunday. Because baking in the home was such a rarity, I had never experienced such an embarrassment of riches. This amazing floating machine had more luxuries than could be imagined in our tiny village.

Perhaps we should have enjoyed this idle more we than we did. By the end of our first week, we were all ready to be off the ship, but were only half way in our passage. Our quarters, previously as fresh as a sea breeze were now a dank cell holding over four hundred people ready for land. First the beef, then the pork ran out. The steady rolls to which we had adapted gave way to a full-blown gale. One morning, I staggered to the deck to be splashed by a huge wave washing the entire length of ship before quickly retreating below. After the storm, the wind died for the calmest conditions of the trip. We were treated to a most eerie sight, a white mountain rising out of the middle of the water. On the horizon were other of these mountains and two other ships, stopped dead. I asked one of the crew, "Do ships ever hit these bergs - mountains?"

"Niet, mariners know to sail as slowly as possible whenever we see them. Only a fool sails through them at full speed, and never at night. We see them here this time of year. They fall off the glaciers of Greenland before floating here. They're immense; you see only a tiny part of them; the rest is under water," he replied before returning to scanning the horizon with his binoculars.

Finally, on a morning later in the month, we clambered up during our time on deck to see the Statue of Liberty glide by to our left. We had arrived! Within the hour, we docked at the tip of an island at the north end of the harbor. In front of us was Castle Garden, the immigrants' gateway. We embarked down the gangways, our legs rebelling against the sensation of firm land. In a harbor busier than Amsterdam's, steam-powered ships of every description crossed in random patterns, whistling insistently at each other. Weaving between the straight wakes of the steamboats, schooners gracefully tacked towards their destinations. A small boy was entranced. We were ashore on Manhattan, the capital of New Amsterdam, the former Dutch colony.

Any chance of this place being familiar or comfortable to a Dutch boy was dispelled stepping ashore. The land seemed to be moving as our gait, accustomed to the gentle wallow of the Zaandam, faltered. Gerke and I staggered like the drunks we imitated back home. Castle Garden was certainly more a castle than a garden. We were directed into the biggest room I had ever been in during my life. A man in a uniform pointed us to seats among the countless rows where we sat for the rest of the day. And into the night; trying to sleep sitting upright. We children lined up with mother, suffering through a long night as sleep was interrupted with cries, snores, and murmurs of the assembled multitude's Babel of languages.

When dawn finally came, the large glass dome overhead illuminated an island of uniformed officials, all with mustaches, who examined our papers when Mother was called forward. She gritted her teeth. "Vader" was nowhere to be found, spending his time searching for us among the rows of Germans, yet another confusion of "Dutch" with "Deutche". In Amsterdam, we understood the language of the "Nederlandische", different from what we spoke in Friesland. Mother spoke German, but father did not. I guess if my language was called Dutch here, it made sense that "Amerkaansche" should be called "English". Here in "Amerika", the officials spoke in an indecipherable torrent I would never understand. Neither did the men in mustaches and stiff hats. Since Mother had her identity card, they wrote her surname, "Sipma" as my last name, and as that of each of my brothers and sisters. Once we finally found father, there was no opportunity to change it since the ink had dried and there were trains to catch.

"The Lord knows the name from your baptism, safely stowed in the trunk in the Bible," father assured us. Yet I wondered if the Americans would insist that I was now "Hermanus Sipma," not "Veenstra".

Though it was spring, and beginning to warm, we were bundled in our winter clothes. Everyone else was wearing as much as they could in addition to what they carried in their numerous trunks, bags, and valises. We made our way out from the gauntlet of officialdom. Once through the massive oak doors, we were now on our own in a completely foreign land. We were now truly eels out of the "kanaal", flapping in the pan. Fortunately, there were agents meeting the waves of immigrants flooding into this country, and they knew enough Dutch to assist us (for a fee) to the Grand Central train station in the middle of the island for our trip into the country. Mother and father were appalled by the run on their meager wallet of dollars that their guilders received at the money exchange. After the relief to our purse of being at sea, now ashore, our savings were under continual assault as nine mouths needed feeding, and nine bodies needed transport across a country whose vastness we were now about to confront. Mother, if not as crafty and thrifty as a Friesian, cleverly carried another brother of mine for free, who would be born the following winter.

Father's cousin, Jan Veenstra, had already immigrated to America. Jan had moved to western Michigan, where Dutch religious dissenters who subscribed to the same conservative tenets as we did established a Dutch "colonie" in the late 1840's under Dominie Albertus Van Raalte. There, Jan was helped by a man named Vander Meulen. Father had also been in correspondence with a Mr. Bosgraaf, a friend from Sujuisterveen, the town where I was born. Bosgraaf lived in Englewood, Illinois, near a big city called Chicago. Both Vander Meulen and Bosgraaf offered to help us. However, when the decision to move was made, no confirming letter was received from Bosgraaf until it followed us to America, nearly a year later. These choices of what would be our new home were completely unknown to me. I thought we would make a short trip like in Holland and be at our new home. Little did I know that the trip west would take five more days and be much more perilous than our two weeks at sea in the tidy confines of the N.A.S.M. Though we children did not know it at the time, I am sure father and mother agonized over this decision, asking God for guidance. They had very little to go on. Englewood might offer better employment opportunities, but this town called the "Rapids" may be more like back home. We certainly did not leave Stroobos to move to Amsterdam. As country people, a smaller town had its appeal. Father may have interpreted the missing correspondence from Bosgraaf as divine direction to head for Michigan. I wondered how water could move so fast as to be "rapid" once I learned the meaning of the word. Water in Holland rarely moved anywhere and certainly not rapidly.

If our old village of Stroobos smelled like the rich muck of the surrounding farms and the "kanaal", my first impression of America is that it smelled like coal. Sure, I was acquainted with coal, appreciating the warmth radiating from our stove back home, but here, mountains of it were burned to power the bustling machinery of transport. Nowhere was this truer than in the train shed of the Grand Central Station. We would now ride on a railroad owned by a Dutch - American, Cornelius "Commodore" Vanderbilt. The "Commodore" was not there to greet us nor did his agents offer a discount to his poor cousins recently arrived from the Netherlands. "Vader" visibly blanched as he counted out the precious dollars securing our passage. We had been advised to secure food for our trip. Sjierd, this time accompanied by "muder", set out to find a market. Klaas and I stayed close to father watching over our pile of possessions before consigning them to the rail agent to stow in the baggage car. We stood amazed at the constant movement of trains, where one empty track was soon occupied by another train in a haze of steam and smoke, accompanied by a racket of steam and clanging bells. As I coughed and wheezed, my eyes could not be drawn away from the spectacle. I saw more activity, power, and people than ever before. Growing up along a canal, I was familiar with boats and barges all of my life, but these were the first trains I had ever seen. It did not take long to understand that the big black belching contraption at front pushed and pulled the impossibly long carriages along the skinny "spooren" on which they ran. I was sure that the whole thing would buck off to our demise. These monstrous beasts made not a move without the clang of bells and the shriek of whistles emphasizing their obvious importance. Later in life I often lived close to train tracks; in America it was hard not to, and I came to appreciate the whistle and bell as a backdrop to life. Who of my age doesn't hear a bell and immediately conjure the indelible image of the steam locomotive? For my generation, it was the most impressive mechanical thing we had ever seen. Little did I know that this would be the first trip of many by rail across this immense newly-adopted continent.

Many of the Dutch coming to America chose not to spend their life savings in reaching the Dutch communities in the Midwest, choosing to stay close to the banks of the Hudson River, where the Dutch had lived for centuries. However, most of us who subscribed to the more conservative branches of the Reformed faith opted, like in Holland, for a more rural life, joining our like-minded brethren over 200 leagues away. Many were farmers, heading where cheap land could be found.

My subsequent trips to New York would be in stark contrast to the filthy loud platform of the Grand Central Station of that day. The grubby platform on which we now stood would be replaced by the soaring Grand Central Terminal. The coal stinging my nostrils became a distant memory with the electrification of the trains. The slums where mother shopped for bread would be transformed into Park Avenue, one of the most fashionable streets in the world when the trains were located below the pavement.

Mother and Sjierd returned in plenty of time before our train clanged up the track. When it lurched to a stop, we clambered aboard to find our seats. There was less space than on the ship. Instead of finding cozy berths, we each shared a seat. Since there was no place to sleep, I thought we would soon be at our destination. I did not know we were embarking on another trip of over five days. In the dark of the train shed, I stared at my dim reflection in the large window, my blond hair illuminated by the sputtering kerosene lamps. The car jerked, moving forward, first slowly, then with gathering speed. My reflection exploded into the vista of a teeming slum outside the window when we emerged from the shed. Not long after, the grimy city gave way to the bright greening countryside of the land that would soon be ours. The view was certainly better than that from our quarters below decks on the ship and more interesting than the monotonous horizon of the sea. Past the city, we rattled alongside a wide river.

Sjierd asked Gerke and me, "' You know the name of that river?"

Gerke hazarded a guess, "Het Manhattan Rivier?"

"No, good guess, but it's the Hudson River, named after a famous explorer from the 17th century. He was English, but he was working for the "Vereenigade Oost-Indische Compaigne - The Dutch East India Company". The "Halve Maen" that he sailed here from Amsterdam was about the size of the ferry we took across the IJsellmeer. He claimed this land for the Netherlands. The English later stole it, but we Dutch have lived here ever since. After that trip, he went back to work for the English, before his crew marooned him on a small boat. It figures, the ungrateful wretches."

At this last bit, "Vader" cleared his throat, bringing Sjierd's history lesson to an end, but I looked at the valley with greater appreciation. I was always amazed at what Sjierd knew, especially since he had been out of school working for father for the past three years. I did not think that it looked at all like the Netherlands, no matter who lived here. In spite of being farmed for over two hundred years, the land was mostly forested, unlike Friesland where the only trees divided the fields or provided shelter in the villages. The forests through which we traveled were clothed in the lightest shade of green, bathed in sunlight brighter than I had ever seen, even when seen through the cloud of smoke from the aptly named "locomotive" pulling our carriages up the valley named for the Anglo-Dutch sea-farer Hendrijk Hudson. Soon the gentle swaying of carriage lulled me to sleep.

Our train continued toward Buffalo, a city named for a type of bull that the Indians of America hunted. I kept a sharp eye for any natives, but did not see any, nor a buffalo, for that matter.

What I did see was an endless succession of towns where we stopped to take on water and coal. These stops gave mother a chance to shop for provisions, where she learned to read a few English words such as "market", which was quite similar to Dutch. I had less success, since I was a novice reader even of my native tongue. To a seven-year old, this starting and stopping became tedious, especially as mother confined me to my seat so as not to bother the other passengers who did not find a little blond boy in funny clothes babbling gibberish to be either cute or appealing. We were no longer in a part of America where the Dutch held any sway. Most of the names now seemed to be derived from the Indians or the Romans or Indio-Romans, which did nothing to mollify my boredom.

My apprehension was well founded as our trip almost ended in Buffalo, but not because of a bull hunted by the Indians. We changed trains, waiting for well over an hour in stifling heat. Opening the window did little to soothe us as I squirmed on the prickly wicker upholstery. I glanced up to notice a man in large hat briskly walk the length of the car, stopping before entering the next carriage. I wondered why he did not take his seat to go to "Chicago", another English word I was learning. He just stood at the end of the car, staring intently through the door's window towards the next car. A moment later, a conductor came in through the first door, loudly asking for tickets. His uniform was different from that of the previous conductors on the New York Central Railroad, but I figured that the new train had new conductors. He slowly made his way down the aisle, collecting tickets from the immigrant families, who, like us, made up most of the car. In return, he gave them an official looking "transit certificate". Just before he reached the rows where we were sitting, the man in the large hat, now pulled down even lower, quickly walked back towards us. The conductor stopped what he was doing, following him in the direction from which they had both come. Right after they left the carriage, another man, this time in what I recognized as a proper New York Central Railroad conductor's uniform, entered from the end where the man with the hat had been stationed, bellowing for our tickets. In the center of the car, we waited patiently until he came to us. He took our tickets, finishing his business in a flurry of punches. He issued no "transit certificates", but if he was satisfied, so were we.

The outcry started two rows after ours. "Transit certificates" were of no value to the NYCRR. After informing a family from Germany that they must leave the train, the conductor set off after the swindlers, who had left with their haul of legitimate tickets. The immigrants without tickets were removed from train, unable to argue in their faulty English against the majesty of a NYCRR conductor. If America was a land of mechanical wonders, the people who ran them could be officious and merciless, especially to immigrants. Those poor fellow passengers were no better off than the people of Judah before the court of Nebuchadnezzar. Father seethed at the injustice, but knew he had no power to stop it. Like Daniel, he would wait his turn, praying that until then that the lions did not devour him. To me it felt more like the Fiery Furnace until we lurched out of the town named-after-a-bull-hunted-by-the-Indians with the windows opened as wide as possible. If this was paradise, it sure was hot.

After Buffalo, we had no choice but to travel on the Lord's Day; the NYCRR unsympathetic to suspending operations for the day, the Dutch Commodore notwithstanding. This tore at father since he tried to obey all of God Commandments that were read every Sunday in our church. He had no choice but to make the best of a bad situation. As the carriage swayed across an endless Ohio, he called us together to lead us in prayer. Our Bible was in storage. Father would never be so presumptuous to offer a sermon, so he then recited the Ten Commandments from memory, then calling on us to recite verses and passages that we had learned. Klaas's Beatitudes brought the car to silence. There was enough commonality in the languages that our fellow German passengers were rapt. As we concluded with the doxology and the Lord's Prayer, almost the entire car joined in their native language.

Suddenly, Friesland, Holland and even Europe seemed very small as we rolled along the vast prairie emerging before us.

Chapter 3

And so our family, which left Holland with such excitement and hope, dragged exhausted into the small city of Grand Rapids in the province of Michigan. While we had not spent 40 years wandering in the Sinai, we identified with the tribulations of the Israelites. We had been underway for twenty-three days. Grand Rapids might not have been the land of Canaan, but it was a welcome sight to nine pilgrims weary of three weeks of hard traveling. None of us wanted to endure that again. Most of the family never would, choosing to stay within a few miles of where we landed, but it was my fate that the changes in my life would result in many moves. Little did I know how far I would travel across this vast new continent with my children. Their children would scatter even further. All we wanted now was to stop moving and restore some normalcy to our transient lives.

We were met at the substantial brick train station by Mr. Vander Meulen, who was taken aback by the arrival of not one small family, but two; with ours consisting of seven children, with my mother additionally beginning to show with what would be a baby brother. It took two trips in Vander Meulen's wagon to carry us and all of our belongings to our new home. I stayed behind at the depot with mother while father, Mr. Vander Meulen, and the older boys left in the wagon, taking our trunks and mattresses to our new home. One more train came through while I sweated in my woolen clothes which I had not removed in weeks. Our new town, a small city actually, was larger than Stroobos and more interesting to a small boy. It was also considerably brighter and hotter. The sun stood higher here than back home. I knew now that Stroobos was no longer home, but this was not either. There were tall trees everywhere. Instead of farms, the "Rapids" was surrounded by forests. As with everywhere else in America, I did not understand a word anyone said except for mother as she cautioned for me to stay close.

After about an hour, Mr. Vander Meulen returned to pick up mother, my younger sisters, and me. Mother rode on the driver's seat with Mr. Vander Meulen, her bonnet protecting her skin from the bright sun. She sat very upright, staring mostly straight ahead with her hands on her lap. Mr. Vander Meulen, his straw hat stained with sweat, pointed out a few sights in Friesian as we plodded north. Sisters Hendrijke and Minke rode with me in back; our backs against rails that read "Vander Meulen Furniture – New and Used". Bouncing along, I held three-year old Minke steady. We followed the river to our left upstream for over a mile until reaching a cluster of houses on a street identified as "Howland". Here we turned, stopping in front of a house across the street from a building with large sign proclaiming "Vander Meulen Furniture - New and Used." Both buildings were quite tall, not so much as those in New York or Amsterdam, but certainly taller than anything in Stroobos except for the church. Both structures were made of wood, not the brick and stucco of a proper Friesland house and were capped by much steeper roofs. Along the gable were decorative carvings painted in bright colors. These tall buildings, besides being Mr. Vander Meulen's place of business, were residences.

Mr. Vander Meulen helped mother out of the wagon so we could follow her inside. There we met father and climbed the stairs to our new home. Our tread and voices echoed as we walked in. Thank heaven we were not in "klompen", but then, they were reserved for outside use anyway. It was larger than our home in Friesland, but the walls were plain. The third floor under the roof was unfinished without the benefit of plaster or insulation. Our possessions, so formidable when carried from ship to train, disappeared in the echoing rooms. At last I could take off the sweater and coat I wore, hanging them in a small room attached to the bedroom. As we peeled off our layers, this "closet" filled up quickly. Klaas and I shared a room upstairs that was not finished, but we were grateful for the space. Come winter, it was very drafty, but on this late May afternoon, it looked like an acceptable place to lay our mattress. Out of the window, I saw a bridge for what I was to learn was Leonard Street crossing the river one block away.

Mr. Vander Meulen made a business helping Dutch immigrants by renting out floors in this house across from his store and selling them used furniture. He gladly extended credit, since he knew that most of his customers thought that the Eleventh Commandment prohibited debt; sooner choosing not to feed their children than to be thought of as a deadbeat. We soon had a table and four chairs, a rocker for mother and father, and some dressers for our clothes. Over the next several years, we added chairs so that we could all eat around the table at the same time. But in that first year, I wondered if it was my fate to forever eat dinner sitting up against a wall as I had during the past month at sea.

When we arrived, my Father Melle Veenstra was 49 years old; mother, Aaltje Sipma was 42. It was near the end of May, 1887. Here are their children who accompanied them:

Brother Sjierd............ age 17
Sister Degina............ age 15
Brother Klaas........... age 13
Brother Gerke .... age 10
Hermanus (me) .... age 7
Sister Hendrijke ...... age 5
Sister Minke .... age 3

Our brother Hendrijkus was born in December of the year we arrived.

Grand Rapids did not flow with milk and honey, but flour was plentiful. Wheat bread would now be a constant in my life; an improvement over Holland. David Vander Meulen, our benefactor's son was my age and we became immediate friends. He had learned some Friesian in his home, so he was invaluable in helping me begin to learn English. Their house across the street was on a steep lot sloping down towards what I now knew was the

Grand River, which would be important in my life for years to come. Their cellar was open on that side, so you could walk right in without walking down any stairs. There, Mrs. Vander Meulen fired a large coal oven from which emerged delicacies that were beyond my imagination. The location in the cellar was a blessing, because in the summer months she could still fire the oven. This was not done in other houses if the oven were located in the house proper. When her windows were open, I smelled bread, cookies, or vanilla-flavored sponge cake. This oven was only the beginning of delights for young boys to explore. There was more to see and more mischief to find than in Stroobos.

As poor immigrants, we lived in a rough part of town, where residences, stores, and factories were all cheek by jowl. If this made for noisy surroundings, it also made for convenient walking. I was pretty noisy myself, so I thought we landed in the right part of town.

Hardwood forests surrounded Grand Rapids. Logs from the timbering were floated down to the factories on the banks of the river. The Michigan Barrel Company was one of these. Michigan grew much fruit (another taste revelation). There was a constant demand for barrels and peck baskets to ship this produce to Chicago and other big cities. Next to the factory, booms floated in the river, corralling the company's logs, placidly floating before conveyance into the mill. When the factory operated, men with pikes guided the logs to the conveyor, where they jumped as if alive, flying up the conveyor. We warned the logs not to go, but such was their fate, evidenced by the constant screams coming from the relentless three-foot diameter circular saw slicing them and their hapless companions. These now poor boards had brief respite as they were stacked in a rick yard to dry before being contorted into the barrels and baskets of their eventual fate.

This was high drama to young boys, not always to our benefit. After the factory shut down for the day during the summer months, we ventured on to the rafts of logs corralled within the booms. I am sure mother would have forbidden this activity if she knew of it. She had yet to understand that Grand Rapids was a far more dangerous place for a boy than Stroobos. Walking across the booms was fairly straight forward for the pike men, who were bigger, stronger, and more experienced than neighborhood urchins. It was only later that we learned that they also benefited from hobnails on their boots.

On a day not long after we arrived, Gerke slipped, falling in before immediately disappearing! The logs callously resumed their previous position where he had slipped, with no sign of him. Fear paralyzed me. Fortunately, his panicked chums thrust their arms in between the logs. Surely guided by Providence, they pulled him sputtering to the surface. They mocked him for being such a poor swimmer, for what, being a Frieslander and all, to which he stared ahead sullenly, shivering. I made myself scarce as he lied to mother about slipping from the bank into the river, which she took in stride, being more upset by the damage to his shoes. If she only knew! We did not even want to think what would have happened if father knew. Gerke might have preferred drowning.

I, too, was young and stupid, but you would think I would have enough sense to give the Michigan Barrel Factory wide berth, but several months later I was playing hide-and seek, crawling around the rick yard on a Saturday afternoon after the crew was gone. I found a spot where no one would find me, a rectangular hole facilitating drying in the middle of a rick pile. While wiggling in, I felt the pile shift, jamming the leg of my pants between two large square-cut boards. I was stuck! I tried crawling back, but my jacket curled back. I was more trapped than ever. I yelled to no avail. Yelling again, my voice became raw, adding to the misery. My friends were long gone. I have no idea how long I was there; I thought for hours, but I am sure it was much less, when I heard a voice, "Hey Dutchie, wha' you doin' in dere?" I was silent, hoping that maybe it was talking to someone else.

Again, "Yo' boy, get outta dere!"

This time, I craned my neck to look up towards the end of the pile to see a black face staring at me. If I were not so confined, I would have jumped out of my skin. After Gerke's brush with death, I thought I too had succumbed: one of Satan's demons had secured his latest prize of a disobedient boy.

"Get your dumb ass outta dere!" Now I was sure it was a demon, because angels certainly did not talk that way.

"I can't," was all I could weakly muster, "I'm..," What was the English word for stuck?

"Well I'm gonna git you' scrawny white ass," he exclaimed, going around to the other end of the rick.

"Well, you all jammed up. I'll go get a po'."

I was completely confused. I was not entirely dead; did people encountered demons on earth? I was still very stuck, but at least I wasn't alone. Pretty soon I could feel him pushing the logs away from my legs, before calloused hands around my ankles dragged me backwards. "I'm a goner now," I thought. "Please Jesus, I will never be bad again!"

Once free, my legs swung down, hoping to find the ground. As soon as they touched down, the demon's hands were around my waist. I prepared to do battle like Jacob wrestling with the angel. "Amerika is a far scarier place than back home," flashed through my head in a perfectly formed Friesian sentence.

At last I was free, but my arms were above my head, confined by my jacket which was pulled inside out. I fell down since my legs had fallen asleep. Looking up at the face towering above me, I screamed. His skin was black! He was a demon!

His language confirmed it, "What da hell ya doin' in my lumba' yard?"

I was speechless, bursting into tears. So much for wrestling with angels or demons!

His face softened as he pulled my jacket down, helping me up on to shaky legs. Then he spun me around, shoved me with his boot, yelling, "Get yo' scrawny ass outta here, boy, and don' le' me eva' catch you again. If I you do, I'll make sho', the debil duz get you!"

I stumbled forward as the blood seeped back into my legs. I made my way through my tears to the hole in the fence before running all the way home. Mother and father accepted that, "I had gotten lost." I felt miserable getting away with another lie so soon after my time of need. I was no better than Peter when he forsook Jesus on the night of his trial. I was very quiet until I got together with Gerke, explaining what had happened.

"No, you dope, that wasn't a demon," he explained. "He's Gus, the barrel company's watchman. He's a Negro, like from Africa." I had never seen anyone with that skin color before. I did not even know that such people existed.

"You're lucky he didn't call the police. You could have gone to jail."

I wasn't so sure. I had gotten away with another lie and felt miserable. That night I prayed, really prayed, finally feeling better. I knew then that Jesus' grace was not merely words floating above me out of "dominie's" mouth, but a real force in life. Exhausted, I fell asleep, wondering what other surprises this new country held in store.

The next day was Sunday. After father finished reading scripture after supper, I spoke up to get attention in the melee that was our table.

"Father, mother, I have a confession," my voice wavered. The table went silent, a rarity as all eyes looked towards me.

"Yes?..." was father's reply.

Continuing in a rush, "I lied yesterday. I was not lost. We were playing hide and seek in the barrel factory, and I got stuck. The watchman, a Negro, pulled me out."

"Herminus, it is a sin to lie. You should have not been where you do not belong. Here in our new country, we must behave so we will be accepted. Since this is the Lord's Day, I will not punish you until tomorrow... Well now, enough of that."

I felt a great wave of relief, fearing no punishment. Having done the right thing, I felt strangely strong; stronger than I ever had before. The next day I don't think he spanked me. It did not matter. I knew I was responsible for myself. I prayed for the strength to meet that commitment. In my little way, I was beginning to understand what it meant to live by faith. That strength was enough for me; I did not need the threat of a paddle to be good.

    A few weeks later, after two days of non-stop rain, the river threatened the banks near our home. In this downpour, from my third floor bedroom, I saw people very active on the Leonard Street Bridge. It was hard to make out what they were doing until I saw they were dipping nets into the river, pulling out large fish. Then I saw that their skin was the same color as the watchman's at the lumberyard. These were not demons, they were only people, people with a funny skin color, but people, none the less, now probably very wet people. When the rain let up, I stole outside. Keeping hidden, I crept closer to hear their banter and laughter. I barely understood a word they said, but was pretty sure that it was in English. At last, I could not contain myself, coming into the open to see their catch. I always loved the taste and color of fish. They asked if I wanted to buy one. I said no, not having any money. Mother said we should not eat any fish from the river because it was essentially the sewer for the city. I hung around for a while, marveling at the immense and tasty looking suckers they were landing, listening to their musical voices. They lived across the bridge in part of town called "Comstock", after the man who had built it. Their proximity to the river and its bounty compensated for the fact that their homes often flooded when the river raised high enough to bring the suckers off of the bottom. I later learned that they had come north after the American Civil War, welcomed as evidence of the North's victory. The Dutch were strong Unionists, cognizant of the rights of any man. Their families were few, certainly fewer than the Dutch arriving daily by train. The large migrations from the South would come forty years later when we all took advantage of the great automotive boom that would sweep across Michigan. Poverty was their plight, but the extreme prejudice of the later time was not rampant in Grand

Rapids at the end of the nineteenth century. I wish I could say that a rainbow came out, but no, the sun did not shine for two more days.

All of the waste from the sewers flowed into the Grand River. Our parents prohibited us from swimming in it. No sane person drank from it. Proximity to the river, however, yielded another advantage to a young boy living in the industrial part of town. The city pumping station was on the route to school. I rehearsed walking the route in anticipation of starting in a few weeks now that my first summer was winding down. A huge flywheel, twenty feet in diameter drove the city's pumps. Two very large steam pistons pushed the flywheel. The boiler inside the brick building fed a tall smoke stack with "Grand Rapids" proudly spelled out vertically in a mosaic of blond brick. Raw water was pumped from the river to a large pipe running to settling reservoir up the hill behind the Ionia Street School. Ideally, there the solid matter settled to the bottom, so that the water delivered to the mains was more clear than green. We knew enough not to drink this water, instead relying on our back-yard wells. The water in the mains pressured the fire-hydrants which were a great improvement over the hand pumping from the canal like they did in Friesland when a house caught fire.

There was nothing better than seeing firefighting in action. Engine House No. 5 was located at the corner of Canal and Leonard streets, immediately to the north of Comstock's Row. Just behind the firehouse was the bridge where I saw the men netting the fish. Each day at twelve noon, the bell rang before the doors of the stables flew open as the firemen led the huge snorting Percherons into their harnesses suspended from the ceiling. At the same time, the fireman sprang from their quarters, sliding down the brass pole polished from years of repetition. As soon as the horses were harnessed, they were driven out the door for a brisk trot around the block. If the alarm was real, we were in for a real spectacle as the horses thundered down the street with the fireman at the rear of the pumper furiously stoking the boiler fire with perfectly-sized small logs, first of pine and then of oak. Nothing matches the sight of a steamer charging down the street, horses galloping at break-neck speed, urged on by the driver's whip, smoke and sparks belching from the engine's smokestack. Maybe this is the origin of the phrase "fighting fire with fire." Hopefully, by the time they arrived at the house, the pumper had enough pressure to supplement that from the hydrant to douse the blaze. Sometimes it was an advantage to be a mile from the firehouse, so that the steam had time to build. Such dramatics were not the usual life of the firemen. I observed them as they sat in front of the firehouse, smoking in their oak captain's chairs tilted against the wall. If lucky, I heard their tales, "...Like the time I was driving so fast, that the suction from the engine lifted the skirts of the ladies on the curb, leaving them standing in their bloomers. Of course, I didn't see it, driving the horses and all, but Michael here can tell you it's true." Though Michael silently nodded his assent between puffs on his pipe, I could not quite accept it as the truth, even if I had seen an engine lifted off its inside wheels when taking a corner too fast.

Mother and Father had spent most of what they owned to come to America. Father needed for this investment to pay. He soon took a job with the Harrison Wagon Works, another of the many factories that grew, literally, from the forests stretching north of Grand Rapids. This was crude unskilled work, in contrast to the high level of craft he practiced in the Netherlands as a painter and decorator. Even though he was almost fifty, father never complained about the physical demands of this job. In the factory, he worked shorter hours than in the Netherlands where he ran his own business. There, he often got up at two hours before sunrise to be at a job before dawn, carrying his tools and supplies. He worked twelve-hour days, so ten hours at the wagon works seemed relatively easy.

Father, as a new immigrant, received his fair share of the practical jokes and hazing that broke up the tedium of the jobs at the wagon works. He often had a leftover in his dinner pail that he shared with me when he walked home from work. This was a treat, both to get a snack before dinner and some undivided attention from the old man. One evening when I opened the pail, I jumped out of my wits as out flew a bird! One of the fellows at the works probably thought this a funny trick to pull on Ole' Dutchie, if not the poor sparrow. It was only later, as I began my own working life with its many opportunities, that I appreciated my Father's gift to his family. He sacrificed his career at its peak so that his children could have better opportunities. Later, he, too, would seize these opportunities. His own business would grow far beyond what was possible in Stroobos.

We stayed on Howland Street for a couple of years. One Sunday, after church and dinner, father announced, "Mr. Vander Meulen suggested, and I agreed, now that we are in America, we should become Americans. We need American names. We all know that when a Yankee sees double Vowels or "J" he will "Kwam terug met hangende pootjes - ...come back with hanging legs." We do not want to do that to our new countrymen. Besides since the authorities think that you are Sipmas here, we can make the switch back to Veenstra."

"Here is what Mr. Vande Meulen and I came up with: Sjierd, you will be Charly, Degina, your name will be Jennie, Klaas, you can be Nicholas, or Nick, as the Americans like to say. Gerke, in English, that would be Gerrit,"

"Where's Hermanus? Oh, over there. We'll call you Harry. Hendrijke is now Reka; Minke, now Minnie; and baby Hendrikus will never know any other name than Henry."

Some of these names made sense. I had no problem becoming Harry, but I thought that Sjierd to Charly was a bit of stretch, but after a month of calling everyone by their old name and then correcting it, we began to get the hang of it. The house was increasingly bilingual as we mixed the languages indiscriminately, except for mother, who was at home more than the rest us, unable to practice her English as much. We adapted to our adopted names as we did to our adopted home, except for Degina who never did became "Jennie", remaining Degina for the rest of her life.

Like most of us, school is where I learned to be an American. If our church and home life still reflected the values of small town Holland, the schools were bursting with American vitality. Our reduced economic circumstance dictated that Christian school was out of the question, not to mention too far a walk, so I enrolled at the West Leonard Street School. However, as this was Western Michigan, the curriculum was imbued with Christian thought to my parent's comfort. We sang overtly Christmas songs over the holidays, including lines like, "Christ our Savior was born today," to no one's objection.

It was there for the first time in my life that I became afraid of a teacher, but not for the reason you might think. Friesians were never the mostly demonstrative of people. Father and mother were kind and considerate. I do not recall Father ever speaking harshly or unkindly to mother, but there was little outward display of affection between them. I never saw father kiss or fondle mother. Even stranger is that I cannot recall mother ever kissing me. The Friesians I knew were the same; it just was not done.

You can imagine my abject terror of my home room teacher who often kissed her children, boys as well as girls. However, she opened her class with prayer, so that was acceptable, as long as she kept her distance. Between black demons and kissy teachers, I wondered if my travails would ever end. I was the oldest child in her room since my poor English was on par with the youngsters. Providentially, I was promoted to the fifth room with Ms. Kettle, who at one time administered a thorough beating. That was not too bad; I was happier with the devil I knew than the one I did not. I appreciated a teacher that keeps her distance. The business end of an eighteen-inch willow switch was close enough for me.

There was little prejudice against us Dutch youngsters. There were enough of us to be a sizable minority. Many of the children who spoke English perfectly had names like deVries or Vander Hough. There was some confusion with our teachers when they asked, "What is the Dutch word for horse?" Having learned formal Dutch in school, I responded "Paard," but David Vander Meulen, having learned nothing but Friesian at home replied, "Hiender". The teachers had no idea how a country as small as Holland could contain two completely different languages. In some cases, Dutch seemed more familiar to the English speakers than Friesian to the Dutch.

My best teacher was Miss Stout, who treated even a rambunctious ten-year old with the respect usually accorded an adult. When caught in a lie (lying being my principal vice as a youth) she chose to ignore it, rather than come unhinged - the normal adult reaction. A friend of mine enjoyed an unusual arrangement to leave class on Thursday afternoons to go to the country to secure eggs from relatives who were too feeble to come to town. Why the school thought this was subject for a legitimate excuse was beyond our feeble ten-year old reasoning, but we reckoned if it worked for him, it may just work for me. He invited me on his excursion, but I would rather stay in class than walk two miles out of town, but did not want to appear the coward. My pal forged a note on my behalf that I proudly presented to Miss Stout.

Looking at the note, she let me know that the ruse had failed, directing, "Return to your seat, Harry." Not another word was said; no switches were brandished, but I promptly returned to my seat. I knew my credibility had been damaged when she later spied me from her second floor aerie, eating an apple as I entered the school grounds. When I entered the classroom, she pounced, "And where is the core, Harry?" thinking I had littered our immaculate hallways. This time I was in the clear, because as a frugal Friesian, I never wasted anything as precious as an apple core. "I ate it," I gulped, not from guilt, but from swallowing the last of the seeds.

As the school year wound down, we were assigned patriotic biographies to research and deliver on the last day before the Memorial Day weekend. Each child was to speak as one of the presidents. Benjamin Harrison, 23rd President of the United

States, held office at that time. I was assigned John Quincy Adams. With great dignity, in a red, white, and blue sash, I took the rostrum for my oration. In the loudest voice I could muster, I proudly proclaimed (in English, of course), "It was during the four years that I was President that the first railroad was built and the first steamship crossed the ocean." So John Quincy Adams is why I was here speaking this funny language. It was his inventions that brought me here. Bully for him! I sat down to what I thought was thunderous applause. After the pageant, sister Degina asked, "Why didn't you speak up? I couldn't hear a word you whispered."

I was an indifferent student, my brilliant oratory notwithstanding. I was as smart as my classmates who took to their lessons, but I could not or did not focus on what was being taught. While I now spoke English easily, its writing drowned in the syntaxes of the three different languages swirling in my small brain. I did not care for the Americans of the last century who were credited with fighting one war or another. I felt no more "free" in this country than in Holland. And our Reformed and Christian life that were the norm in the Netherlands, were here regarded as "foreign" and old-fashioned. I managed learning my sums and long division, blessed with the Friesian gift of making sure transactions balanced. But there was one thing I loved to do: whenever I found a scrap of paper, I was always drawing pictures, whether of the fire engine from Station No. Five or the boom-men on the Grand River. These brought great amusement to my brothers, and every so often, even father took a look.

The school year ended and we were off for the summer holiday. The length of school vacation in America concerned parents who had grown up in the Netherlands. The summer sun stayed up so long in the Netherlands that you could go to school and complete your farm work before retiring to bed. The American summer vacation was a perfect time for Christian education which had been missing from the curriculum in the various public schools that the Veenstra children attended. I missed formal Christian education since our move. It was hard to pick up on the whole span of the Bible from the snippets of the text read during the service every Sunday.

Our summer lessons were not as rigorous as church school in Friesland. Over the summer, mother enrolled us in Vacation Bible School. While the basement of the Clearbrook Christian Reformed Church was cooler than it was outside, the classroom was stuffy. Seminary students from nearby Calvin College taught these courses, their first opportunity to expound on the gospel before their whiskers grew in and they would manage their own consistories. We were good practice. Adolescents and grumpy old men are probably the toughest audiences they would ever face - one doesn't pay enough attention, the other pays too much, and both are obstreperous.

Only sister Reka and I attended; Minnie and Henry were not ready, and the older boys and girls were working. By this time, father had restarted his painting and decorating business, needing all the help he could muster. I don't think Gerrit attended much school after the time he was the age I was then, ten. The seminarian delivered his lessons in Dutch, so that we would retain enough to follow the Sunday sermons still delivered in the mother tongue. Occasionally a visiting minister preached in Friesian, a special treat for young and old. Teaching us was probably not a plum assignment, though I thought than any young seminarian should be thrilled to spend a summer in a muggy church basement with me and fifty of my closest friends. This young man seemed well on his way to being the type of preacher so wrapped up in his work, that if not for his wife, he might preach in the pants he wore painting the kitchen. He was, however, kindly and God-fearing, so I did not mind listening to him if it was not so uncomfortable in the basement.

I soon discovered that I could do as I pleased. There were too many students for one instructor and the recording of attendance was sketchy at best. Reka and I lived too far from home to return for lunch, so we brought it with us. If the weather was nice, after the noon devotional, we ate outside. On a hot afternoon, rather than return to the basement, I suggested to Reka that we walk up Canal Street. We kept going, arriving at the Michigan Soldier's Home, full of the last codgers from the American Civil War. It must have been a terrible war because they looked awful; many missing their limbs, hobbling around on crutches or in chairs with two large wheels in front and small ones on casters in the back. We enjoyed our trips up there, missing the afternoon class once or twice a week. I followed my nose to the bakery, where if we hung around long enough, the bakers shared a treat fresh from the oven.

Though we never were caught and Reka was my co-conspirator for life, the pastor must have realized something was amiss, because next year, we were placed under the tutelage of a professional Christian educator who needed the money. He was not happy spending three more months of the year among howling towheads instead of reading on the porch of a shack by one of the many lakes dotting the forests north of town. Trips to the Soldiers' Home bakery were now out of the question, but there was a smithy across the creek behind the church. One day we spied the front end of a wagon - the wheels, axle and tongue. I cajoled my classmates to haul two of us across the creek with it. Accidentally, or as we believed, purposefully, they let go of the tongue, unceremoniously dumping us in the creek. Soaking wet, there was no escaping our crime. Not having his usual tools of discipline at his disposal, the teacher grabbed what was handy, the consistory's gavel. Peter, my partner in crime, took his punishment first, seriously misjudging his role in the drama, stoically taking his beating. The schoolmaster hit him increasingly harder to elicit a reaction until a blood-curdling scream resulted. I think the schoolmaster knew that he had over-reacted or knew that the consistory would not approve of such an undignified use of their emblem of office, giving me a perfunctory whap. I bellowed like a bull being led to slaughter. Peter did not return the following day and I did not return to Vacation Bible School the following year.

Corporeal punishment (a fancy phrase for spanking) was the norm. My father was as good and as kindly a man as you would ever met, but he was a father. In those days, fathers brooked no disobedience. A mere misdemeanor warranted a few well-placed slaps of the slipper to the fanny, but it was backed-up by the "Klabots" hanging near the back door as a reminder to all boys as they left the house. I cannot translate "Klabots" – I think it was a brand name, since it was written on the handle. Attached to this handle were a number of leather straps, a quarter of inch wide and a foot long. The "Klabots" was among the effects that came to my father from his older brother who had fallen from a troop transport in route to the Dutch East Indies. In the service, this misbegotten tool was used to beat dust from blankets. It was just as effective at beating the bad out of misbehaving boys. When I felt the wrath of the "Klabots", I readily identified with the scourge applied to Peter and Paul preaching in Antioch.

I escaped punishment for my most serious crime, but the beatings one gives oneself are the most effective for learning a lesson. A new house went up next door. One of the families that moved in came from a farm in Zeeland, Michigan. I loved going over there, as their mother was far less strict than mine. We could jump on the beds, after which there was an endless supply of cookies coming out of the kitchen. On baking day, we were given slices of bread fresh from the oven, slathered with butter and sugar. Even to this day, the first slice from a loaf is a special treat.

Like us, they had eight children. I do not recall that the oldest of the bunch ever did much of anything except shoot sparrows, for which the city paid two cents per head. Men earned a dollar or a dollar and a half per day, so a young man who was a good shot could earn a living as a penny-ante bounty hunter. People tolerated the noise of the twenty-two caliber rifle because it was for a good cause. In was inconceivable that he would miss, harming something else.

Their youngest son, Peter, was a year older than me, and we began to pal around. Peter and I became fast friends after the incident of the wagon axle and the creek, since he had bravely borne the ministrations of the schoolmaster. We were the best of friends until a new boy came to our neighborhood, a handsome lad with curly hair, a winning personality, and popularity with the girls. Since I was a little younger, this last dimension to his personality had little appeal to me. We formed a threesome, but I wasn't too happy, a bit jealous I suppose. John, the new lad, got an after-school job helping in a drug store owned by a white-haired elderly gentleman. Peter asked me to keep a couple of dimes and a quarter for him and John. I was pleased that they trusted me. I stashed it in a slot between the stud and the wall in my bedroom. In a few weeks, Peter had another two dimes for me.

One day, when walking to Brice's Slaughter House, Peter and I ducked into the drug store where John now worked every day during summer vacation. We briefly chatted with John until the old man went back into his living quarters for a cup of tea. Saying not a word, Peter pointed to the candy he wanted, which John obligingly handed to him. After we left, Peter told me that I could help myself to the candy, too. I must confess, I took him up on it, but then I worried about the money, becoming afraid. I gladly returned it when Peter asked me about it. I knew where it had come from and was totally petrified. I learned that a filched piece of candy, which has hard to resist, could easily escalate. Morality was not relative. I didn't need the "Klabots" to scare me into becoming the kid I wanted to be. Playing around with a wagon axle was one thing, stealing was entirely another. It was OK to challenge the arbitrary authority of adults, but not God's strictures. I committed to never do it again, even for something as minor as a piece of candy.

Chapter 4

Seven people stood under borrowed umbrellas in the Washington Park Cemetery. It was the first rainy day in months. Summer ended abruptly, and the squall off of Lake Michigan propelled the sheets of rain in torrents.

Why did it have to be him? He was only four years old; he never did anything wrong; he never lied, or filched muffins. I was just starting to take him outside to play. Why does it have to be stupid raining? Not all of us were there. Minnie and Reka were home with diphtheria, the same disease that had taken baby Henry from us. I could not bear to lose them, too. Henry safe in the Lord's grace was far from my thoughts; all I wanted was to keep my baby sisters safe.

Only the undertaker accompanied us. Rev. Hulst did not come, either due to his fear of diphtheria at the advanced age of 67, or perhaps the law prohibited him from coming to stem the contagion. The undertaker, experienced at these things, quoted the appropriate words, but the hearts of this family of believers were too heavy to take much consolation. I saw father, for the first time in my memory, wrap his arm around mother as they staggered down the hill to the buggy where he helped her in. Our faces were all streaked with tears indistinguishable from the rain.

We returned to our new home that we had built on Jennette Avenue. I knew, for the first time, that we were truly home. Home was where you were born and now where you died: our family was now firmly rooted in America. Only Charly would ever return to the Netherlands, and then, only for a month. That summer, diphtheria spread throughout Grand Rapids, striking indiscriminately, taking young and old, Reformed and Catholic, Dutch and Anglo-Saxon. The disease stuck our house, and the three youngest, the most innocent, succumbed. I was spared.

Our grief did not divert us from doing all we could to save Reka and Minnie. We initially did not believe that diphtheria was a killer, but our hearts now carried evidence to the contrary. How could we save the girls? Please God, let it be thy will that they live. Since the disease was highly contagious, I was not allowed to see them. I knew that their throats were swollen, strangling them in a cruel, slow death. God in his mercy sent us hope. Father heard of a certain Mr. Prins, who, while not a doctor, had worked for a physician in the Netherlands. This doctor had devised a remedy that if applied in the early stages of diphtheria had proven effective. At last, a shipment from Holland came to Mr. Prins and he could now share it. This was all done surreptitiously, in conversations whispered in Dutch, since he had no license to practice medicine. Our doctor would not take kindly to what he would think of as a quack meddling with his patients. My desperate parents were not willing to expend their daughters' lives for the niceties of medical protocol. Even if he proved to be a fraud, we had nothing to lose; this strain was lethal, that is all we knew. Mr. Prins came by night. In our part of town there were no streetlights, so one could easily pass unrecognized. The days were shortening. Father persuaded Mr. Prins that he would make it worth his while to come, even to our West Side location. Would he be soon enough?

The girls' reaction to the treatment was immediate. The swelling in their throats subsided. When the legitimate doctor arrived next to examine them, his face lit up with joy and disbelief. So few of his cases had enjoyed any success. He was a Christian; we would not have employed a doctor who was not. No doubt he thanked God in his heart. He came to our house a few more times before pronouncing his patients out of danger. Father used the medicine Prins had given him, but the doctor garnered the credit. However since the prayers of father, Prins, and the doctor were answered, they all acknowledged God as the source of this miracle.

After the girls' miraculous recovery, Mr. Prins looked to Father for help. Mr. Prins lived in southeast Grand Rapids, far from us on the northwest side. Like us, he did not have a carriage or a horse. At the time, there were no streetcars.

"Melle, you must help me, I cannot do it all by myself," Mr. Prins, implored Father.

Father had his own business and was reluctant to do anything that risked running afoul of the authorities, harboring the fear held by any immigrant.

"Melle, who helped you when your daughters were near the end?"

Father could not refuse, so, for as long as people needed help, he became an after-dark angel, helping other Dutch families in northwest Grand Rapids. Along darkened streets, outlined only by the lamps of the houses and the stars in the sky, a mysterious figure lurked, not as a thief, but as a bearer of mercy. Father took not a cent for his mission, neither tiring of painting by day nor tending to the ill by night. Our lives blessedly returned to normal after the epidemic ran its course, but the house was markedly quiet without the boisterous four-year old so drastically taken from us.

With such devastating epidemics a possibility, The Grand Rapids Public Health Department was invested with considerable power. A few years after Henry's passing, another infection entered our house. While this was not as fatal as diphtheria, the G.R.P.H.D. deemed it necessary to post warnings on our house alerting the general public of the danger of the infection within. After the inoculation period, they returned to fumigate the premises. They moved us out before moving in, closing the windows to set off smoke bombs. Knowing the toxic nature of their mission, they promptly left. Mother was beside herself. Ever-enterprising Charly was not going let anybody do this to his mother. Holding a handkerchief across his mouth and nose, he ran in, throwing the offending bombs outside after opening the windows. Our skepticism of the public health authorities was shared by our neighbors, none of whom reported us for what, I am sure, was a serious violation. Again, taking medicine into our own hands proved to be the wisest course.

We did not escape the doctors' tyranny forever. Brother Nick had a weak respiratory system, often needing a prescription to clear his lungs. The doctor came to our house during one of his attacks, writing a prescription for a very bad-tasting compound. In those days, you relied on doctor's prescriptions because patent medicines were entirely unregulated, often doing more harm than good. I took the prescription to the drug store. The pharmacist, knowing that the stuff tasted awful, carefully poured it bit-by-bit into small gelatin capsules. We thought these capsules were of non-dissolvable glass. At home, the patient dutifully emptied each one into a spoon to gag down. Our doctor laughed when he discovered that his patient did not take advantage of the gelatin capsules. Nick was on the mend, so it was hard-earned lesson. The only recompense was the occasional orange that father gave him. The rest of us only saw such a treat at Christmas.

Charly, Nick (when he was able) and Gerrit joined father's painting and decorating business. Our congregation, the Coldbrook Christian Reformed Church, hired him to paint the interior. He was determined that it showcase the breadth of his skill. I was not alone gasping at his transformation of the dingy old interior with the grained oak and faux marbling on round pillars supporting the organ gallery. Many visitors wagged their tongue that it was ostentatious for a Christian Reformed Church to spend money on marble pillars, thinking that they were real stone. I knew that it was not wise to be overly proud, it going before a fall and all, but I could not help it when this work was for the Lord's House. His talent was appreciated and his appointment book soon filled.

With the added income we could buy our own house. We had been renting since moving from Holland, having spent most of our savings just to get here. Now, however, with so much lumber nearby, and so many capable sons, it made sense to build a house. Gerlock and van Bree, a couple of prominent west side Dutchmen subdivided new lots not far from where we lived on Crosby Street. We were by now confirmed Westsiders, as were many other Dutch families. We may have lived in a growing city, but we rarely strayed more than a mile from our church or the cemetery where Henry would be laid to rest. Father was one of the first to purchase these lots, securing a prime location on the corner of Jennette Avenue and the new Myrtle Street. Father paid $600 to have a house built.

The interior was completely unfinished, so essentially we bought a wooden box big enough to live in, but this had been normal in our American houses before this. We four boys slept in our dormitory on the second floor. Our parents wisely rarely ventured into this aerie. Though good God-fearing young men, we were still boys. If our speech and thought modeled "Cleanliness is next to Godliness," our hygiene sometimes did not. In this, we were not alone. Upstairs, our house, like most, had no sink or facilities. We went to the outhouse to relieve ourselves. Our space was one step up from living out of doors: it was stuffy in the summer and drafty in the winter. There were more than a few mornings when upon waking, we found that a fine dusting of snow had blown in onto our blankets.

The main floor of my parents and the girls was finished in a more civilized manner featuring the latest convenience, gas lighting. With the gas jets built into the wall of the house, you never needed to fill lamps, knocking over kerosene and starting a fire. However, we were still not immune to fire. One Christmas, Charly (our family hero, once again) extinguished a blaze ignited by the candles on the tree, but not before the lace curtains erupted in flame, disappearing in a nonce. If he had run into the room a moment later, the whole house might have been lost (but I would have got to see the fire engine). I doubt if my father had purchased anything as frivolous as fire insurance. Our belief was in God, not in men.

On the first floor were a front parlor (for entertaining important guests like the "dominie", who visited annually to assess the spiritual life of the home), a living room, two bedrooms, and a kitchen, supported by a pantry. Attached to the back was an unfinished room where mother did the washing. In this room was a cast-iron pump above the sink. This pump drew water from a cistern below the house, so it did not take many pumps to draw the water. Rainwater from the roof fed the cistern. Even though the new cedar shakes of our roof were relatively clean, the cistern needed yearly cleaning. During the summer dry spell, after we had drawn down most of the water, I, being the right size, was commissioned to scrape out the malodorous mud that accumulated during the year. It didn't dawn on me until much later that I had been drinking this same mud. When I put it on the garden, it did wonders for the tomatoes, which were delicious, so I guess it was all worth it. At the beginning of a rainstorm, we diverted the first few minutes of the runoff onto the lawn. This cleaned the roof, protecting the cistern from dirt and leaves accumulated in the gutters.

The parlor was closed off from the living room by a wide sliding door. It was rarely opened, especially during winter, except for special occasions like weddings, Henry's funeral, or New Year's Day parties. I thought it strange that we never used our best furniture, but understood Mother's logic, because we were pretty hard on the kitchen table and chairs. We spent most of our time in the kitchen. We ate all of our meals there when the entire family gathered. It was the warmest room in the winter, where the wood-fired stove did triple duty heating, cooking, and warming the laundry water. We sat around a table with four sturdy turned legs, supporting the extended leaves drooping on the long cantilevered edges. You dared not put your full weight on the table when excusing yourself from the table for fear of having the entire dinner joining you on the floor. Four matched chairs seated Mother Father and the two oldest girls. The rest of us enjoyed an assortment of sturdy wooden chairs that, over the years, conformed to our personalities. Furniture was easy to come by in Grand Rapids. This is the only town where wisps of sawdust, blown from the nearby factories, littered the gutters. You could not walk around our part of town without a whiff of the pungent smell of wood burnt by a saw.

Sometimes, I think this house was a big decorative box for our stoves. They were the center of the house, a surely a blessing in the winter. Both dominated the rooms they occupied. The kitchen stove was a lovely affair, the source of the baked goods that I adored now that we could afford finely milled flour and sugar. In winter, it was the source of all good things, making the kitchen the center of our family's life. If mother had to bake in the summer, well, I would find something to do outside. Bread would be ready soon.

The living room stove was a far more temperamental beast, haughty in its polished nickel trim; self-important in its job of heating the whole of a very drafty house with no insulation. Michigan winters, if anything, were colder then than they are now. This stove burned anthracite, pulling its weight the entire night without stoking. It extracted its vengeance every spring after a winter of faithful service. Our drafty house consumed a mountain of Pennsylvania anthracite every year. Not all of this combustion made it up the flue. Come April, we disassembled the stove and pipes for a thorough cleaning, so that it would draw well when called upon the following winter. There is no dirtier job.

My brothers and I argued about which was worse, removing the stove in the spring or putting it up in the fall. There is no question where father came down in the matter. In spring, the soot had built up all winter. He had to do the job in the midst of spring cleaning, when there were plenty of decorating jobs to be undertaken. This was the one time when I heard my father say words I had never before heard cross his lips. In order to prevent leaks, the stovepipe fit snugly into the chimney. Being above father's head, it was hard to exert enough leverage to pry it free. As it came loose, he fell back across the room in a cloud of soot. My mother's concern with the mess now to be cleaned (she did have the proper Dutch sense of spotlessness being the only acceptable standard) did nothing to improve father's disposition.

"Die duivelsche pipe! - You devilish pipe." To my young ears, it was the most profane thing I had ever heard him say, but seeing the disarray of the room, I was amazed that he did not say more.

Father was not alone in being confounded by this beast. This stove had isinglass windows through which we observed the coals cheerily glowing inside. Isinglass, processed mica, is quite expensive. Unfortunately, it frequently needed replacement. I had found pieces of celluloid that I thought made a superior stove window since it was cheaper and clearer than isinglass. My thrift went up in smoke, or rather balls of flame, when we lit our first fire of that season. The cold house was soon full of bellowing smoke as one by one, each of the stove's windows erupted in flame. I learned a harsh lesson in flammability, especially regarding celluloid, one of the most flammable materials made. We shivered through a chilly smoky night until I returned to the hardware store the next morning to buy the proper isinglass.

There were no refrigerators then. We chose not to buy ice, which father regarded as an extravagance, so we relied on a "Michigan" cellar for food storage. Under our house, we dug a small room about twelve feet long and ten feet wide into which you could walk. We poured a concrete floor, plastering the sides, leaving a ledge about halfway up upon which we built shelves. On the floor, in a wooden bin, we loaded a winter's worth of potatoes. A smaller bin contained apples. Over the cooler months on the shelves you might find a side of pork (now purchased, not home-raised and butchered) or a tin milk container from which mother skimmed off the cream for her coffee.

After a few years in our new house, father's business continued growing. He and his sons could no longer carry their brushes and materials in the long tool boxes strapped to their shoulders. At first they used a push cart, but this was difficult to maneuver when the streets softened with the slightest bit of rain or snow. A delivery wagon would let them work throughout the entire growing city. He purchased a used closed delivery wagon that soon had "M. Veenstra & Sons - Painting and Decorating" painted on the side in smart gold leaf. I was more interested in the feeble horse we conscripted to pull this enterprise. A horse did not make such a fine friend as a pig, but he was better than nothing. As new horse owners, we unimaginatively called him "Dobbin", a name that fit as well any. His main claim was that he did not die within the year that we bought him, which happened to many a used horse in the neighborhood. The other problem with horses is their large capacities on both ends. They also need shelter appropriate to their rather large size. We put together a rudimentary barn in no time, since the older boys were becoming skilled woodworkers, but the care of Dobbin's alimentary canal was overwhelming, especially since it was assigned to me who was about a tenth of the creature's size. Our fly population, already doing quite well due to our privy, exploded with a new food source, which I shoveled into the bin daily. Why could we not have a nice clean animal, like a pig?

Fortunately, we disposed of this waste before it buried the lot. Farmers were willing to pick up composted horse manure, since there was no commercial fertilizer. The soap factory accepted our ashes. How did something so dirty make you clean? The contents of the privy were a different matter altogether. This was task for the "Honey Dippers", whom we paid. They tipped over the outhouse, extracting the "honey" with a long bucket. The awful smell of the undertaking was masked, with no success, by a pot of burning rags. Everyone had an excuse not to be home on that day, but someone needed to be there to pay for the service, making sure that our vault was ready for another six month's service. I was very impressed with my brothers' successful eloquence convincing my father that I was old enough for this important family duty. I was old enough to hand over the cash, but was no match for my older brothers' rhetorical skill.

Maybe our ignorance protected us. Our privy was no more than forty feet from our shallow well. Grand Rapids is blessed with ample rain, so the rain-fed cistern met our needs for potable water. We drew from the well to wash our clothes with no problems.

Flies were a fact of life. Their diminishment was one more blessing of the first frost in late October. Before then, mother cut one-inch strips from flour sacks and attached them to the stick from a worn out broom. With this shoo-fly, she herded the hordes towards the door that I opened at the last minute. After repeating this several times, the house was relatively free of the incessant buzzing. Later, we had installed screen doors, yet another marvel in America, but you could never free the house completely of the pests.

> A fly and a flea in the flue were imprisoned,
> Said the fly "Let us flee,"
> Said the flea, "Let us fly,"
> So they flew thru a flaw in the flue.

At this time, I played on a baseball team organized by some families in the church - no gloves or uniforms, but a chance for kids to do something other than get into mischief. Our baseball team was challenged by the nine from Zeeland, a small town to the west. I do not recall how the game turned out, but I do remember that our hosts treated us to a meal at the small hotel in their town. This was a big event, since I had rarely not eaten in my mother's or someone else's kitchen. One of my team mates asked that I pass the raisin bread. He was very disappointed when the raisins all flew away.

In the fall, the Dutch farmers hauled their potatoes to town. Families in the neighborhood hastily cooked a sample (Father was our judge) to be sure the taste and texture would survive winter in the cellar. This would be the basis for our dinners until spring, and no one wanted mealy potatoes. The risk went beyond poor flavor, because this was a major investment upon which our nutrition relied. When we lived on Howland Street, we barely gagged down the load we had purchased (our "cellar" there was far more rudimentary), but mother was very creative in doctoring them with vinegar until spring and fresh produce arrived.

Farmers also brought loads of wood to town. Michigan was blanketed by a forest of trees nearly fifty-feet tall. Every year, farmers slowly cut back a little bit more of their woods into productive farm land. They waited until the first snow after Thanksgiving before loading sleds pulled by oxen. These sleds carried a much heavier load than a cart or wagon. The farmers let us attach our sleds for a free ride. You did this at you own peril with a horse drawn sleigh because even though the high speed was a thrill, if you fell, your sled disappeared far down a snowy Michigan road. As in the Netherlands, winter was a time of speed.

The winter night sky was magical. Walking at night, you could make your way by the glow of the sky. A clear night was brighter, because of moonlight or the Milky Way arcing across the sky. In summer, I came in for bed as the last rays of the sun faded. Mother and father relaxed on our front porch, chatting with neighbors, enjoying the profusion of morning glories vining up the trellis. He rocked and smoked while mother cooled herself with a stiff paper fan (maybe courtesy of the local undertaker). Lemonade was a special treat if the train had brought a load of lemons from the South, made with the cool water from the crock in the cellar. The fireflies were borne along by the piano practice of the girl across street who also sang. Her talents were put to good advantage when her suitor joined in duets of gospel and popular songs. For me she was too successful, because they soon married, ending our impromptu concert.

Dim kerosene lamps at each street corner lit the neighborhood. A few years later, gas light brightened things up a bit. Both types of lights required that a lamplighter come by in the evening to ignite them and return in the morning to extinguish them. I watched him silently, but we never said anything to each other, although I saw him several times a week. Grand Rapids had many more strangers than Holland.

I managed the family's kerosene lamps. Maybe father realized that I had a pyrotechnic bent from an early age. I assiduously trimmed the wicks, filling the lamps with a funnel, carefully not spilling a drop. The wood box by the stove needed constant refilling, especially during the winter, when each pie meant two more arm loads. The logs were dropped off at the house sawn, but not split. Each log needed quartering; a chore all of the boys shared. We competed as to who could most precisely split the center, chopping the most uniform quarters in the shortest amount of time.

Socializing with church members was the extent of my parents' leisure life. No time was this truer than around the holidays. Snow and darkness slowed the pace of life, so people readily took time off from the grind that was their lives. This amount of levity struck most as the right balance, because people took great pride in their work, and did not, the men particularly, put great value in chit-chat. However, even the most dour knew that it was kindly to greet the neighbors they had not seen for a while in the dead of winter. Christmas Day was spent at church and at home, but New Year's Day was a time for house visits and socializing, just as it had been in Holland. Apples, hard candy, and cookies were given to the kids. The less conservative families served "Boerejonges - Farmer Boys" an old-country tradition where raisins were soaked in whiskey for several days before serving. Most of the men, not having had a drink all year, were soon looped, thinking it good fun to serve the kids. I suffered the whiskey to get to the raisins, but before long, I was as tipsy as my server. At home, my brothers had a good laugh as I stumbled down the stairs to the outhouse to surrender the mess sloshing around inside my stomach. From that day, the appeal of alcohol has eluded me, a blessing for which I will be forever grateful.

I had to live with that bad taste in my mouth, since at this time we had not learned oral hygiene. While visiting a friend, I noticed his older sister put some white powder on to a small brush that she shook actively in her mouth. She explained that this cleaned the food from her teeth. Oh, how wished I had such an elixir on that fateful New Year's Day, but God obviously had a more punitive plan for me. I suggested to mother that we might want to take advantage of such modernity, but it was not until I was adult that I brushed my teeth regularly. Childhood remained a succession of toothaches, fillings, and the killing of nerves. Mother was oblivious to this because dental problems never bothered us in the Netherlands. It was not until we moved to Michigan that we could afford sugar.

I became aware of life beyond our home. There were churches other than our own, and other people than the Dutch in Grand Rapids. These sectarian divisions were pronounced. People jealously promoted and protected the values of their ethnic group. If America was a "melting pot", there were still many solid clumps within it. Nowhere was this truer than in the politics of the day. Men took their party affiliations seriously; or if not seriously, at least dramatically. Candidate's parades were spectacular, one of the few forms of entertainment available to us with our strict religious practice. The participants marched in tall stovepipe hats provided by the parties - the Democrats wearing gray, the Republicans in a more dignified black. Parades took place at night. The marchers carried torches made up of a six-foot long stick with a burning kerosene soaked rag on the end. I delighted in all the flame, smoke, and smell. Some of the torches had a little tube through which the carrier blew a stream of flame another three feet above the torch. Voter turn-out in America would improve these days if we brought back the delight and danger of burning kerosene. I recall the year that Grover Cleveland ran against Benjamin Harrison. I did not know a single Hollander who was a Democrat. I did not believe that a person could be a Christian and a Democrat. Walking to school we chanted:

Harrison on a white horse,
Cleveland on a mule,
Harrison to the White House,
Cleveland going to school.

We were the only ones going to school; Harrison served his one term; Grover Cleveland returned to the White House for his second.

Father, hoping that I would learn things more important than the presidents and politics, joined a committee organizing to build a new Christian school. He was elected treasurer, but with his expanding new business, needed help performing his duties. Made up mostly of immigrants, the Dutch community was of modest means. In order to undertake such an ambitious project as building a school, a subscription campaign was initiated, whereby families pledged to give a modest amount weekly. As father now worked every Saturday, he asked me to collect the pledges. This was a chore, especially when I heard through the window of one of the homes on my route, "Daar komt die kliejne aap weer aan – Here comes that that young ape again." I knew that anyone collecting money among the thrifty Dutch would be unpopular, but I thought this was bit extreme. Father had a book where I recorded the weekly dues, sometimes amounting to a dime, a trifling figure now, but then part of a family's weekly budget. Occasionally I was asked to come back later in the week when the dime would be available. Men worked sixty hours per week for a dollar a day, so a dime represented an hour's worth of work. Through this sacrifice and determination, we raised enough money to build the school. In my case, they should not have bothered. One girl and I comprised the seventh grade. The teachers were so disorganized that I learned next to nothing. Being part of the oldest class in the school, I assisted with the younger children but got to be with my younger sisters, Reka and Minnie.

Other than being with the girls, I was miserable and angry with my Father's poor decision regarding my education. Questioning his judgment was not permitted, especially after all his work in the founding of the school. If there was anything to be gained, it was in the friendships that I would value for the rest of my life. Richard Broen was the son of the Rev. Gert Broen, pastor of the Crosby Street CRC. When I first started attending school, mother did not let me walk barefoot. In the Netherlands we always wore "klompen", removing our shoes at the door to scoot around inside in stocking feet. Only the poorest children were barefoot. When she saw a minister's son walking to school barefooted, her son could too. Of course, Richard and I were ready to be re-shod come the end of September. Walking to school with us was Lee Huizinga, who was a year younger. For amusement, Lee brought two pet white mice to school. Our teachers never discovered his contraband, or were too overburdened to care. Little did I know that this fun loving kid next to me would go on to become my pastor and a martyr.

Eventually, my father realized that the school did not live up to its promise. After a semester, he re-enrolled me in the public school back on the West Side. Before, I enjoyed good grades, but now struggled in grammar after the wasted semester. If I had been blessed with attending high school, no doubt I could have caught up.

My religious education grew out of the church and home. When we first arrived in Grand Rapids, my parents documented that they were communicants of the "Nederlandse Hervormde Kerk", joining the Coldbrook Christian Reformed Church. In America, not dependent on state support, the conventicle congregations had split from the Reformed Church in America to form their own separate denomination, the CRC. Coldbrook had been formed because the congregants were not pleased when their former church permitted members of Masonic orders as members. We are taught that the Lord our God is a jealous god. Many CRC members believed that the secrecy and mushy divinity of Masons ran counter to the monopoly on theology that was central to our faith. My parents were more comfortable in this more conservative branch of Dutch religion, as was I, with some exceptions, for the remainder of my life. We worshiped at Coldbrook until the year Henry died. Maybe because the new church was closer to our new house, or maybe because father was not pleased that Rev. Hulst did not come to Henry's burial, father and mother joined the Alpine Avenue C.R.C. In any case, I was ecstatic. This church had a great Sunday school; was growing and dynamic, and to my mind, Rev. Ekster was easier to understand as a preacher. His sermons were straight-forward in the explication of God's action in the world, not branching into half-dozen supporting points in scripture. His sermons illuminated how God's plan affected our daily lives. He let the Calvin professors display the theological wizardry, citing over eight supporting texts in any one sermon. Instead Rev. Ekster focused on "Are you saved? Here's how to know, and if not, what to do about it." Though CRC pastors cite the entire Bible, Rev. Ekster made sure that our focus was on the gospel, augmented with the Epistles.

Mother still asked, "Heb je centenen en Pepermenten?" as we grabbed our pennies for the offering and the fat round peppermints. The mints were a Saturday gift from our grocer. Mom said that her father did the same thing at his store in Groningen. Once we were in our pews, the consistory, led by the pastor, walked in single file, sitting in the front pew facing the pulpit. The pastor before taking his seat facing the congregation, shook the hand of the chairman of the consistory. A consistory of the most revered men presided over each church, making sure it met its obligations and that the preacher followed the doctrines of the church. At the end of the service, the pastor shook hands with each of the elders. If one of them refused to shake the pastor's hand, indicating displeasure with the sermon, he and the pastor met privately. Pastors walked a fine line, being spiritually responsible for these men, but also answering to them. Dutch Reformed Churches are among the most vigorously democratic religious institutions you will ever encounter. During the congregation prayer, aptly referred to as the "long prayer", the elders and men all rose and remained standing the length of its duration. Fortunately, this was not required of children, women, and the other less exalted of the congregation. Keeping your eyes closed was hard enough.

Men sat on one side of the aisle, women and small children on the other. When we boys reached an age when we were no longer to sit with our mothers, we selected pews as far back as possible. The pastor probably appreciated this courtesy, as well. The services were still in Dutch, but if you spoke this language since age five, this was completely natural. I consider Dutch as my liturgical language, like Latin with the Catholics. Alpine Avenue was billed as the Friesian Church, because many of us hailed from the northern part of the Netherlands, but as it grew, so did the representation from Groningen, Zeeland, and Drenthe.

Many newcomers were not acclimated, complaining about the extremes of heat and cold. In the summertime they found the heat oppressive. Coming to church, they drank from two pails of water, using common dippers, not worrying about the germs. Church here was as cold as in Holland. I guess the Reformed tradition believed that we would be warmed upon hearing the Lord's word. Spiritually I am sure this was true, but my flesh itself was immune from the blandishments of the Holy Scripture. After services, congregants brought their frozen faces to life by washing with a refreshing mitten full of snow.

The Alpine Avenue Church grew until there was not enough room to hold everyone in the sanctuary for services. To accommodate the crowds, wide boards were attached along the outer walls with hinges so they could be swung up to hold the overflow. A hinged triangular brace swung out to support these boards. These seats were swung out of the way later in the day for the afternoon or evening service when attendance diminished. These seats were not comfortable by any means, but were popular with boys and young men. No one could look over your shoulder, allowing many a boy to while away the service reading a more interesting story tucked inconspicuously into his derby, the hat style popular at the time. The "koster - custodian" sat with us to keep order, but he could not patrol behind us, so sitting in those seats was pretty safe.

Reverend Esker elicited a good response from the expanding flock, in spite of the lack of creature comforts. Twice the sanctuary was expanded. For all that I liked Rev. Ekster, I missed the elegance of our old Coldbrook church with father's graceful decoration.

I loved this church, because for the first time, there were programs specific for children. A "Sunday School" was instituted, rectifying the void in my religious education since church school in the Netherlands. In addition to hearing Bible stories in their entirety, not just chopped up into verses as part of "the lesson", Sunday School was an opportunity to meet new friends. I was amazed that something associated with church could be fun, but once a year, in the summer, the church took us on the Sunday School picnic. The picnic was located on an island in the Grand River, so the church engaged a small steamboat to take us there. I was thrilled to once again return to "sea", so the trip was as much fun as the picnic. As with my other experiences with water-borne craft, my joy was to be short-lived. Since the steamboat was not large enough to carry all of us, some of us were pulled behind on a barge. Too many rushed to the bow of the barge, yelling and waving to friends in the boat, until it foundered below the surface. The weight of the water coming over the bow pushed the barge toward the bottom. I was about a third of the way towards the bow. My first thought was to protect my shoes from the oncoming water. I no longer wore wooden shoes in Grand Rapids. Even if my high-topped leather shoes were cheaper here through the mail-order catalog, my first duty, once out of the house, was to protect them. Growing up along the canal and river, I knew to bolt for the stern. Right next to me was a girl a few years my junior, decked out in an innocent white smock that would be ruined by the mud up swirling the deck. I grabbed her, yelling "Come on!" accidentally in Friesian, but she understood immediately. In four or five steps, we were safe for the moment. It dawned on me that she had understood me, but in all of the confusion I did not think of it again. A crew member on the boat saw the problem. Immediately, he chopped the tow rope, averting a catastrophe. Adrift, the barge floated to surface, as the other children scrambled to join us in the stern. We were soon reattached and properly distributed, to make our way to the island grove. The girl was gone, off with her chums in a cloud of white lace.

What fun we had on shore! I was not old enough to be interested in the games where girls participated, but competed in three-legged and gunny sack races. I was fast enough to garner a blue ribbon or two. With this superior speed, I also caught a small furry native of the island, but was not quick enough to elude its bite, nursing a bleeding finger on the trip home. In those days, nobody gave a second thought to rabies, figuring that any kid dumb enough to be bitten got what was coming. However, the fun was worth cost of near swamping and rodents bites. I marveled at how different church activity in America was than back in Stroobos. There, church consisted of the services and nothing else. You can imagine my delight in finding a church that cared about me as a child, combining lessons with a chance to have fun with my friends without getting into mischief in the lumber yards.

Chapter 5

"Question 20: Are all men then, as they perished in Adam, saved by Christ?"

"Answer: No; only those who are ingrafted into him, and receive all his benefits, by a true faith."

Rev. Ekster was asking the questions; we, a group of young people, were answering them. In preparation for joining the church we undertook the program of learning the correct responses to the 129 questions of the Heidelberg Catechism. This educational program, drafted in the year 1563, is a pillar of the Reformed faith wherever it is practiced. It sums up and elucidates the tenets of the belief in salvation through God's grace, and God's grace alone. Memorizing the answers to the catechism is a major rite of passage for the young men and women of my church. One cannot join the church without being able to answer any question in the catechism before a panel of elders. Not joining the church is unthinkable. Though the rest of my life outside the church is conducted in English, these classes, as are our services, are conducted in Dutch, with a large helping of Friesians asides in recognition of the large number of immigrants who make up our congregation. By the end of this instruction, I will have a thorough understanding of Reformed doctrine that will hold me in good stead for the rest of my life.

Rev. Ekster, overworked from growing our church and preaching three sermons every Sunday, chose to teach boys and girls simultaneously. The difference in the range of pitch of the voices would be amusing except for a subject matter that lends little to hilarity, no matter how hard the minds of teen-aged boys might try. The time after catechism classes was one of the few times that young people could flirt and socialize without interference from their parents. Rev. Ekster minimized the peril of such a reckless situation by dismissing the girls fifteen minutes early, but they are as motivated as the boys to mix, so they wait outside until we were released. Later I realized that Rev. Ekster walked a fine line between keeping his young flock separated, but not too much so that they did not find potential mates with the proscribed circle of our church.

"Question 21: What is true faith?"

"Answer: True faith is not only a certain knowledge, whereby I hold for truth all that God has revealed to us in his word, but also an assured confidence, which the Holy Ghost works by the gospel in my heart; that not only to others, but to me also, remission of sin, everlasting righteousness and salvation, are freely given by God, merely of grace, only for the sake of Christ's merits."

Satisfied with our response, Rev. Ekster releases us for the evening. I make my way to the door with as much casual haste as I dare. Hattie Lindemulder, the girl whose hand I grabbed on the barge was chatting in a circle of her friends. There, she briefly glanced my way. Hattie was no longer in a girl's smock with a large bow, but was now in a smart shirt waist with her hair drawn up under a brimmed hat. Just like my mother's, her family was from Groningen. I knew she thought I was still "country", but that she appreciated my quick action on the barge. I stood with a circle of five boys, glancing furtively her way, elicited a glance. As her circle broke up, she walked by saying, "Hello, Harry." My heart skipped a beat, as I bleated, "Oh, hello to you, too, Hattie." She continued on her way. I was thrilled to have spoken with her but mortified by my awkward response. Hopefully, under the gaslight, she did not notice my flushed face. I had noticed her again earlier that year at the Sunday School picnic. This time, I was not chasing rodents; now an eager participant in the games with the girls. Again, a little of Rev. Ekster's magic was at work. Our favorite was drop-the-handkerchief, which was an ideal way to denote an innocent interest. We both dropped the handkerchief behind each other; but not too often as to suggest any exclusivity amongst our friends.

Later at the picnic I experienced a very scary moment. I saw Hattie talking to a very severe looking woman. My heart sank. If she was her mother, what chance would I have? What if she grew up to look like that? I left the picnic confused. I might have felt better with a rodent bite. My little heart was still thumping, but now with ice water. Maybe drop-the-handkerchief was a little too high stakes for me. It wasn't until we were leaving the park that I saw her real mother, a perfectly lovely woman. My heart soared again. But this time, I was a little more circumspect, standing quietly as I observed them walk away.

Father was not feeling well. All of the early mornings and late nights carrying heavy loads in damp climates had taken their toll. He could barely move, confined to his chair for days at a time, wracked with pain. The doctor came, directing father to grasp two handles connected to a device made up of a spool of coiled wire a little over a foot in diameter. The doctor whirled a wooden handle extending from the center of the wires. Father grimaced as his arms stiffened. After an endless couple of minutes, the doctor relented from this torture. Father relaxed, gently putting the handles down. He experienced relief for several hours from this treatment, but soon his arthritis would flare again.

The nation as a whole was in a "panic". The U.S. Mint no longer minted silver into currency free of charge. Jobs became hard to find in the previously booming city of Grand Rapids. Back in Friesland, where nothing ever changed, bad times were marked by bad harvests, meaning fewer life-sustaining potatoes. Here in America, cash was king. Everything depended on a family's income. It was now time for me to do my part.

Because of father's condition and the Panic, our family's financial condition was again perilous, so I took advantage of summer vacation from school to look for work. I was thirteen. I joined brother Nick at the Kent Furniture Company where he worked as a cabinetmaker. We worked 60 hours a week, from seven in the morning to six at night, with an abbreviated lunch hour. Saturdays, we worked only until five o'clock. That extra hour seemed like a holiday. This was the time for men to be shaved at the barber to be ready for church. Before his arthritis, father shaved daily with a straight razor to look presentable for his clientele. The men in the factory cared not if they impressed the foreman with their grooming, shaving maybe once a week. Many Dutchman still favored beards, unlike the English speakers who opted for mustaches or going clean-shaven. At thirteen, my whiskers were yet to come.

I was paid $3.50 for a week's work; less than nine cents per hour. I gave my seven dollars to mother, proud of contributing my share to the family. Of this, she returned seventy cents as my own. I think the factory owners favored Dutch employees since we were all Republicans, regarding unions as a tool of the Democratic Party. Rugged self-determination was not just a Friesian trait, but extended to all Dutchmen. Collective action took place only within the church. Each family looked after itself with dignity and pride. The native English speakers in the factory were more interested in organizing around labor issues.

The work in the factory was rough for anyone, but particularly for a boy. I tended a deafening rip-saw. I stood behind the saw, sorting and stacking the boards coming off the blade. This was not difficult if the saw operator worked at a steady pace, as did the other rippers. Unfortunately, my ripper spent a lot of time on the toilet, breaking the tedium. The toilet was a long structure, cantilevered over the river, so that all waste floated off as someone else's problem, the prevailing attitude of the day. On a summer's day, this was a quiet respite from the factory floor. There I heard tales that first confused and then embarrassed me. Not all of my fellow employees belonged to the Christian Reformed Church. It dawned on me that some did not belong to any church, the first time in my life that I ever confronted someone ignorant of God's grace. My ripper's habits put him so far behind the production schedule that upon his return, he shoved the trunk sections through at a furious pace. Being small, I had a hard time of it keeping up with the speed. My work piled up, making me, not him, look lazy and inefficient. The pay came too slow and the lessons too fast. I grew quickly, in more ways than one.

I should not have even been there. Newly passed laws restricted factory work to boys fourteen and older. Nobody asked, knowing that a Dutch kid would get the job done without asking too many questions. From the ensuing carnage, I soon found out why I was so easily hired. Many of my fellow workers were missing fingers, a commonality in Grand Rapids. I kept my wits about me at all times, but it was difficult as fatigue set in near the end of the shift. That summer, I saw all the fingers on a man's right hand sheared off in a "buss planer" faster than you read this sentence. One moment he was a whole man; disfigured the next. It did not end there. A sander grabbed the sleeve of one man's jacket. Before the machine was disengaged, his arm wore off in a pink mist. For once, I was glad the din of the machinery muffled his scream. Near our rip-saw, another man operated the cut-off saw, which cut the logs into lengths we could manage. This saw was driven by a large leather belt connected to the whirling power drive above us. These belts extended throughout the factory, never stopping. One Thursday, a belt snapped, felling the man as he stood. He was back at work on Monday, needing the income to support his family.

A primitive elevator carried carts loaded with lumber between the two floors. Late in August, on a brutally hot day, Bill Harmon, too old for any job but as a "lugger", rolled a fully loaded cart of lumber onto the elevator. No sooner did the cart clear the floor than the cable snapped, dropping Bill and the car directly to the basement. When we arrived at the basement, his bald head was split open, reminding me of the globe in my classroom; only now the oceans were drawn in blood.

Returning to school that fall was a relief. I was actually happier for the endless amounts of free time, especially on Saturday, than from escaping the carnage. As young as I was, I barely recognized the impact of the daily bloodshed I had witnessed. I was now the "hard man" amongst my classmates, but they did not relate to my blood-soaked tales, and soon we all returned to more mundane subjects like construction of a new streetcar line to the Westside, or Rev. Ekster's hair.

The extension of the streetcars to our neighborhood led to an interesting theological discussion with my parents. We and everyone in our church strictly observed the Sabbath, not performing any work. I polished my shoes on Saturday night, so as not to perform this "labor" on the Lord's Day. This prohibition extended to not riding streetcars, because our fare required the motorman to work, operating the car. No one in our church could be a motorman or conductor, since the job required working on Sunday. This was disappointing to me, because, for a while, I thought that riding the rails around town collecting money from people could be a very interesting career choice. One Sunday morning, while standing near the corner of Leonard Street and Alpine Avenue, I was shocked to see Professor Rev. Gerrit E. Boer step off of the streetcar to walk the short distance to our church where he was guest preaching. That the most honored and revered minister in our denomination could ride the streetcar on Sunday and my parents would not posed a dilemma to me. After church, I asked my parents about this discrepancy. After what felt like a minute, father replied, "He was on the Lord's business and he had no other way to get here from where he lives on the East Side near the Calvin Seminary. Our church was honored to hear him. Didn't you think he gave a good sermon?"

"Couldn't he have walked?" I suggested.

"Harry, it is not up to you to determine how our ministers spend their time," father concluded, but I was pretty sure he was as conflicted about this as was I. No matter what issue of church protocol arose in the future, or had arisen in the past, our family was more comfortable in the certainty of the more conservative side. However, my parents would never criticize a minister in front of their children.

Near our home lived a man who bought rags, iron, bones, and other scrap material that he collected to resell to the factories. Brother Gerrit explained that he was a "Jew" with a bit of a sneer. While I understood that Jews were not Christian, I knew that Jesus was a Jew, in addition to all the heroes in the Old Testament, so I thought he should be treated with respect. His son was my age, hanging around with my gang of neighborhood pals. We named him "Raggy", which he accepted with quiet grace. He was an immigrant, too, from where, I am not sure. He certainly was not Dutch and his English was worse than the rest of ours. Scouring the neighborhood for scrap to sell to Raggy's dad was a way for us to earn a few pennies. We ranged about, looking for anything not tied down that Raggy's dad might buy. The railroad tracks were good pickings to the point where some of the older boys climbed up on a boxcar, wrenching off the cast iron brake wheel from the top. They then hurled the wheel with all of their might at the adjacent track in the hope of shattering it. Iron brought a better price than rags, bones, or other scrap we found. If the rag-picker recognized the source of our iron, he made no mention of it. We delivered our finds to the barn behind his house where he weighed it. He wrote the value on a scrap of paper that we took into the house for payment by his wife. One of my friends, who went on to be an elder in his church, occasionally slipped a 1 or 2 in front of the amount, garnering an extra dime or two. People like to accuse Jews of their sharp business practices, but they do not hold a candle to a pious Dutchman. When my friend, the elder, later ran his grocery store, I asked if I could erase a 1 or 2 from the front of my total.

Walking along the tracks of the Grand Rapids and Indiana Railroad was not for the faint of heart. If the rag-picker did not know the source of our iron, the railroad bulls certainly did. We waged an ongoing turf war with them over the tracks. What they had in age, size, and authority, we countered in numbers, speed, and guile. They might drive us off momentarily, but this was our neighborhood, so we always returned. They were tied to the tracks, we were not. We executed a major coup in this struggle when Raggy loosed a pebble from his slingshot at a handcar whizzing by. When hit, the railroad man had pushed his handle to the bottom of its arc with his dungarees tightly stretched across the target, which Raggy solidly struck, if the reaction was any indication. The railroad men could not let this indignity go unpunished, but by the time they arrested the momentum of the heavy handcar, we were long gone.

Our free time was not spent entirely in unproductive pursuits. Charly and Nick built a shanty in our backyard. This was the perfect clubhouse for boys. We cobbled it together from scavenged scraps of the plentiful wood. Harder to come by were the necessary tools, but these, too, could be found or purchased used for a few pennies. We equipped the shanty with a small stove and a bench, permitting year-round occupancy. We convinced father that this was a good place to perfect the skills we would need to further our careers. I suppose I did learn some good handiwork, but to me, it was just a perfect hangout. Patterns for a great variety of household products were available then in hardware stores. Following these patterns, the older boys started small scale, but before long, they made real pieces of furniture. Never had a street-gang turned out such a high level of craft. Nick built a bookcase indistinguishable from a factory-built piece. In service of his skill, he had great patience, not stopping until his work was perfect. He sanded the pieces endlessly until they fitted together on their own. Glue was just an afterthought. Charly's masterpiece was a floor clock, five feet high. The pediment featured very delicate scroll work, laboriously cut by a hand jig saw. The sides were bent wood. Charly soaked the boards in hot water until he could bend them in his jig. However, the wood would not be willed, and the elaborately carved piece snapped in two. He bought another piece, again spending a week sawing and sanding, only to have it snap again. Grabbing his hammer, he almost smashed the nearly completed work, before Nick grabbed his arm. The third time and Nick's help were the charm. The piece keeps time to this day in the home of one of Charly's sons.

Not all of our hi-jinx ended so well. The abstract lessons of life and death on the factory floor would now strike much closer. A small creek in open farm country near our home was a favorite swimming hole. It was a clear, cold spring-fed stream. After the first shocking plunge, it was very refreshing to our skinny naked bodies. But it was big enough for us to learn to swim. Or what we thought was swimming. I did not take a formal swim lesson until I was an adult. We all taught each other more or less how not to drown as we cooled off on those hot summer days, but we made sure we never got too far from the bank.

Swimming in the Grand River, with its currents, snags, and muddy smelly demeanor, was strictly forbidden. After my work breaks at the furniture company, my parents did not need to tell me twice. However, brother Gerrit, being older and bolder, dragged us to spot that he said was safe and clean. The location was near a sawmill whose booms allowed our easy access to the water. When would Gerrit learn to steer clear of sawmills? In a moment, we piled our clothes on the logs in the booms to dive in. Here we could really swim, not just splash around. Raggy challenged me to swim across the river to the far bank.

"Come on Harry, I swam it before," he implored in his accent.

"No, Raggy, it's too far."

"No, there's a place to stand in the middle."

"You mean a sand bar?"

"Yes, a sand bar, I'll show you and then you come."

Everyone else was already in the water so they did not hear him to stop him. He set off. After paddling out to where he thought the sand bar was, he was still in deep water, drifting away in the current. He called for help, realizing that any refuge was a long way off. His cries became more plaintive as he drifted further. There was nothing we could do to help. He panicked and started thrashing. Then he disappeared. Forever.

We all stood for in dumb silence before yelling wildly to the men in the mill who ignored us. Previously, other boys who were good swimmers had gone out to the middle of the river to call for help, only to swim back when they received the desired reaction of the launch of the mill's boat. Now just like in the story, the "wolf" appeared for good when the guard was down. Raggy was gone and we were scared to death because it happened on the forbidden river. We dressed hurriedly, before realizing that one ragged pile clothes remained unclaimed. Bravely, Gerrit picked them up as we hurried back to our neighborhood. Shocked out of our wits, we left Raggy's clothes on his back porch before running all the way the home.

At home, Gerrit and I did not know what to do, so we did nothing. We were sure that a long session with the *Klabots* was in the offing. But nothing happened. We were not going to go to the police to tell them we had been swimming in the forbidden river. I am not sure that Raggy's parents contacted the police either. Maybe they were afraid of the authorities as we were as teenaged boys. Perhaps my parents were grateful that their "baby boy" (now me with Henry's passing), had been spared. More likely, they didn't know we had anything to do with the "missing Jewish boy". Raggy's body was never found, so the authorities lost interest quickly. Drowning is what happened to boys who swam in the river.

Having lost my own brother, I felt for Raggy's parents tremendously. I agonized over this, but I had no one to whom I could confess. My parents and pastor were all too scary. Our older brothers would just tell our parents. Instead, it festered in my heart for years. A boy is lost; a family is shattered and all that remains is guilty glances between five boys. Would I ever be strong enough to be a good Christian? I prayed for forgiveness, but without a public confession, I was unsure if God would forgive me. For the first time in my life, I felt the lash of Satan's whip and beseeched Jesus for the power to overcome it.

Chapter 6

Though I was still a very young man, I feel that my life as an adult began when we moved above father's new store on West Leonard Street. Father had always sold painting and wallpaper supplies to supplement his livelihood as a painter, but the sales alone, especially in Friesland, had never been enough to sustain us. Besides, his skills were often in high demand. However, his arthritis now prevented him from working the long days that were the norm of his adult life. Grand Rapids and our community on the West Side had expanded enough that he believed it could support a retail establishment dedicated to decorating.

We rented our Jennette Street house before moving into the second floor of a building on Leonard Street, a major thoroughfare in northwest Grand Rapids. It was in this new location that I formed my ambitions for life, cultivating whatever gifts I have as an artist. I had always loved to draw. I could now experiment with an endless supply of scrap paper and paint. Mother and father indulged my passion, often wondering what I was doing, but I was still the "baby" boy. The older boys were mostly out of the house, seeking their own fortunes.

I started out assisting brother Nick on our family's painting jobs. The biggest thrill was harnessing Dobbin to pull the wagon to the correct location. This was not a difficult task, since as an old horse, Dobbin responded to the tugs and pulls of a rookie driver. However, he was anything but spirited, so we planned our workday accordingly. Owning a slow horse meant for many an early morning to arrive at our job site on time.

Though I possessed a steady hand, learning to "cut-in" a contrasting edge of paint as well as anyone in the family, father needed me in the store. As the youngest brother, my English was the best, so I was valuable in serving our English-speaking customers. Once his factory life was behind him, father spent most of his time in the Dutch community, little needing to learn more English. My school life was entirely conducted in English, but church kept my Dutch sharp. Father managed well enough in English, but it was hard work. I overheard him once waiting on an "American", as we called our English-speaking customers, impressed at how well he did. However, he was a perfectionist, hating to do any job, even selling wallpaper to a customer, that he had not mastered. He believed in giving his best to each and every customer. This he considered his Christian and professional duty. Though he tried to do each job as smartly and efficiently as possible, he never took a short cut in his life. He considered that overheated emotion, whether being too angry or too happy, conflicted with his focus on getting the job done. Although he was not overly demonstrative, I thought that he was the best and fairest father a fella could have. Sometimes, I wish I could quiz him on what he was thinking, but in those days, the gulf of privacy between parents and children was just not crossed. Though I lived with him every day, there were many parts of his life that I did not understand, but I appreciated that he was fair, kind, and God-fearing.

I must have tried his patience as I showed as little aptitude for clerking as I did for papering and painting. True, I was only fourteen at the time, so I did not have an aptitude for much except hanging out along the train tracks or the river. I was now of an age where my presence in those places would garner a lot more attention from the authorities than I had at age nine. I was now old enough that I could get into more mischief than previously, which was plenty. Besides, I was now a family asset and expected to pull my weight. I just needed to find something that I liked to do.

I could not abide showing wallpaper to women. The patterns all looked alike to me as the women pawed endlessly through the pattern books before making a selection. Wallpaper was the wall covering of choice back then because paint, made with linseed oil, was expensive and slow drying. People preferred the exotic patterns of wallpaper, which decorated their walls with repeated scenes or designs of infinite variety. Houses of this era featured rich visual interest, full of as many elements to catch the eye as the homeowner could afford. Mother was no exception, as our once simple Dutch house became cluttered as she could afford more furnishings. Everything remained spotless, however, in spite of the need for more dusting. She was relieved that we now lived on a soon to be paved main street.

Father adapted to American business ways. A printer friend in our church convinced him that if he distributed handbills, customers would flock to the store. The printer failed to mention that distribution was needed. My father, now with a stack of handbills neatly bound in manila twine, looked about the store where his eyes fell on me. I thought this was the most unpleasant task that could be imagined; worse than wallpapering (which was pretty dreadful) and worse than hauling out wallpaper books for a disaffected customer. I am not sure why I complained since it got me out of the store. My brothers claimed that I was lazy and good for nothing. I felt like Joseph, banished from his family to the far reaches of Egypt. I would show them! If I did not return with a coat of many colors, at least I would distribute the handbills in record time. I set out, avoiding dogs and the housewives who thought that the offer of the most excellent services of M. Veenstra and Sons was nothing more than litter. Did they not know they insulted the very honor of my family? Judging by the tone of their voice and barks, they did and intended to. After first running, then walking, and finally trudging for eight blocks, I realized that my stack had barely diminished. I saw that the entire span of my life consumed with the distribution of one printer's run of handbills. I could never outpace the speed of the printing press.

Deliverance was at hand. Next to our building, a new house was under construction. One afternoon, as I set out on my detested rounds, I noticed that the carpenters were gone. I sprinted up to the second floor in the partially completed structure. In this part of the house, I spied a gap between the outside wall and the floor that seemed ready for handbill distribution. Surely, if someone looked into this gap, they would need the services of a nearby decorating firm. A few extra flyers, say a hundred or so, would drive home the point. Later in life I learned that repetition is an important part of advertising.

My entire day's quota of handbills was gone before I confronted the enormity of my crime. First, what would I do for the rest of the afternoon? Anybody who saw me would know I was not distributing handbills. Going through the motion of distributing handbills would be just as bad as if I had not stuffed the lot down the wall. Even worse, what if the bills were found? I developed a new found interest in the pace of construction. Every single piece of paper had the name and address of the litterer and could easily be returned if found. I noticed the progress with great satisfaction when the carpenters returned. I have always thought of it as "my house", doing anything to keep it standing. Last I looked, it was still next to where the paint and wallpaper store stood for many years. I considered that if it came on the market, I would have to buy it to protect its secrets. I knew that if my father occasioned to show mercy, my brothers in the business would not. Somehow our business survived without all of the handbills being distributed, and I knew that my talents would be better utilized elsewhere.

Father was awarded the contract to paint the new Reformed Church being built at the corner of Jennette and Leonard, a few blocks from our home and business. It was here that I formally joined the family in undertaking a job. I was to learn that my brothers' jobs were not so easy and that distributing handbills was the lark that they said it was, dogs and housewives notwithstanding. Painting is constant stress because it is so easy to splash paint somewhere it is not intended, such as on the floor or in your hair. Each mistake costs time and money. As a teenager, I was prone to many. I began to appreciate the stolid attitude and concentration of my father and Nick as they focused on their craft. As the job wore on, I became better, if not accomplished; performing the simplest jobs competently. I was awed by the amount of work we had to perform bringing the job to completion.

The church was a wood-framed building. As a church, especially a Dutch church, it was made from the most economic materials possible, which is a polite way of saying that the pine boards were complete "shitte", which even if not taking the Lord's name in vain, I heard Nick mutter only when out of father's earshot. The boards were full of knots, the "veins" of the former tree, which bled sap when nailed into place. Sap repels any paint applied to it, vexing us to no end. Nick assigned me to apply liberal doses of shellac to these knots hoping we could build up a layer thick enough to staunch the torrent of sap.

Fortunately the family's instincts to protect the baby brother still extended to me (they still did not know about the handbills). We hoisted Gerrit up to paint the steeple, even if I was smaller. Gerrit, small for his size, was always the family daredevil. For once, I forgave him for his constant teasing, watching in awe as he focused on each brush stroke high above while Nick and father anxiously manned the supporting rope. I shellacked the exterior boards with one eye on the wall and the other on the aerialist high above me. His experience of being closer to God had no effect on his personality. Once on the ground, he reverted to his vile older brother's ways.

After the church job, I continued helping in the business, primarily assisting Nick and Gerrit in wallpapering. I applied the paste as they hung the paper. I would have joined my brothers as a full-fledged member of the firm with the skills necessary to make a living, but did not have the desire, even if my aptitude had progressed. I recall only one other painting job with the family. This was for a big house in East Grand Rapids. I was up on a steep roof when I started to slip. The ground was over two floors below. I would have fallen to certain broken bones or death if not for the protruding nail that tore my trousers, holding me up at the last moment. After the summer in the factory, I thought that life and death were normal for work. In the years since, rarely a day goes by when I do not say a silent prayer for my deliverance. Of course, it was Gerrit who quickly scaled the ladder to rescue me. Maybe an older brother was good for something after all.

After that, I returned to work in the store. Ours was a cash-and-carry operation. Customers came in, made their purchases, and departed with the goods. On larger orders we also performed the labor, so that necessitated delivering the goods to the job site.

Much of our custom in the Dutch community was done for barter since everyone was short of cash, especially during the Panic. I do not think we ever paid cash for milk during the whole time when we had the store. There were several older men in the neighborhood who kept cows. They walked around the neighborhood with carts carrying canisters of fresh milk. Nothing was refrigerated or pasteurized, but we drank it within a day or two after it was milked, so it rarely spoiled. The temperature in our cellar reduced it to a drinkable temperature. I still prefer a cold glass of milk that was then only available in the winter. It's even better if the cream is separating, with ice crystals forming across the top. The dairyman came by, ringing his bell. One of my sisters or I ran out with our pitcher to refill, as the dairyman carefully ladled the milk from the canister.

During the course of the year, we bought milk from Dhr. Schuur (Mr. Barn), Dhr. Naaktgeboren (Mr. Born Naked), Dhr. Neiuwstraten (Mr. New Streets), Dhr. Vroeg in de Wey (Mr. Early in the Pasture), or Dhr. Vreugdenhavel (Mr. Joyful Hill). English names should be as fun and descriptive. My surname, Veenstra, indicates that we had once been peat cutters. Farming and peat cutting pretty much sums up the industry of early Friesland, so my name was not all that unique. In Grand Rapids, the Americans did not have too much trouble pronouncing or spelling my name, as they did, say, the names of our dairymen. These were all respected elderly gentlemen. Back then, it was the old who held position and respect, not the young. The greater the head of whiskers; the greater the wisdom that had accumulated. Any oaf could be strong, but only a man of discernment and wisdom could be a saint. Starting out in my career, I admired the skills of these men.

I knew that only through hard work and application would I achieve their status. I was proud that my father stood among them as the foundation of the Dutch community. We may be new in this country, but we earned our place in the society of Grand Rapids. While we did not participate in the entertainments of the American crowd downtown, we were one of the pillars on whose hard work the community was being carved out of the Michigan wilderness. Life was different from that in Friesland and there was more opportunity for all us. How much change and how much opportunity I scarcely imagined in my limited teenaged perspective, but I did know that I drank a lot more milk than I ever did before. I am not sure if the land was overflowing with honey, but the milk part certainly was true.

Even the Dutch were caught up in the American penchant for invention. Dairyman Schuur had been a carpenter before retiring to his cows. He now devised a box that he claimed would wash clothes, then a back-breaking chore that consumed all of one of my mother's and sisters' days. We did not have too many clothes. We wore what we had until it stood on its own, making the eventual day of reckoning even more onerous. Mr. Shuur's device consisted of a long box, about four feet long by perhaps eighteen inches in width. The wooden box was supported by rockers on the floor. These ran the length of the box, instead of across like on a cradle. Inside the box, a concrete block on small iron wheels rode on tiny rails attached to the bottom. A long wooden handle extended three feet above the rocking box. I was intrigued by the contraption so that mother promised me the first opportunity to use it, gladly taking advantage of my teenaged enthusiasm.

We tried it without water where it rocked merrily to and fro. For the maiden voyage, we added clothes and hot soapy water from the stove. I secured the lid, rocking it back and forth. The action was no longer free and easy. I soon tired as the block no longer freely moved. Opening the lid, we found a tangled dirty soapy mess. The delicates were shredded. It took me a half hour to unsnarl the resulting knot of clothes. The beautifully crafted device was relegated to the basement, where an occasional youngster tried it for a hobbyhorse. I doubt that in the history of civilization something so well made was of such limited utility.

Mother, for being so conservative in her personal life, was very progressive when it came to taking advantage of the many "labor-saving" devices that were coming on to the market. Other devices were well conceived, contributing to the family immediately. It was this promise that kept Mother on the lookout for the new and useful. Before then, our stockings were knit by hand. Now, mother owned the first knitting machine in the neighborhood. She could now knit a stocking in a day. I especially appreciated this, since as a young man, I no longer went around barefoot during the summers.

She bought an apple peeler and corer from a new store in Chicago called the Sears & Roebuck Company which promised, "Satisfaction or your money back," an entirely new concept at the time. Until this amazing promise, it had been "Caveat emptor." Even our Dutch merchants considered it a personal affront if you questioned the quality of their goods. The Sears & Roebuck catalog became the second book in our house after the family Bible. Novels were forbidden (including Gerrit's contraband "dime-novels" stuffed under his mattress). Other books were too expensive. I was entranced by the wide variety of goods for sale, spending hours leafing through it until mother imagined a chore she needed done. I liked the numerous illustrations, studying the line work very closely. I saw that good pictures sold these products.

Unlike the washing machine, the girls enjoyed the peeler immediately. There was no reason to mail it back to Chicago for the refund. After fresh vegetables ran out in October, we ate from the preserves we put up at the end of summer. For the princely sum of ninety-five cents, the device from Sears made the preparation of apples for applesauce a snap. Now, our supply of apple sauce no longer ran out in February.

The Dutch love "sny boonen - pickled green beans". Before the beans can be blanched, they need to be sliced and, here again, another little wonder from Sears did away with hours of young hands on the cutting board and the inevitable cut knuckles. Before long, we preserved beans for the entire neighborhood. We filled the other women's crocks for a dime. The girls now joined the boys in augmenting the family income. Those beans, cooked with potatoes, barley, and a chunk of pork, are one of my favorite dishes.

Mother's most popular purchase from Sears was an ice cream freezer, the only one in the neighborhood. On a hot summer evening after catechism, we bought a quart of milk for a nickel and some ice (which was more expensive, stored from the previous winter in an insulated warehouse). At home, mother boiled a mixture of the milk, corn starch, sugar, and vanilla extract until it thickened. Setting it aside to cool, we chipped the block of ice into small fragments that we packed tightly into the wooden bucket surrounding the tin churning pail. We poured salt on the ice and the cooled cream mixture into the tin.

Then began one of the hardest half-hours of our young lives. I have worked in factories and pushed lawn mowers in the blazing sun, but nothing is more arduous than cranking an ice cream freezer in anticipation of the glorious treat within. Our scrawny arms rebelled in pain long before the sweetened glop thickened, yet we continued manfully taking our turns on the crank. We did not enjoy many luxuries in life, but I think my parents allowed this one as a metaphor for the sweet salvation awaiting a life of Christian struggle. Just when we thought we could not continue, the cream thickened, so that the task became even harder for the last few minutes. But, oh, the delights contained within! Nothing beats a bowl of well-earned hand-churned ice cream topped by Michigan raspberries. At first bite, I knew that our transition from Holland to America was now complete.

While the ice cream maker was the best new addition to my life, there was one new invention at the time that would have far-reaching impact, not only for our family, but for the nation as a whole. Gerrit, like mother, was on the lookout for devices that might improve lives or business. We did not buy our first telephone for the home. Since our friends did not have one, whom would we call? However, Gerrit convinced my father to install one in the decorating store. Before long, it paid for itself with increased efficiency and business. At first, it seemed a convenience when we called in orders to the paint distributor instead of mailing them, but the faster turnaround led to more profit. Customers called with questions, leading to more sales and jobs. This meant more time in the store for me, and less time handing out handbills or painting, so I was all for it. I learned that communication was an important part of a successful business.

Michigan in general (and Grand Rapids in particular) grows magnificent fruit. Fruit has to be handpicked. There is always a shortage of pickers. Teenaged boys were in demand since we bounced instead of broke upon the inevitable fall from ladders set up on uneven ground. We soon took up with Mr. and Mrs. Webster, returning to their farm for several summers. We were paid 75 cents a bushel, which was good money. These were big Michigan bushels that I could barely wrap my arms around. Webster's customers insisted these bushels be rounded at the top, not merely leveled off. I picked about three pecks in a day, but Gerrit filled an entire bushel basket, a most impressive skill. I liked cherry picking. It was cool and shady in the trees, and I liked crawling through the branches. I could eat as much as I wanted. Looking back, maybe that is why Gerrit always filled his basket faster than I.

Gerrit had a secret weapon: a bicycle, which to me as a boy was a greater invention than the telephone. We would leave home at the same time, but by the time I had walked to the Walker's, the bottom of Gerrit's bushel was already covered with cherries an inch or two deep. He left later, too. As an older brother, he had a two-year head start on saving enough money to purchase this miraculous transporter. Mother let him keep a dime from the three quarters he usually brought home for a day's work. My daily half-dollar and Gerrit's were a good addition to the family budget at a time when men in the factories earned a dollar to a dollar and a half for their day's labor. Nobody's head split open in the orchard, which was a welcome improvement to my working conditions. As the summer wore on, the cherries ripened faster than we picked them. Mr. Walker suggested that we stay overnight for a spell, so we could get an earlier jump on the day and work later, too. This was the first night I had ever spent way from home. That, in its own right, was a novel experience. I was old enough not to be scared, but it still felt different. Sleeping next to Gerrit was no different than before, though, since we had shared a bed for years.

Mr. Webster seemed to me, as a boy, to be an old man, but maybe because he rarely shaved. This was not that outside the norm. Straight razors were nasty bits of business needing constant stropping to be effective. Most men relied on a professional barber and then only weekly. Why waste a nickel when you did not have to? Professional men shaved on Tuesdays, Thursdays, Fridays, and Saturdays. Believing that most men in the Bible grew facial hair, Christian Reformed men trimmed once a week, always on Saturday, never on Sunday. I don't know when Webster shaved, but certainly it was not often, to the detriment of his appearance. Let us just say that grooming did not come as second nature to him.

Mrs. Webster was an entirely different matter. She was only a little older than Gerrit, probably not much over twenty, and let's just say, definitely knew how to use a comb. One night after supper, she told her husband that she was going visit her parents, asking that Gerrit and I accompany her. I was thrilled, since the farm was dark and boring once the sun set. Gerrit did not say much, keeping his eyes down, except for one furtive glance at Mrs. Webster while the excursion was being discussed with the old man. Gerrit was subdued as he and Mrs. Webster walked off together in the lead, me trailing. The mystery of the discrepancy in the ages of the Webster's was additionally compounded when I met her father who was obviously younger than Webster.

On the trip back, Gerrit maintained his silence until Mrs. Webster queried,

"Gerrit, what do you want to do with your life other than to pick my cherries?" "Oh, I don't know. I like it here on the farm. And I would like to be with a person like you."

"I am afraid there is only one of me."

"I know that," was his choked reply.

We walked along again in silence until Mrs. Webster suggested a race to the corner that marked the edge of her farm. We took off down the sandy Michigan road barefoot, until reaching the corner, out of breath. As we turned into the farm, she warned us to say nothing about the footrace to her husband, whose racing days seemed well in the past. That night I asked Gerrit, "So what gives with the different ages of Mr. and Mrs. Webster?"

"It was a shotgun wedding," he replied. In my innocence, I had no idea what that meant, but he said no more. Later, I learned that the former Mrs. Webster had passed away and the new Mrs. Webster had come over to help with housework. The old Mr. and the soon to be Mrs. became too familiar, resulting in an unplanned wedding. I doubt if our parents would have consented to our spending the night if they knew the education it afforded Gerrit and me.

A year later, Ransy, a school chum, and I worked for a Mr. Sanford whose 80-acre farm was not far from Webster's. These farms were close since they were within walking distance from our home. Though not Dutch, Mr. Sanford looked the part; tall, taciturn, bewhiskered, and tobacco chewing. His domestic situation was more settled than Webster's as he lived with a short, chubby cheerful wife, who was offset by their vinegary adult daughter, Elizabeth. She taught school in a nearby one-room schoolhouse. Her left arm was atrophied but she had no trouble driving the two-horse team when she helped on the farm. Her brother Frank, a few years older than Ransy and me, took after his mother and was good company. He did not make a big deal of being the boss's kid, pitching in on the chores.

We worked by the week, picking berries before cutting the corn, labor that was very tiring after an hour of hacking at the thick stalks. We finished the fall picking cucumbers. This was miserable as we crawled along the rows cutting off the green fruit. The cuke patch must have been only half of an acre, but to me and Ransy, it looked as infinite as space. Picking cherries was a one-time job; you climbed up into the tree, cleaning it out. Cucumbers were different; continually bearing until the first frost. No sooner had we finished the field than we started again, picking what had ripened since we had gone through. If you heard of the Greek myth of Sisyphus forever pushing the rock up the hill, you have an idea of what harvesting cucumbers is like.

This back-breaking labor was compensated by the best food I had ever eaten. Mrs. Sanford and Libby were awful housekeepers, but they could cook, with a bounty of fresh ingredients right outside the kitchen door. Mrs. Sanford served us each a quarter of a pie with the cherries we had just picked. Her crust melted in the mouth. Ransy's and my mom cooked just standard Dutch fare, which was nothing much. Maybe the difference was the fresh churned butter that Mrs. Sanford used in her piecrust instead of my mother's lard.

Mornings and evenings on the farm were glorious. The birds outside made a racket long before the sun came up, which would have been charming if not repeated ad infinitum. When it comes to calling to their friends, birds have no terminal facility. The melodic selections in the evening were more tolerable. Frank leaned against the corncrib, serenading us with his harmonica. I never tired of "My Old Kentucky Home", or "Carry Me Back to Ole Virginny". We didn't have any instruments in our home. The only music I had ever heard was in church. I am afraid those hymns in the Psalter did not sound as good as the plaintive notes coming from Frank's mouth organ. That fall, with my earnings, I bought a harmonica. I never achieved Frank's mastery, but learned enough to squeak out a few simple tunes like Home Sweet Home, and one I found a bit more difficult, Jesus is a Shelter in a Weary Land.

As we sat beside the corncrib, the heat of the day radiated from the ground beneath us. The fiery orb of the Michigan sun set with few accompanying clouds. Old Sanford and Frank chewed tobacco, which for the life of me, is a completely absurd habit. Why would anybody knowingly stick something so evil and foul tasting into their mouth? The only thing that made sense was spitting it out, which father and son did with great accuracy. For a spittoon, they used a flat metal pan, 12 inches across, filled with sand. This pan sat near the big heating stove that looked as if it had never been polished, exhibiting rust, in spots. "Quelle horreur"; in contrast to my mother's pride and joy on which she lavished as much attention as she did her children. Mr. Sanford exhibited as much skill and dexterity with his precision expectoration. He simply turned his head, and with unerring aim, hit the pan. During the length of the summer, I never saw him miss. People took great pride in whatever their chosen craft in those days.

After the sun went down almost instantaneously the stars came out by the thousands. Soon after, we dragged our tired bodies off to bed. We slept in the unfinished second floor of the house. I am sure it was stifling except for the faintest of breeze wafting through the tall, narrow window but Ransy and I fell asleep as soon as our heads touched the lumpy pillows.

Even with the cucumbers, I wished that summer would never end. It was my first taste of freedom, living with a friend without my parents or older brothers. One day, I was sent into the pasture to bring in the old buggy horse. Having spent the past few years as Dobbins's principal caretaker, I thought I was well suited for this task. Their horse was docile as I guided her by her mane to the fence. There, I jumped on to her broad and comfortable back. I gave her a little kick in the ribs with my bare heels. She started willingly for the gate where the buggy was waiting. But, having no bridle, she was unresponsive to my tugs on her mane, taking me into the barn. I was sure we would halt there when she found her manger. As my eyes adjusted from the bright outside to the dark barn interior, I made out a man door at the other end of the barn from where we came in. Surely, she wasn't heading for that? I found the answer as she ducked through unencumbered, scraping me off with the lintel to land unceremoniously in a pile of her manure piled by the door. Ransy thought this was the funniest thing he had ever seen. I was just sore, dazed, and stinky, none of which I thought was very funny.

Eventually, frost curled the cucumber vines and our summer idyll came to end. My back would recover. Ransy and I rode with Mr. Simpson as he took his final load of cucumbers to town. He gave us our money, thanking "Harry" and "Clancy" for our good work. I do not know why he could never remember Ransy's name, but he was still a good boss for a summer I will forever cherish.

That fall, after Ransy and I returned town, we were in catechism class together. It was here that I learned that he was not just a fair-weather friend but one I could count on. Our teacher was a kindly, well-mannered man but not a very strict disciplinarian. This was a combustible situation with so many teenaged boys in the room, many rebelling at being force-fed Reformed doctrine. I am not sure his attitude made much of a difference because teachers in many of my classes had trouble. In one of them, the older boys wrestled the teacher to the floor when he tried to eject a student.

I sat in the same pew as a boy whose pockets contained an arsenal of peas. He was so skilled at shooting them that he could hit any target at several feet with a flick of his thumb. As soon as our kindly teacher turned his back, he was pelted with another pea. At first he ignored this indignity, but after a while, the barrage demanded his attention. Finally in a shaking voice, he demanded, "Who is doing that?"

The room was silent, as snitching is a cardinal sin among teen-aged boys, so extreme is the fear of being shunned by the group. He resumed his teaching and I assumed that the culprit, having humiliated his prey, would persist from his torment. But no, he loosed another pea from his unerring thumb. I could not stand it any longer, identifying the culprit.

After class, we broke to go outside where I was surrounded by the ruffians who were going to administer school-yard justice on the "squealer". Who should I find next to me but Ransy, ready to take them on with me. With such a force protecting the weak (both me and the teacher), the bullies backed off. A better friend could not be found.

What we did not know is that the matter had been reported to the church consistory. They determined that more drastic measures were needed. At a subsequent catechism, things were again out of hand, with the troublemakers paying no attention to the calls for order. What happened next would have made John Calvin proud as he restored order on the unbelievers of Geneva. Catechism was held in the church basement. The classroom was separated from furnace room by a door with a pane of glass in the upper half. What only the teacher knew is that behind that door sat two Grand Rapids police officers. There were no lights on in the furnace room, so that two officers observed everything comfortably from the dark.

Possibly they waited for a signal or when they had seen enough on their own, they sprung forth, promptly taking two of the boys to jail. The rest of us sat in stunned silence while the teacher calmly resumed the lesson. After our class, there was much discussion, pro and con. After, catechism was conducted with more decorum.

One of the boys hauled away was the son of the "kloster - church custodian" who ruled the back of the sanctuary with an iron hand on Sundays. There, he identified the mischief makers in a hoarse whisper, loud enough to attract the attention of the congregants in the rear pews. Naturally heads turned to see whose son was causing the disturbance. Maybe the boy thought he could get away with misbehaving when away from the watchful eye of his iron-fisted father. The rest of us in the back pews thought that het "kloster" had received his just deserts with his own son now in the clutches of Grand Rapid's finest.

Though my friendships centered on catechism and the pals I met there, this was not always true for the rest of neighborhood. Though all of the Dutch were affiliated with one Reformed church or another, attendance and belief ran the gamut from the devout, which our family tried to be, to the less so. Sons of the "less so" hung out on street corners at night under the gas lights, developing allegiances to their locale and to each other. Elsewhere, these might be called gangs, but these swarms of young men were fairly benign except when they tested themselves against the fellas from a few blocks away. Near our store, the "Corner Gang" congregated at the corner of Alpine Street and Leonard Avenue.

There they took up a collection to buy an "eighth" (of a barrel) of beer. The local saloon sold them an "eighth" for about a buck. Each was able to get a pretty good buzz for about a dime a piece. The strongest of them hoisted the barrel onto his back, ambling off to the "Boneyard". There, on the outskirts of town, under a canopy of oaks, they whiled away the hours drinking beer and playing cards. I never joined them, but their activities were common knowledge. Adults were too busy earning a living to interfere. Besides, confronting a pack of drunken teenagers is not for the faint of heart.

It was called the Boneyard because it was a convenient place to dispose of animals. In the days before the automobile, there were plenty of animal carcasses, especially of horses, needing disposal. The hilltop must have been an old dune from an earlier lake, because the soil was all sand, making it worthless for agriculture, but easy to dig. The easy excavation and drainage also made it attractive for the dumping of the "honey-wagons" that serviced the backyard privies. They scraped off a bit of soil surrounded by a foot-high dike before pouring in their load. We were in the vicinity one day when a friend was drawn to the perfect smooth sheen of brown gloss in the overgrown woodlands. It took no more than a few steps before his bare feet were running at full speed towards the nearby creek and its soothing cleaning water.

The Corner Gang was willing to live with the obvious drawbacks of the "Boneyard" for the privacy it entailed. They accepted the dangers under foot that they could see rather than the occasional slop bucket hurled their way from a second floor window when their carousing became out of hand at the corner. This gang was not entirely innocent. A rival outfit held turf three blocks south under the gas lamp near the Lindemulder Store. I do not think there were any gangs until gaslight gave them enough illumination to assemble. Our side of Grand Rapids was gradually filling up as a neighborhood of two story frame houses with small stores like my father's on the corners. I knew little about this gang, rarely venturing south of Leonard Avenue, but knew that they were named after the grocery store on the corner. That store was owned by the father of the girl I had noticed at our church, Hattie Lindemulder.

One evening, I saw a number of toughs surround a couple of the fellows of the Lindemulder bunch before punching one of them in the face. I was shocked by such a cowardly act without any provocation. Later, I was doubly aghast, as the young man assaulted was to be my brother in-law. Fortunately I was about to begin working full time, spending even less time with these wastrels who offered me nothing.

Chapter 7

It was time to think about a career. I was about to enter the swirl of greater Grand Rapids after what, I found, had been a sheltered existence in the ethnic enclave of Dutch west Grand Rapids. Jake Feenstra had been a pal since on Jennette Street. He now helped me secure the first job that I really liked that was more suited than fruit picking or wall papering. Jake worked for a luggage dealer downtown about a mile south of our home on Leonard Avenue on the east side of the river. One of Jake's duties was to take trunks and suitcases to a sign painter who lettered the owner's name, assisting in identification in the stacks on a Railway Express wagon. Knowing I liked to draw, Jake told me that the sign painter had an apprenticeship open. Father gave his permission to apply.

A day later, I joined Jake walking across the Leonard Street Bridge to downtown. I worked for Daniel Powers, a former captain in the Union Army during the Civil War. He recounted endless stories from the conflict. I did not believe half of them; except that the way he told them, they all sounded true. He claimed to be the "black sheep" of the noted Powers family. His half-brother owned the Powers Opera House on Pearl Street where the most notable plays in town were mounted. Or so Mr. Powers claimed, since as a good Christian Reformed boy, I never would have darkened the door of a playhouse. Mr. Powers did not go either since his brother would not have him - something about "His wimmen keep me away from him, my own flesh and blood." Black sheep or not, Mr. Powers owned the building where our shop was located. Our shop occupied the entire second floor. The first floor was occupied by a saloon, one of many thriving at that time. Most people did not keep liquor in their home, so men ducked into such an establishment for a drink. I was too young to drink, but this was more of a guideline than a hard and fast rule. This was just as well since I did not like the taste, nor cotton up to the effect. Besides, I needed a steady hand as a sign painter.

Powers had foresworn the bottle himself, claiming he previously needed it to forget the war, but was beyond that now. To avoid temptation, he sent me downstairs every day at noon to fill our jug with root beer from the bar for our mid-day break.

Mr. Powers was an excellent marksman, a skill I found completely amazing as I had seen very few guns in my life. I did not know a single Dutchman who owned one. There was a nice horseshoe of bullet holes in the brick wall about three and half feet above the floor in the sign shop.

When I asked Mr. Powers about it, he replied, "In my drinking days, Willy and I came in after quite a bender. I was feeling frisky when Willy nodded off in the captain's chair over there. I thought it impolite that he should find my company so uninvigorating that I thought I would wake him up a lil' bit, taking a shot just above his right shoulder. He didn't wake until I circumnavigated his head by emptying the entire cylinder of my Navy Colt. Willy did not take well to this as an opening gambit to resuming our previous conversation, promptly falling back asleep after brushing the red brick dust from his shoulders. Willy stayed stock still for twelve hours. I never had a drink again in my life."

I cannot say as much for Willy. He still came by the shop to sleep off a drunk. We covered him with newspapers as he lay on the hard dirty wooden floor, as inert as if Mr. Powers *had* shot him.

I had learned the rudiments of sign painting from my father. He was not a sign painter per se, but since he had all the necessary paints and brushes, our Dutch neighbors called on him for their simple needs. He was often called on to paint grave markers. Stone markers were beyond the budget of our neighbors. My father took a good pine board one inch thick and about eighteen inches wide and four feet long, covering it with two coats of high-grade primer to delay the rot from contact with the ground. On this, in stark black letters with a graceful script, he lettered the epitaph ordered by the grieving family. When he was busy, I did this lettering over his penciled outlines. I learned how to make the brush stokes for all the letters which was fairly easy for my small hands after practice. I was proud of this work, concentrating on doing it perfectly. I was not entrusted with doing any gold leaf work like on our family's wagon, but was happy to contribute to the family business, since I never again scaled the heights required to paint buildings.

I learned my chops under Mr. Powers. We painted nearly one hundred signs for Standard Coffee, many of them identical, so I repeatedly practiced the same stroke, holding a steady edge. At this time, all outside advertising was hand-painted, so we had all of Western Michigan to fill. Big national outfits like Standard used the rail network to ship their products across the country, needing advertising to attract customers. Having mastered this repetitive sign painting, I tired of it, especially when brother Gerrit signed on as a temporary employee during a rush. Gerrit was older and more confident than I. He asked and received seven dollars per week, twice as much as I was making, even though my work was faster and better. Gerrit's arrival was probably sent by God since Mr. Powers was an unbeliever. Mr. Powers was strong, interesting, and happy, but Christ played no part in his life. His magnetic personality sowed doubts in my steadfast faith. How could a non-believer be so successful and satisfied? In our church, we believed that God worked in our lives in meaningful ways, but that was not the case here. It was time to thank him for the job, the improvement to my skills and move on.

"De Standaard – The Standard" was a twice-weekly newspaper printed in Grand Rapids for the many Hollanders in the region. My parents were faithful readers, as it was the source of what was happening in our community, the nation, and back home in the Netherlands. "De Standaard" had an opening for an intelligent boy who spoke Dutch wishing to learn typesetting. My mother was vehemently opposed. This surprised me. Until now, she supported my employment ventures outside of the house, even in the furniture factory. She believed that print shops were unhealthful. There may have been health hazards associated with printing presses, which were dangerous. I explained to her that the job had nothing to do with the presses, but with typesetting before printing. She was under the impression that I would work with inks and other nasty volatile liquids. I assured her that a typesetter had no contact with those substances, but the safe (so we thought then) alloy of lead, tin, and antimony. In fact, the newspaper's offices were located in a downtown office building and were no more hazardous than our decorating store. At last, she reluctantly consented. The next day I called at the "De Standaard", was interviewed, and landed the job.

The paper was run by the owner-publisher, Mr. Schram, one of the best men for whom I have ever worked. I served the two typesetters, as a "printer's devil", the industry's nickname for an apprentice. The five of us put out an eight-page broadsheet in Dutch every other week. My duties were not all that difficult. Every morning and at noon, I fetched a pail of fresh drinking water from "The Arcade", a narrow passage between the buildings connecting Lyons and Pearl Streets. An artesian well with a clean but slight mineral taste continually flowed near Pearl Street. At the well I met the other apprentices on the same mission. The rest of day, under the watchful eye of the typesetters I was introduced to my future trade as a compositor, another word for typesetter.

First, I was taught the "case" – the location of each letter in the large wooden case containing the entire alphabet. The most used letters were near the top, easy at hand. Speed was balanced against accuracy and correct spelling. Nimble fingers overcame the early stress of performing the job as soon I was reaching for the correct letter before even thinking about it. I was given a definite number of stories, called a stint to set. Once this work was complete, I was free to return home for the rest of the day. Wednesdays and Saturdays, I usually got home by mid-afternoon. The paper went to press on Mondays and Thursday afternoons. On those days, immediately after lunch, I took the forms - iron frames of type to the printing company. Good to my promise to my mother, I had nothing to do with the actual printing. These forms were for the outside pages of the paper, 1 and 8, 2 and 7.

While these sheets were printed, I returned to our offices to help set the inside pages. The interior pages had the latest news stories. One of my duties was to buy the latest copy of the "Grand Rapids Evening Press" as soon as it came out. This I handed to Mr. Schram, who quickly translated the important stories into Dutch. This hot news was immediately set in type and locked into the last forms. This was timed to coincide with the completion of the printing of the first forms. I then carried the last forms to the printer. I stayed there, until the last sheets came off the press. When there was as much as I could carry, the pressmen softly folded them, tossing the 24" x 36" sheets over my shoulder to carry back to "De Standaard's" office.

The paperboys folded their own sheets into assembled newspapers. The typesetters folded the copies for mailing while I ran back and forth to the printer. I wrapped up the mail run, pushing the loaded cart to the post office. I think we spent as much time assembling the paper as we did writing and typesetting it. On the way back from the post office, I stopped by a local saloon for the latest baseball scores posted inside, grabbing a bite of free lunch that was available for the purchase of a nickel mug of root beer. The cool and dark of the saloon was a nice break after the frantic pace of putting out the paper, even without a beer.

The "Grand Rapids Evening Press" was probably unhappy about our lifting of their latest stories, but there was little that they could do. The Dutch-only readers were a market that they could not serve. By the time we printed one of their "hot" stories, it was lukewarm after our translation and cumbersome production. The big daily had mechanical linotype setters, printing many more sheets than we could. Their paper hit the front porches all over town at a speed we could only envy. The poor Dutch-only reader was always behind when it came to current events. My father took all of his news from "De Standaard", at the mercy of the laborious production schedule. Once, sitting down to read the "De Standaard", he exclaimed to the family, "De koening van Engeland ook dood! - The king of England is dead!" The king had been dead for several days. The news was wired to Grand Rapids immediately after it happened. "De Standaard" released the news about a half-week after the English language press since it happened long before we went to press. The news was so old it made the outer pages of our newspaper. The rest of us in the family, now reading English, already knew the news, chuckled at the old man only now finding out. Working at the paper, I saw that my generation was the first to have instant access to news from all over the world. Telegraph wires not only extended across the country, but were laid under the Atlantic Ocean. The European politics that we had escaped followed us now to our new backwater corner of the world. I may never have the thorough grounding in a trade as my father, but in the short span of two decades, I was better connected with the world than he ever had been.

Our editor, Mr. Visser, wrote all of the editorials. He included a definite Christian perspective that was popular with his readership since almost all Dutchmen were affiliated with a Reformed church. His outlook proved a good knowledge of Calvinist principles. My father read these editorials with pleasure, comforted by this application of Reformed doctrine to modern issues. Mr. Visser maintained a dignified bearing. I considered him on par with the ministers who were the leaders of our community. But there was an incident that proved that he still was an impudent newsman not relying on the Bible as his sole text. Coming in one day after lunch, it was evident that he had more than one beer with the free lunch at the saloon. He was unaware that the phone in the office was out of order. After several unsuccessful attempts to contact the operator to place a call, he let out a string of Dutch curses, the like of which I had never heard. Having never heard such thing before, I was unsure whether to be afraid, appalled, or amused. It was a great blow to my father when I told him about this incident. I then learned that discretion is an essential element in the dissemination of the news, since my father never again derived the same pleasure from the reading of Mr. Visser's doctrinally correct editorials. Printing the legend is indeed sometimes more important than printing the truth. Later I learned that Mr. Visser was the son of devout Christian parents who had entertained fond hopes for his entering the ministry. Even with a first-rate education, his calling was, for them, something less exalted than the pulpit. Even with his feet of clay, I looked up to him, marveling how he could spin words as fast as he typed. I learned how a man could still live a Christian life in the hurly-burly world of newspapering. His good heart and right thought were as exceptional as many preachers I would meet.

I worked at "De Standaard" for three years, carrying my weight as typesetter, but determined that there was little room for advancement. I was still the principal "donkey" on whose back the production of the paper depended. There was not enough work to hire a new apprentice and the two typesetters were not going anywhere. Reading the English language paper everyday on the prowl for news, I became aware of a much larger world. There was a whole range of characters who did not attend church every Sunday. Even among those who did, I encountered a range of belief beyond our Reformed doctrine. I began to appreciate Catholicism as something other than a complete heresy and historical rival as was taught in my church.

However, there was little opportunity to discuss these finer points of theology. All of the religious communities stayed amongst themselves. The Dutch had a leg up over the Catholics when applying for jobs controlled by the Episcopalians and Presbyterians who ran most of the town's businesses, since we shared a Protestant background. We were still primarily an immigrant community, without the capital or management experience to organize or own the larger business concerns in the city. However, our fellow Protestants were more than happy to take advantage of the strong Dutch work ethic.

While reading the "Evening Press", I came across an advertisement placed by the Dickinson Printing and Engraving Company for an apprentice in their art department. I called on them to show some of compositions from the newspaper and drawings I had made. They offered me the job. However, the terms of employment were such that I hardly dared ask my parents if I could take it. At the age of nineteen, I was expected to support the family's income. Father was now almost sixty and slowing down. He stayed off of the ladder whenever he could with his rheumatism flaring up regularly. Charly helped with the business, but he could not cover the store and jobs at the same time. I earned a respectable wage at the newspaper with the promise of further raises and the eventual recognition as a journeyman typesetter. If I accepted the Dickinson offer, for the first six months I would be paid nothing and the rest of the year, a dollar per week. Father consulted with the older boys before giving his consent. I guess that as the "baby brother", they thought I was contributing nothing anyway. The terms of my acceptance did not surprise my father since he had served an unpaid apprenticeship in the Netherlands. He knew that there were stiff barriers to entry in the most desirable trades. Mother accepted my choice, too. I think there was some forbearance as the "baby" boy in the family, though I now needed to shave occasionally. I think the family did not have much faith in my career record to date. I certainly did not care for painting or papering, nor clerking in the store. Since these were the focus of everyone else in the family and our principal livelihood, I was out of sorts. Now I wanted to sacrifice my own perfectly good typesetting trade with good potential. I guess mother knew that I liked to draw, so Dickinson's made as much sense as anything. Before this opportunity came along, I was attending art school in the evenings for two nights a week, so maybe I was guided towards this outcome.

 I am happy to say that I made good on my choice, being promoted after the lean first year. I soon contributed as much as my brothers to the family coffers. I showed some of my work to my father. He was pleased and impressed. This was greater compensation for him than any financial contribution I was making. He lived his life doing his best in whatever he did, and it made him happiest when his sons and daughters did the same. Nothing in my life made me happier than pleasing him. He was not terribly strict, but was very sparing with his praise. Something had to be exceptional for him to comment positively. His high standards are what made him so effective at what he did.

In those days, at the turn of the century, duplicating photographs in newspapers or magazines was still an imperfect art. It was difficult for a photograph to match the range of tone found in a good engraving, so advertisers relied on art scratched by hand onto a brass plate to illustrate their wares. There was ample need for illustrators like myself. From my days at the newspaper, I understood the rudiments of printing. After the year, I could scratch out a presentable image on the engraving plates. There was little room for error, since a scratch could not be erased, but it took many scratches to build up an image, so a less than perfect line could be hidden by scratching a better one next to it. I had no problem with the intense focus required for this work. The days sailed by as my hands bore down, cutting the shiny plate in front of me. Soon, from an incoherent bird's nest of lines, a picture emerged. Mr. Dickinson said that I probably sold more women's shoes in Western Michigan than anyone else with my realistic representations.

At last, I had found something that I was good at and I truly loved. During my first year with Dickinson, I entered three decorative pieces in the fine art judging of the Western Michigan State Fair. I scraped up enough money to take Hattie Lindemulder to the fair with me. We hopped on the new electric inter-urban trolley that rambled out to the fair grounds. I wore my derby, but she did not seem to care that the other boys looked more stylish in their straw boaters, more appropriate for the season. As a grocer's daughter, she was perfectly turned out in a shirtwaist and large brimmed hat held on with a chiffon scarf. I was amazed that she liked me better than the other fellas, but it had to be obvious I was completely devoted to her. Though she certainly was "classy", she never lorded it over anyone but was very straight-forward and sensible. She liked that I was modest, paying rapt attention when she spoke. She had a very good sense of humor, or at least appreciated my jokes, which was good, because I was often not without a quip. I was not ribald, but saw humor in almost any situation. I think it helped me survive in a world where death or dismemberment was not out of ordinary. I was relieved that her parents were willing to let her spend time with me, like this trip to the fair. Certainly, I would not have had a chance if my parents had not been respected members of our church.

Naturally, I wanted to show her the pieces I had entered. My heart jumped when I saw a second place ribbon on each one; not for the recognition, which was nice, but for the three-dollar prize that accompanied each ribbon. After a year of virtually no income, nine dollars was a princely sum. We celebrated with ten-cent ice cream cones, an extravagant treat on a summer's day.

I now attended a more advanced art school taught by Mathias Alten, a talented Grand Rapids artist from Germany. He had returned from Paris showing us the broad brush strokes of the new "Impressionists". Mr. Alten's work varied from very modern impressionistic work to refined copies of the French Academy. From him I learned to paint in addition to the engraving that I practiced at work. I continued to practice his lessons in the composition of landscapes for my entire life. Mr. Alten also had entered the Western Michigan Fair, of course winning first place with his entries. He concurred with me that second place was more desirable because of the cash prize. First place was awarded the ribbon and the glory but no cash. I realized that no matter how much talent one might possess, the plight of the artist was to always be scrambling for money. Commercial art paid something; fine art, less.

My first duties at the studio were very much like those at *I* Morning and noon I trudged back to the Arcade for a fresh pail of water. This was the best water in the city. The entire business class in the city ran on the water and news from the well. The Arcade was the center of the city where boys and men gathered to briefly get the news of the day and gossip. I enjoyed meeting with the other apprentices sent on the same chore, but I wanted to advance my career to where I was no longer called upon to tote water. My new employers also had me wash dishes, something that I did not even do at home. Sweeping was ridiculous. The stubby broom I was given bounced over the dust, firmly embedding it in the floor. A job that should have taken five minutes took ten, but at my rate of pay, the Dickensons did not care. Father had told me that you have to take the bitter with the sweet, so I persevered. When I complained to the head artist, he replied, "Julia isn't ready to buy a new broom yet. Maybe Miriam will notice the floor is not clean and put a little pressure on Julia."

Julia, the bookkeeper did not pressure easily. Instead, she handed me a small drafting brush to sweep the floor on my knees. I could not believe she was justified in such a ridiculous use of my time, but ours was a small business, short on money. This was often a false economy because she bought the cheapest materials for our work, making our jobs all the more difficult. This was remarkable since the cost of the artist's time far out-weighed the cost of the materials in production.

Originally there had been two Dickenson brothers, but one died, leaving Albert as the owner of the company. It was a family affair; his three maiden sisters were also partners, with Julia, the oldest, as bookkeeper and major-domo of the whole affair. Irene ran the pressroom, and Miriam, the photo-engraving department and art studio. It was quite unusual for a business to have so many women managers. Albert was lazy, seldom coming by the studio except to hand out work. Most of the artists were competent and conscientious, needing little supervision.

Earning a reasonable living was a struggle for the entire time I worked there. In the summer we worked a forty-nine hour week instead of fifty hours. I am not sure why. In my first pay envelope (we were paid in cash), I received ninety-eight cents instead of a dollar! Julia had pro-rated my princely rate of pay at two cents per hour. However, Julia was absolutely fair in all of her dealings. She treated everyone in the same penurious manner, protecting the firm's solvency.

Only Mr. Dickenson had the authority to give a raise. Naturally, it was impossible to meet with him. When I did get in front of him, he gave me his stock reply "Harry, you have great stay-ability, but not so much a-bility." I will talk with you later and see how you get along." I fell for that line initially, but then learned he used it on all of the employees, even the best artists in the shop. I do not think he was even aware of our individual work or talents. What he excelled at was delaying any decision. I finally cornered him so that he could not shine me on. Our studio was served by an elevator controlled by a pulling up or down on rope. This was one of the first examples of the use of electricity that I can recall. Electric lighting was still a few years in the future. The elevator was a slow moving affair. One morning we were the only two passengers when I thought, "Here's my chance, he cannot get away from me now."

"Mr. Dickinson, I have been here over two years. I am pulling my own weight and I am making you money, I think it's time I share in that profit." Not being able to escape, dependent on my control of the elevator, he consented.

The studio was led by some of the best engravers in the city, whose work attracted the attention of unexpected admirers. The best, Mike Ross had a winsome personality but was also an alcoholic. When his hands were steady, he could cut brass with the best of them. One day working drunk, he deliberately threw his tools out of the window, one by one. "I'm through for good. I am too good for this stinking shop!" he exclaimed precisely without slurring a word. Fortunately, neither Miriam nor Dickenson were on the premises. If she had been on our floor, Julia probably would not have cared since the tools were his, docking him a dime for the time. Once a bit more sober, he skulked downstairs, retrieving his tools scattered in the alley below.

A couple of months later, Secret Service agents called on our place of business. To me they were a complete secret, because I had no idea that such a force existed. I learned more about them when they were assigned to guard the President of United States after the assassination of President McKinley the following year.

On the day they visited our art studio, we were all agog. They had not come to buy art. Counterfeit five-dollar bills were circulating in Grand Rapids. After an extensive search, they had traced the source to Dickinson Printing and Engraving. Any of the engravers was suspect. We stood by our drawing boards, proud that someone in our shop had the skill to duplicate a complicated federal note. Our pride was justified when, after an hour's search, the offending plates were found under Mike's drawer. He did not have a drink for the next five years, but not by his choice, as he spent the time in a federal penitentiary.

I spent time away from work, too, though in my case, voluntarily. Vacations were becoming accepted as a way of refreshing workers, preventing them from getting too restive. My parents never took time off except to go to a funeral. I was not paid for the time off, but was ready for the break. What twenty-one year old would rather not play than work? We were not the only ones taking advantage of the new-found leisure time. Many factory owners took off most of the summer, disappearing to their "cottages" on the Lake Michigan shore. Such deluxe accommodations did not appeal to me or my chums as we rented a rowboat to explore the upper reaches of the Grand River (or what we imagined were its upper reaches). We left the cares of the city behind to explore the wilderness of Western Michigan. We set out from the boat livery near the Leonard Street Bridge, our gunwales barely above the water, loaded as we were with supplies and gear. The load and the opposing current made for slow going, even as we took turns manning the oars. After rowing for the greater part of the day, we reached the mouth of the Rogue River. Here we set up camp on the adjacent bank. With no experience as woodsmen, even pitching the tent was difficult, but at last, it was up with our gear stowed inside. Then we got down to the real business of our trip: cooking food boys like to eat. After dinner, we smoked corncob pipes, not because of any affinity for tobacco, but that it seemed like the right thing to do on a camping trip. We documented our masculine bonding by taking snapshots of ourselves with the pipes clenched in our jaws at a rakish angle with one of the first Kodak Brownie cameras that had been introduced for one dollar. This was the first opportunity for people to make their own photographs instead of relying on a professional photographer with his bulky bellows rig and glass plates.

That night, I was awakened by ferocious beasts outside the tent, pawing and snorting outside the flimsy canvas. I could not imagine what beast made such sounds, but was sure it did not have my best interests at heart. I was certainly not going to open the flap to give it entry into our precarious domain. Probably aware that we were just scrawny kids and not very good eating, they took their leave. Once the walls of our tent lightened at dawn, we dared look outside to confront our nemesis. About two hundred feet away stood a small herd of Holsteins peacefully grazing, paying no heed to the interlopers.

This night of imagined terror stimulated our appetites. I set about boiling water for the oatmeal, while Jake made "flap-jacks". He claimed to be using "his mother's recipe," but I doubt if she cooked them in a half-inch of sizzling lard, even if she did include apple slices in the batter. The resulting cakes were crispy on the outside, soft on the inside. They may have been life-shortening, but to young woodsmen, they were simply the best. After breakfast, we extinguished our fire, struck our camp, returning to the river.

Another good day of rowing took us to the "Devil's Elbow", a delightful backwater where we planned to spend the week. All alone, we had a good time swimming, fishing, frogging, and, probably unique to our group, sketching water colors. Again, I marveled at the American sun. Netherlands never had days delightfully warm and sunny as these. There, it was always too cold and dangerous to swim in the "kanaal". But here, you dried off in seconds sunning yourself on a log like a turtle. After a few days, the girls came from town for a visit. The fellas' sweethearts joined Hattie, my girl, and another pair of sisters in the Lindemulders' horse and buggy. They left the rig at a nearby farm where we met them for the walk through the woods to our camp. They brought a large lunch to share. They were happy not to partake in our fare since our big pot doubled as a frog repository. Everyone was on their best behavior. We wanted to show the girls the wilderness paradise we had found. Of course, they couldn't swim, but they marveled at our rustic camp and our willingness to sleep outside. Eating lunch was a perfect opportunity to flirt and laugh without the nervousness that would have attended each couple being alone. We were all good friends, growing up together at the Alpine Avenue church. After the girls left, several of the fellows returned home as well, taking one of the boats. John and I planned on spending the entire week, but we too rowed back to town after a cloudburst soaked our entire camp, making for a miserable night. The next day dawned sunny. What had been arduous two-day row upstream became a delightful cruise downstream returning to town. My mother was very glad to see me, as camping was completely unknown in the Netherlands. She wondered why anybody would leave a perfectly good house to live "like a savage" in the woods. Unrolling my soggy blanket, I understood her point of view, but I still appreciated our adventure and manly test. She gladly warmed a large kettle of water on the stove for my overdue bath. The world had proceeded without us as President McKinley had been savagely gunned down in Buffalo, New York. To me, Buffalo was no longer a town named after a type of bull, but one more place in the larger world that was opening up. What was it about that place? Nothing good happened there. In comparison to sober President McKinley, his Vice-President, Theodore Roosevelt, seemed like a madman. Sure, he may have been Republican and maybe he was Dutch, but he appeared more interested in hunting and shooting than in maintaining a sound currency or the other policies supported by our party. However, just having come back from the woods myself, I appreciated his outdoors perspective a bit more than before I dipped the oars in the river. We would see how he would do.

Chapter 8

After several years, I knew Dickinson's would never pay enough. However, there were not many other art opportunities in provincial Grand Rapids. The bustling metropolis of Chicago was around the shore of Lake Michigan, a little over one hundred miles to the south. In 1901, I boarded the train to the big city with brother Nick. Frank Godfrey, formerly the head artist with the Dickinson's, had moved there to run the George Benedict Art Studio. When he lived in Grand Rapids, we rode out into the country on his tandem bicycle to sketch watercolors. He was a good artist and a good boss. I dropped by the Benedict studio soon after we arrived at the LaSalle Street train station. Godfrey was happy to see me, saying that I could come to work for him at any time. I was now twenty-one years of age and looking for new adventures. I also hoped that, in moving to Chicago, I could earn and save enough money to move out of the house; hoping that Hattie Lindemulder would be interested in being more than just friends. This would be a big step, so I hoped that my parents would agree to let me depart to try life on my own. Early in October, Nick and I set out on a scouting trip. We felt like small town boys out of our natural surroundings, which, of course, is exactly what we were. In downtown, we climbed the stairs on Wells Avenue to the elevated streetcars above us. We were impressed that traffic was so intense that the streetcars were relegated to their own iron "street" twenty feet above. This city was busier than Amsterdam, which had been overwhelming while we were there. I was older now, so I took the sound and congestion in stride, if not entirely.

We waited for a streetcar to take us to Lincoln Park and its famous zoo, north of downtown Chicago. One car after another came by, but they all headed south. After four or five cars went by, we mustered up enough courage to overcome our unwillingness to look like rubes, asking a man where we could catch a northbound car. "Why, right here. Get on the next one," he replied. We were along the famous Chicago "Loop". After we boarded the car, it turned east for five blocks before turning north towards our destination.

The Lincoln Park tiger was not the only marvel of this trip. Away from our parents' supervision, we took in a "show". I was skeptical if it was the right thing to do, but Nick persuaded me that "Ben-Hur" was a "story about Christ". Even with the safe subject matter, going to a theatrical production was too outside the Reformed norm for our parents. They expected the same behavior from their children. "Ben-Hur" was very popular. The only way we could enter the theater was as "standing room only." Either I was younger and stronger then or was totally entranced, but I had no problem standing for the entire performance. The climactic chariot race was like nothing I had ever seen. The charging horses reminded me of fire engines rushing to a fire. An elaborate treadmill was built into the stage, permitting the horses to gallop at full speed without going anywhere. I wonder what the horses thought of not moving while at full exertion. As exciting as the chariot race was, it was more thrilling to see the Bible come to life. The story takes place at the same time when Jesus lived. Jesus is never seen in person, but is depicted offstage by a shaft of light. I was very moved but frustrated that I dared not share these wonders with mother and father. Even if they saw the show, their innate fear of the theater would not permit them to enjoy it. Where they grew up, there was no entertainment or it was strictly prohibited. Now, theaters were safer and the choices of shows like "Ben-Hur" were more wholesome. Previous theaters like the Powers in Grand Rapids were illuminated by open flame, first with whale oil and kerosene and more recently with carbolized gas. Lighting a large theater and its stage required hundreds of open flames, any of which could cause a conflagration of the entire house. When our preachers proclaimed that wages of sin are death, the numerous theater fires were their favorite example. The usual loss of life and hell-like flames drove home their point. This was my first encounter with electrical illumination. It had not arrived in our homes. My parents were still marveling at the use of gas to light the first floor of their home. Though the light given off by the electrical bulbs was dim and cool, I saw that safety would promote its adoption. Once I learned that the "bulbs" could easily be switched on and off, I saw the great potential. At this time of life, I was glad there was not wide-spread electrification, since art work required good light. During the winter, we scheduled our work so that tasks requiring less detail were undertaken as the sun was setting. This meant that we worked longer hours during the summer when we longed to join our friends outside on porches or street corners.

Returning home to Grand Rapids, I had a bigger item on my personal agenda than this theatrical marvel. I had to talk to my parents about another job change; this one necessitated me leaving home. Although I am sure that they would rather that I stayed in Grand Rapids, not in the big metropolis, they consented. I think that they believed that drawing pictures for a living was not real work, though my contributions to the family's cash box were real enough, at least to me. Writing to Frank Godfrey at the Benedict studio, he replied for me to come to join his shop. I bought a trunk, loading it with mother's loving help. Once in Chicago, I found that I had brought much of what I did not need, and little of what I did, but that is how we learn. I did not regret my shoe-shine kit. Every nickel for a shoe-shine that I saved was a nickel that I could use to be independent to propose to Hattie and her parents.

Setting off, I had a job but no place to stay. Fortunately, friend Jake Feenstra was attending dental college in Chicago. He met me in the vast waiting room at the LaSalle Street Station. That first night, he invited me to stay with him and his roommate. They both had dates, telling me to crawl into the bed when I was ready to retire. I took them up on the offer, going to sleep early after what had been an exhausting day lugging my trunk to their lodgings. I did not realize the full extent of my hosts' hospitality until the next morning when I awoke with two other snoring bodies in the bed with me. Jake was such a good friend that he willingly shared an already crowded bed with me.

After breakfast, we went to the YMCA where they handed out a list of approved rooming houses. I landed in one on the north side of Ohio Street with a middle-aged German couple. I hauled my trunk up to my room to arrange my possessions before walking down the street to see Mr. Godfrey. He delivered on his promise, telling me to report for work the following morning. We worked by the piece, and he gave me good work. I earned more money than I did in Grand Rapids. In fact, I made more than the highest-paid salaried man in Grand Rapids, even though I had only two years' experience.

But I was not happy. I was an unsophisticated fellow from a small town. I had spent my entire life with other young men like me who came from Christian families. In this studio, the men were at a minimum ungodly, and more than likely, actually wicked. Their minds were open sewers through which ran Satan's effluvium. I ran for the door. Mr. Godfrey, also from Western Michigan, understood. God protected me, as I signed on with the best agency in the Midwest, if not the country, the J. Manz Company. Here, I had to be on top of my game, since they employed some of the best commercial artists in the country. One of those was J.C. Leyendecker, who traded illustrating *Saturday Evening Post* covers with Norman Rockwell. Getting the cover of the *S.E.P.* was the ultimate in our trade. Rockwell, in fact, probably learned much of his technique from Leyendecker. "Joe", as we knew him, was startling handsome. Although an immigrant like me, he was wealthy, since his mother's family owned a brewery. He wore the latest styles with an urbanity I never knew existed. He bore his talent easily, not lording it or his wealth over us. I never a met an artist who drew a more convincing line. His work exuded a "style" as sophisticated as the artist. After that summer, whenever I picked up a magazine, his work just jumped off the page. His images were the source of countless campaigns. Through the power of his work alone, Arrow Shirt Collars became recognized as a chic national brand. His work defined the image of that era. Few artists possess that talent or power, especially one who sat at the drafting board just behind mine, as he did.

My first job was far more prosaic than what was assigned to Leyendecker. I was to layout and draw a new flour sack for a Grand Rapids milling company. Ironically, this had been one of my assignments before I left Dickinson, so at least I knew what they did not want. I am sure the flour company would be surprised that they hired the work of the artist whose last design they had rejected. Only now, they paid three times as much for it. Maybe I had improved, or more likely they thought big city work was worth it. Before long, I saw "my" bags showing up on grocery shelves all over town. I am pretty sure it made the flour taste better.

The distribution of groceries was changing. This was good news for a young artist. Back in Grand Rapids, my mother would send me to a corner grocer like Hatties's father. I secured bulk goods that he weighed out, charging them to the Veenstra family account. We settled our bill every month. Here in big city Chicago, there were "cash and carry" grocers like Atlantic and Pacific. They sold packaged goods on a cash and carry basis. You were served by hired clerks who you rarely knew. Since you could not trust a strange clerk, these stores relied on you trusting the "brand" on the label. This new packaging required artists to make them look appealing and trustworthy. Additionally, more advertising was required to "pull" these goods off the shelf. More advertising meant more newspapers, with more page space that needed filling. Commercial art was a burgeoning business, and I was having fun being part of it.

I had no family to return to in the evenings. After growing up with a large family, I felt lonely. I especially missed seeing Hattie. I continued my art studies after work, so that occupied several evenings each week. Sundays I spent with the Bosgraafs, a family from Friesland with whom my father corresponded before we came to America. If Mr. Bosgraaf's letter to my father had arrived a few days earlier while we were still in Holland, we may have moved to Englewood, the suburb of Chicago where they lived. I joined them there at their Christian Reformed Church. Unlike in Grand Rapids, CRC churches were rare in Chicago, so I relished this respite from the toils in the ungodly world of Chicago to worship with my own kind. They welcomed me warmly, so I got to know their daughter who was about my age. Perhaps Mrs. Bosgraaf thought we might be a good match, but I remained interested only in my sweetheart in Grand Rapids.

Later, after returning to Grand Rapids, I was describing the wonders of Chicago. My father reminded me that he was acquainted with Chicago. With that, I vaguely remembered that he took a brief trip there when I was thirteen. At that time, Chicago presented the Columbian Exposition to commemorate the five-hundredth anniversary of the discovery of the New World by the Old. I guess father thought he should attend because he was a beneficiary of Columbus' daring. Even as a kid, I had heard about the "Great White City" being built on the shores of Lake Michigan. Some even had the temerity to compare it to heaven. Though I knew this was close to blasphemy, it sounded like it was pretty wonderful. Father had set off only to return a day later. The trip itself took a day each way, so we knew he had little time to take in all of the promised wonders. He never shared why he returned so abruptly and we dared not ask.

Mr. Bosgraaf finally enlightened me why the trip had been so abbreviated, inadvertently spilling what had been father's secret. Father had been the victim of a pickpocket before Mr. Bosgraaf lent him the money to return home. Father was mortified that he had to beg for rides just to get to his friend's house to ask for money. This was behavior that he had warned his sons against. He dared not confess it to us, maintaining the picture of probity in front of his family. Mr. Bosgraaf saw nothing wrong with my father's action, pleased to help the victim of his adopted city. The "Great White City" was certainly less celestial than we had been led to believe. Mr. Bosgraaf assumed that my father felt no shame, thinking that I already knew. I assured him that his secret was safe, knowing that my father would be doubly mortified now to be caught in his prideful refusal to share the misadventure with us. I did not care either, knowing the old man tried to do everything right for his family. You certainly could not fault him for that.

My visits prompted Mr. Bosgraaf to reminisce about Friesland. Maybe he just enjoyed the opportunity to speak in Friesian with someone other than his family. Or maybe he thought that I might be interested in his daughter as we all shared the native tongue. On one of these visits, he told me about the day I was born. Again, this was another tale that my own father had neglected to tell me. He was making the rounds, wishing neighbor acquaintances the felicitations of the New Year, enjoying toasts of Boere Joeges - Farmer Boys, a potent concoction of spices, raisins and brandy. My father met him at the door with a woeful, "Wie jouwe joet net- We are not treating today."

Mr. Bosgraaf recounted, "You had been born earlier in the day and your father was a complete wreck. Even if he hadn't been drinking, he seemed like it. Maybe he was completely exhausted. Why he wasn't toasting such a splendid addition to his family escaped me, but considering his condition, I forgave him. Besides, if the truth be known, I certainly had enough from the neighbors."

For the most part, the Dutch in Grand Rapids did not join unions. Organized labor ran counter to the strong conservative and independent streak inherent in the Dutch community. The church was jealous of any other organization that diverted its members' attentions or affections. I was surprised, then, that Mr. Bosgraaf was a union man, to the point where he was an officer in his local Chapter. I was even more amazed that the unions met on Sunday afternoon, a time reserved for the second church service of the day.

Mr. Bosgraaf boasted of the disciplinary methods that his union Chapter employed. Describing tactics for a strike at a steel mill: "If they get out of line, we send the Salvation Army after them." I didn't think bell-ringers in bonnets had much affect at the Homestead Works until he informed me that this was his euphemism for his strong-armed guys whom he turned on the scabs, sometimes breaking an arm or a leg. In reality, Mr. Bosgraaf was a gentle man, but confronting the powerful corporations took backbone. Having worked in the factory, or even in the art studios, I knew how the companies took advantage of their employees. My father would have been shocked by the attitudes his friend adopted in Chicago, but then, my father was an entrepreneur and small business owner, only having to deal with disgruntled ladies picking wall-paper, not the blood-sucking corporate tyrants loose in the world at the dawn of the new century. It wasn't long before President Roosevelt reeled them in with his "trust-busting".

Mrs. Bosgraaf babied the mister to the point where she bought his clothes for him. Maybe this was to avoid going to parts of town where the cops might rough him up. It was not unheard of for the police to be in the pocket of a company with a large presence, and hence a large pocket book. It was well known that Armour & Company ran the stockyards, meaning to keep it that way. Whatever the reason, Mrs. Bosgraaf's sartorial shopping for her husband led to some amusing consequences. She was larger than the mister. As a result, his clothes were all too large for him, but too short in length. However, his derbies fit perfectly since they shared the same hat size. Unfortunately, she never modeled one of his derbies for me. I would have even sketched it.

I was not immune from the burgeoning movement to organize labor. Soon there was agitation to organize the artists at the J. Manz Company. I had never felt the need to organize since we were paid a living wage, and I had a fairly easy time of securing a new job if I was discontented. But as a youngster, I went along with the drive. What resulted was like a comic opera.

Two organizers came to our office, where one-by-one we joined them in the janitor's closet. There, among the mops and the brooms, I was sworn in as a loyal "Knight of Labor," to be given the secret grip. Soon after, to exhibit their clout, the Knights called a strike. I took the opportunity to return to Grand Rapids. I had achieved what I set out for - a big city experience. I had sharpened my skills, now knowing I was equal to all but the best of the big city talent. If the truth be known, I was ready to see my sweetheart on a more regular basis if she concurred. Dickinson's was pleased to have me back. I used the prestige of Chicago to command a better salary. Without the increase, I would have not returned to Grand Rapids. I never did learn how the strike turned out. I was happy to be home.

My folks welcomed me back to my room above the paint store. I contributed more to the family's purse, so there was newfound respect for my career. I was making almost twice the rate of the aristocrats of the furniture factory, the hand carvers. I paid mother rent for the next two years I was under my parents' roof. The "Panic" was long past. Under Roosevelt, the country boomed. Railroads now delivered Grand Rapids furniture to any part of the nation. My advertisements helped fuel the demand. Looking back, the next two years were the end of my childhood. Only now, I may have not been shooting at the railroad "bulls" with my slingshot, but I was involved in as many hi-jinx as ever. There was a great group of artists at Dickinson's with whom I broke up the tedium of etching by devising ever more elaborate practical jokes.

Mr. Dickinson hired a head artist from out of town to give the studio a higher level of sophistication. Having just come from Chicago, I knew that except for the top men like Leyendecker, our shop was equal to any in the big cities. The new head artist was single, boarding in a nearby mansion that was converted to a boarding house. He kept to himself. Rather than go out to free lunches and nickel beers at the saloons, he returned to his residence where he dined with his fellow boarders, mostly "old maids", as he termed them. Mice were plentiful in my corner at work, where I caught them at will. Using a little home-made trap baited with a bit of cheese, I caught them alive and uninjured. I put the captured mice to sleep with ether from the studio photographers. One morning, after anesthetizing my captured prey, one of my fellow artists asked if he could have the mouse, putting it in the pocket of the head artist. Lunch hour was soon upon us, as the head artist grabbed his coat, running out the door towards his luncheon. While seated at the table with his proper luncheon companions, he felt a movement in his pocket, pulling out the dazed mouse much to his companions' chagrin.

I was not safe from the ink-stained wretches with whom I worked. Once, I quarreled with Hattie. To make peace, I brought her a box of her favorite chocolates. Only in this case, the "chocolate" was wood blocks, perfectly re-wrapped to fool the discerning eye. She was shocked for only a moment, realizing that we were both victims of the so-called "professionals" with whom I worked. She also liked it when I brought her the real candy a day later.

We sent Tom Bos on his way to his out-of-town wedding happily and carefully carrying a heavy, bulky, expensive present from all of us to the lucky couple. This gift was as heavy and bulky as a pile of worthless scrap metal can be. He laboriously lifted it onto the luggage rack on the train, daring not to sleep, lest this expensive package be stolen. When he arrived at his destination, his fiancée, Betty, took the gift upstairs where the gifts were to be displayed. Soon she returned, whispering in his ear to come see the lovely gift he had brought on our behalf. After recovering, Tom knew that the real gift would be delivered later. Early next morning, the day of the wedding, he returned to the depot to see the precious cargo on the floor of the baggage car when the door slid open. The express agent wheeled the freight wagon up to the door before the baggage man unceremoniously shoved the precious cargo off the train with his foot. The packaging might have been a little the worse for wear, but the gift itself (a lovely gas lamp) arrived undamaged at the new home of the bride and groom.

I am astounded at how juvenile we were, in that dumbest of jokes supplied endless mirth. It seemed that the dumber, the better. One never returned to his drafting stool without checking to see if it had become inadvertently damp. Soon even this precaution was not adequate, as we rigged rubber hoses to deliver the water lovingly warmed up to body temperature. Jim Kruger's stool's location was the easiest for this treatment. He remarked that, "If you fellows are still in your diapers, I might as well join you." Our fellow artist in Grand Rapids said if you saw a man come into a restaurant who always checked his seat before sitting down, he must work for Dickinson's. It's a wonder that any etching ever got done.

We sent the errand boy to the office to replace our studio towels that were fouled with ink from rubbing off proof plates. Inevitably, Julia sent them back saying they were not dirty enough to be retired. We all chipped in to buy a dozen small towels, painting funny faces on them, to tack up on the studio walls. No one said a word when Miriam came into the studio with an assignment for us, nor when Mr. Dickinson himself graced us with his presence soon after, but at any rate, clean towels soon appeared, although not until Julia made sure our cartooned towels had been used wiping plates.

When we got busy, Dickinson's hired extras to help take up the slack. These fellows did not break into our regular gang, soon leaving, but not before participating in the mayhem that made up a day in the studio. One fellow wore a derby, which was not so unusual in that day, since it was the hat style of choice. However, he never removed it. When I asked if he slept in it, he glared at me with such malevolence that I dared not press the question. I hoped that his silent answer did not mean yes. He was a pretty hard guy and I did not put it past him.

Mose was the best. I had met him at one of Alten's life classes. He was a perfect specimen of manhood, paying for his lessons by posing for the class. He was not much of an artist, the main criterion by which one joined our inner circle, but we liked him since he was friendly enough. He could pull what seemed to me to be an infinite number of chin-ups on the gas pipe running across the studio. I hate to think of what might have happened if our gymnastics pulled the pipe loose, but in those days we were immortal, or least we drew like it. We conspired as to how we could take advantage of this new power in our midst. The men in other departments mocked us as puny artists, but now we had a ringer to challenge all comers. We soon bet with our former tormentors to try to beat the new "puny" artist in a contest of who could do the most pull-ups. We trained Mose to beat his challengers by only one pull-up, performed with the maximum amount of apparent effort. From then on, we had a constant line of challengers, many of them repeaters who had done more training. Mose always won, but alas, our busy streak ended and our golden biceps sought work elsewhere.

Jake Feenstra and I joined the YMCA. Following the lead of our robust President in Washington, young men all over the country sought a more vigorous life. Twice a week, we walked downtown for gym classes. Becoming stronger and faster was not the only reason to join the "Y". There was no bathroom at home, so the showers and the pool were important reasons to join. What a luxury it was to bathe without having to heat the water and drain the tub! It was there that I finally learned to swim with the newly introduced "Australian Crawl". If only we had been taught this as boys! Every time I entered the pool, I thought of poor drowned Raggy, saying a little prayer.

We liked to compete at what we did. I discovered that I ran faster than almost everyone else. I set my sights on the annual "turkey-day" five-mile run that the "Y" sponsored. Since Thanksgiving occurs on a Thursday, and not Sunday, I was excused from church services for the day. I started training out on the road with my fellow competitors. There were no athletic or rubber shoes back then, so I found a pair of broken-down oxfords that fit my feet with thick socks my mother had knitted. A cobbler fit a special heal that was straight and chamfered at rear, so it would not be knocked off by the heal strike.

Thanksgiving Day dawned sunny and cool, ideal for the race. We rode out South Division Street in an open horse-drawn wagon with improvised benches along the side. To stay warm we sang, to the tune of "My Native Country Thee, Sweet land of Liberty,"

There are no flies on us,
There are no flies on us,
No flies on us.
There may be one or two,
Great big fat flies on you,
But there are no flies on us,
No flies on us.

This bit of doggerel did wonders to set a steady pace when the running began in earnest. The initial jocularity of young men quieted as the horse plodded mile after mile. Grand Rapids was now far behind us. I tried to remember where the interurban line ran south of town in case I needed its help to return to town.

At last we stopped. We stripped off our outer layers, leaving them in the wagon, which followed us back into town. Nervously assembled at the line, we jumped at the sound of the gun, setting off north. I took off, believing that my fast pace reflected naturally superior speed, but this was a rookie mistake. Faster in the shorter distances, I should have paced myself. After a mile, I flagged, now being passed with some regularity. Humming on about flies, I settled into a sustainable pace to see the first houses at the edge of town. Running down a closed-off Division Street was a thrill. At last I crossed the finish line, putting my hands on my knees to catch my breath. Only then did the blister begin to really hurt. I did not come in first as I had fantasized (what runner doesn't, when grinding out those training miles?), but at least I was not the last. The winner delivered the Evening Press on foot, so he put in many miles every day. Jake was there to greet me, throwing his arm around me. His disappointment was greater than mine, because he was sure no one would beat me. Turkey dinner that afternoon sure tasted great. Is it any wonder it was my favorite American holiday, centering on dinner? My athletic career was not entirely futile. The next spring, I participated in the YMCA's Olympic style games at the Western Michigan fairground. There, my speed paid off: I was awarded a bronze medal in the pentathlon of hundred yard dash, pole vault, high hump, long jump, and a mile run around the horse track.

I was not the only one growing up. Our family changed as the siblings looked beyond our home, starting their own families. Our parents aged, relying on us more frequently, slowing from a life of constant toil. I am sure they were pleased with the opportunities that Michigan afforded us. This is why we had come. Even though life changed, and changed rapidly, they appreciated that our church-centered Dutch culture remained strong. Here in America, religion was not dominated by the state-sponsored church, so every congregation was a laboratory for doctrine, theology, and governance. Though we stayed loyal to the Alpine Avenue Church, others opted for different near-by Christian Reformed congregations suiting their fancy. Choice of one's pastor is a very personal thing. During this time, I became aware of the Presbyterians, who share our Calvinist heritage, taking root in Scotland and now here, like us, in the United States. Throughout my life, I attended Presbyterian services when I found the CRC too cloistered and self-absorbed in matters pertaining to the interests of the Dutch, and not bringing about God's Kingdom.

The older siblings married, leaving home. Though the extra space was appreciated by the remaining members of my large family, we missed each person who left. We had been through so much and spent time so much together. At night, we had gathered at home or at church to avoid the temptations and expenditures found outside the door. Together, we listened to father's readings from the Bible (in Friesian), sharing our fears and aspirations. Home life was never as cozy as when we gathered around our monstrous stove under the gas lamps. But now it was time for this faith and fellowship to extend beyond our nuclear group. We welcomed each new spouse, although they had not shared our unique arc from our little Friesian village to burgeoning Grand Rapids. If the President was "bully", we were too. I had grown to be large and strapping. With my etching tool in my hand, I was ready to take on the world.

In the flat above the store, we now had room to install an indoor bathroom. Grand Rapids had grown to the point that a sewer system now extended outward. We still relied on our kitchen pump for the house's water, and our new bathroom featured a large pitcher and basin. It was a treat not to have to retreat to the outhouse early in the day, especially on a frigid January morning. However without the benefits of a two-hole outhouse, or the motivation of cold wood, it seemed as if the door to our new room was closed for hours on end, frequently occupied by two younger sisters, who, too, were growing up.

Chapter 9

A custom among the young Dutch Westsiders was to stroll along Leonard Avenue, the main street in our community, to the old bridge across the river that led to Grand Rapids proper. As young people are wont to do, this was an opportunity to couple up and learn something about each other.

On July 12th, 1896 - funny how I remember the exact date - Jake and I went down to Leonard Street in the evening to see what might be happening. At the time, I was sixteen and pretty raw. We had been to church and had our eyes on a couple of girls, but could barely muster the courage to ask if we could walk them home, until it was almost too late. I knew that I wanted to walk with Hattie Lindemulder. Jake did not care since he thought that both girls were nice. As it turns out, he walked home with Lena Ruster who later would be attracted to an older man in the form of my brother Gerrit. As I said, we lived a fairly small and tight community.

After that night, Hattie and I sought out each other's company. It was not like we were dating or anything, but we had ample time to see each other whether after church services or catechism. I kept doing my usual things like playing ball, but found reasons to spend time at her house. Everyone was comfortable to let a good friendship blossom. Hattie brothers were my age, and I joked with them. Since they all worked in their father's grocery, they were at ease in social situations, making me feel comfortable, even if they were not above pulling a joke on me. Though I had grown up with plenty of sisters, I had spent none of my time outside of the house with other girls, so it took some practice to learn how to behave around one. Hattie was a patient instructor, and soon I was smitten, hoping that she felt some affection for me.

Hattie worked at her father's grocery store for a while. I visited her there or later at the fine china section at Wurzburg's department store where she clerked. I stopped there on my own way home from work, waiting for her to wrap up so we could walk back to the Westside together. Seven years after the first stroll home together from church, I gave her a ring inscribed "H.V. to H.L. April 7, 1903." By then, I was pretty sure she would accept it. We had grown up together, and would do so for the rest of our lives.

During those seven years we had wonderful times, as only young people can. A favorite trip was to take the streetcar to the end of the line at Reed's Lake. There we boarded the steamboat Charles E. Belknap for a trip around the lake. Or we rented a row boat, feasting on peanuts and Cracker Jack. We rowed up the Grand River to the North Park Pavilion. Hattie always brought a picnic basket with enough food for four. I probably would have liked her even if her father was not a grocer, but the laden hamper did not hurt.

As dumb kids, not all of our excursions were successful. One summer day, we boarded an excursion train to Ottawa Beach, on the shores of Lake Michigan. We hiked over the dune to the lake, returning to the station after the returning excursion had departed. I knew that stranding their daughter thirty miles from home would not make me popular with her parents. Fortunately, a through train from Chicago was due within the half hour. Unfortunately, our excursion tickets would not be good for this express. Working at Dickinson's at the time, my pockets were empty. I hocked my watch with a sympathetic gentleman on the platform who had been young once, too. He loaned me enough for the fare, until I could repay him the following day. Our misadventure ended well when we steamed by the sidetracked excursion train. Hattie's parents had been skeptical of the excursion in the first place, so I was relieved to return her home before the promised hour. This made up for the long streetcar ride to southeast Grand Rapids the following day to retrieve my watch and repay my benefactor. He pointed out that there was not much point in having a watch if one did not make use of it.

Bicycles swept the nation. Hattie and I each owned one. On Saturdays, we headed out on many an excursion. Especially fun was the day we rented a tandem bicycle. Hattie took the front while I provided the power as the stroker. Together that day, we were as fast as any of the other cyclists on the river road.

For a real outing, however, a young man rented a horse and buggy to take his sweetheart for a ride into the country. This was fine, except that I was not especially partial to horses. They were big, often doing what they, not I, wanted. As a boy, as I curry combed our Dobbin, he would push me up against the side of the stall. This was nothing compared to my adventures with the rented buggies. The livery stables where I rented the buggies loved me as a customer. Most young men asked for the most spirited horses, running them hard and lathering them, or crashing the buggies. For me, the livery brought out the most wooden-legged nag in the stable hitched to a freshly polished buggy that I could proudly drive to the Lindemulder corner of Alpine Avenue and Ninth Street. In spite of the spiffy buggy, Hattie's brothers laughed when I pulled up in front of her house with this broken-down horse. The Lindemulders had a stable full of beautiful horses that they used to deliver their groceries. Each member of the family was proud of these magnificent animals and knew how to drive them. With a good eye for horseflesh, they knew I was driving a dog. No doubt Hattie told them to hush in commenting on the nag that was about to pull their sister.

The brothers' approbation to my horse and carriage was nothing compared to what happened when we hit the open road. Crossing the Grand River by ferry, my rented horse spooked, trying to jump off. Fortunately, she was restrained by the other passengers. Then, our horse bolted from a bunny running across the road. These city horses quickly spooked at the sights and smells of the country. We were off and running. Hattie helped me slow the runaway, but only after I had let the situation get completely out of control. On that ride, I learned how a good relationship is a true partnership.

The Lindemulder brothers welcomed me into their home, but were not above taking advantage of me. Hattie's grandmother was in her nineties and stone deaf. She still liked to go to church; not hearing a thing, but still pleased "to be in God's house, in the presence of God's people". One evening, when I called on Hattie, her brother John let me into the front room. The only other person in the room was Gram Lindemulder. I had never met her before, since she spent most of her time in a little place of her own behind the main house. I was somewhat taken aback, seeing only John and the old lady. Seeing this, John had a little fun at my expense. Taking me over to Gram, he shouted at the top of his lungs, "Dit is Hattie's frijer – This is Hattie's beau." She stared at me kindly, not understanding a word, but reached out to take my hand. John kept hollering as I looked meaningfully at Gram, keeping my blood from rising. She finally understood who I was, but not before Hattie had rushed downstairs, taking my hand to lead me out the door.

We had our most serious adventure together in the year before we married, on Decoration Day, or what we now call Memorial Day. We celebrated the onset of summer by renting a rowboat to cruise downstream on the river. I reserved a boat at the rental located on the west shore near the Wealthy Street Bridge. Early on the morning of the holiday, we rode the streetcar to the dock with a picnic. On a placid morning, we set out downstream. Before long, we located a shady grove on the southeast bank of the river. We pulled to shore, finding an ideal spot for our picnic. As noon approached, I gathered some of the copious driftwood, building a small fire to roast wieners and marshmallows. These foods were a big treat, so I helped myself to several portions. I hoped Hattie did not think of me as a glutton. Although we were relaxed and alone in this little corner of the world, I would never take advantage of her under such a circumstance. It was only after lunch that we noticed that the sky to the west was turning ominously dark blue, verging on black. We both had lived in Michigan long enough to know that the storm bearing down would be a doozy. I said that we should find shelter immediately. Hattie was more scared than I as we left everything by the river to run for a distant farmhouse.

Thunder and lightning punctuated the sheets of rain that hit us before we reached the house. We would be splashed by buckets of water, then momentarily recover before being slammed again. Our once sure footing became perilous as we helped the other keep balance as we slipped on the mud. We momentarily lost sight of the farmhouse, splashing across a now swollen little stream. Our clothes and shoes were now soaked through. Two elderly sisters owned the farmhouse (and our picnic grove). Any suspicions they might have had regarding the young trespassers were overcome by our soaked plight. They had watched us stumble across their field, opening the door when our feet hit the porch. They took Hattie into a bedroom to re-dress her in their clothes. It may not have been the latest in style, but it was dry. In the meantime, their hired man took me into a little shed where I took off everything I was wearing except my underwear. We hung my duds around a blazing small potbelly stove while we watched the torrents outside the door. Less than an hour later, the rain relented before an odd patch of blue appeared in the sky. Returning to the house, I bit my tongue not to laugh at Hattie's outfit, but my wool trousers did not smell all that great either. An interurban ran nearby so we could ride back to town. I now knew to have carfare with me at all times.

The next day was Sunday, but father allowed me to return to the farm to retrieve the boat. I took the interurban back out of town, returning Hattie's borrowed clothing. I labored against the swollen current, the Grand still flowing strongly from the storm. I had my best times on that river and the worst. Pulling my way upstream, a thousand memories of life on the river welled up - of Raggy, the logging booms, the fishers. My sore muscles prompted me to keep looking over my shoulder for the Wealthy Street Bridge. I guess I was a true Dutchman at heart, with one foot always in the water. At last, the bridge hove into sight. The owner of the boat concession was open for business on Sunday. Happy to see that I had not lost his boat in the storm, he did not charge for the extra day's rental, but pointed to the sign suggesting that patrons should always row upstream first.

Hattie and I had spent enough time together and had been through enough that we realized we could live together. Though our families were not particularly close, they both attended the same church, recognizing each other as God-centered families. Both of our fathers were small business entrepreneurs, though the Lindemulder grocery store was more successful financially than my parents' paint and wallpaper concern. The Lindemulders were partially Friesian, coming from the same northern end of the Netherlands. They also had some German blood, since the border with that country was only a few leagues from their hometown.

Soon after our time on the river, I added up my savings, priced some furniture, estimating that I could support a household of my own with a young bride. Next, I consulted with my parents. They were delighted with my choice of Hattie. We hoped that her family would accept my proposal. I earned twenty-one dollars a week; in those days, a perfectly adequate wage, especially for a twenty-three year old. My father said that we could lease our former home on Jennette Street for nine dollars a month.

With these arrangements, I went to the Lindemulder house on Alpine Avenue. After a brief consultation with Hattie, where I received her consent, I visited with her father. He could tell by the entertainments that I showed his daughter that I was a young man on the make but he needed to be sure that I was not spending all of my income. He was sufficiently impressed with my plans and financial wherewithal that, after talking it over with Hattie's mom, they, too, gave their consent. We set the date for the first day of September of that year.

Father visited his tenants to notify them that I would be moving into my boyhood home, giving them two months to find a new place to live. The tenants agreed. I contracted to buy two tons of mixed coal (soft and hard) for fifteen dollars, so I could keep my bride warm for the entire winter. However, nothing is easy. When

I arrived at our new house for the furniture to be delivered, the premises were not vacated. Father immediately visited the tenants who threatened not to leave unless they were returned the last month's rent. I told Father not to surrender to this obvious extortion; Hattie and I would muddle through. Father, not wanting our marriage to start under such an ominous cloud, or perhaps saving face in front of the Lindemulders, relented to the tenant's demand. What disappointed us both is that a Dutchman had so little honor as to renege on a promise. Like everyone else in our community, our word was our bond. It made the community function, setting us apart from Grand Rapids as a whole. Father and I both knew that while he would never have an extra house to rent to one of his children back in Friesland, this incident would not have happened there either. Everyone here was preoccupied with getting ahead, not getting along. There was nothing wrong with that, as long as it was not at the expense of others. We tried to extend the lessons from Sunday to the other days of the week, expecting it from others.

Hattie's uncle Hedrik Van Hoogen was the pastor of the Central Avenue Christian Reformed Church, a large congregation in Holland, Michigan. Many of the preachers in our denomination could preach in English or Dutch. Reverend Van Hoogen used only his native Dutch. Hattie wanted him to marry us, so one Saturday, we took the interurban to Holland. Holland is a small town about twenty miles west of Grand Rapids, located on a lake that feeds into Lake Michigan. Though small, Holland was important to the Michigan Dutch because it was where the first colony of Netherlanders landed in Western Michigan under Dominie van Raalte. We stayed with the Van Hoogen family over the weekend before departing on Monday. They were very devout. Before retiring, each of us said our prayers while kneeling at our chair. This was an observance that I have not encountered before or since.

Hattie's aunt and uncle were happy in America, primarily because they were free from class barriers and restrictions inherent in the office of a minister of the Gospel that were observed in the Netherlands. When you have a state religion, a minister becomes an officer of the state, and hence, a politician. Most ministers had enough trouble managing their consistories, without answering to a bureaucracy. The American denomination is very democratic, with each congregation independent. The classis of ministers who govern the entire denomination decide by majority rule. Mrs. Van Hoogen liked to go to the grocery store and carry home her purchases. Even a small liberty like this would have been out of the question in the Netherlands. A woman of her station was expected to have a servant perform this menial task. When someone asked Rev. Van Hoogen what he liked about America, he replied, "Because it is the land of "hurry up" and "I don't care". Even a saintly gentleman like the Reverend relished the free air of our adopted country, even though he had been a respected *Dominie* in the Netherlands. They adored Hattie and thought I was just good enough, so the Reverend was happy to come to Grand Rapids to marry us later that summer.

As a couple, we kept a diary of our marriage. Here's the excerpt from the first entry dated September 1, 1903:

> We were married at Hattie's home at 6:30 in the evening by Hattie's uncle Rev. Hendrik Van Hoogen…Supper was served immediately after the ceremony. The waitresses were Mrs. John Suit, Mrs. John Lindemulder, and Mrs. Gerritt Lindemulder. Our wedding was strictly a family affair, none present besides our parents, brothers and sisters, and their children. The only exception being my friend Martin Kruizenga, a talented artist-musician who played the wedding march and Mr. and Mrs. Herman deBoer, business partner in the Lindemulder grocery store.
>
> The evening was pleasantly spent playing games, etc. after which we left for our honeymoon. At 9:40, amid a shower of rice, we took a hired carriage to Union Depot. Took the 10:15 train to

Ottawa Beach, connecting with the Graham & Morton Steamer Puritan, sailing for Chicago.

The diary is silent on the rest of the overnight trip to Chicago.

Our life together as man and wife began bright and early the next morning in the bustling Midwest metropolis. As an old Chicago hand, I was eager to show Hattie the sights. We took the Wells Street cable car to Lincoln Park, visiting the zoo and the beautiful pavilions in the park grounds. My bride looked very fetching in her brown traveling suit. Hattie was soon to find that her "man of the world" was not as experienced as she might have thought. We walked into the Saratoga Hotel asking for a room. The clerk asked if we had a reservation. What was that? I did not know there was such a thing. I thought you just walked into hotels where they would be eager for your business.

"I am sorry sir, no room is available." We settled for Thompson Hotel, several blocks away. Looking back, I think that the Saratoga thought we were a young couple seeking a liaison. As reputable establishment they would not countenance it. The Thompson was not as choosy. I remember being very self-conscious when asking for a room for myself and my wife. I was so modest and thrilled by the escalation in our relationship that I am sure I blushed.

After this incident, I hoped Hattie did not think of me as a complete dunce. If she did, she did not let on. The respective quality of the hotels made no difference to her. She was excited to be married and in Chicago. Me too, however, I mourned the loss of my third bowler within the year. Granted my head is round, so that headgear does not adhere particularly well, but this was getting ridiculous. After we boarded the Puritan at Ottawa Beach, we went on deck. Soon after our steamer cleared the channel on to Lake Michigan proper, a gust lifted my hat where it sailed up among the gulls before sinking ingloriously among the waves. My first loss of the year occurred on the Pearl Street Bridge, where, intently negotiating the multiple streams of traffic on my bicycle, I did not notice the wind until it lifted my hat over the guardrail into the murky river below. On Decoration Day, before renting the boat with Hattie, I joined Jake for an experiment with his canoe. He had mounted a mast and sail, picturing himself effortlessly proceeding upstream. This did not happen as the wind promptly knocked the canoe over, depositing both passengers unceremoniously in the river. We swam back to dock, pushing the swamped canoe, but the current carried paddles, seat cushions, and yes, my bowler, downstream. I concluded that headgear and water were not a good combination.

The following morning in Chicago, having forgotten to draw the curtains in our room, we awoke early, and brazenly kissed before setting out for breakfast and shopping. There was far more to buy and wish for here than in our small city. Soon after, we boarded the steamer Christopher Columbus for a trip to Milwaukee. We arrived in the afternoon, walking around the downtown before catching the eight o'clock overnight Pere Marquette Line steamer to Ludington, Michigan. We arrived early the next morning in a drizzle that promised to continue for the day. The early frisson of our days in the big cities was replaced by a day of hard traveling. Hattie and I ran to the train that was fortunately waiting across from the steamer dock. I ducked into a restaurant to buy a basket lunch for our trip. The train left at seven so we settled in briefly before arriving in Baldwin to connect with the local running south to Otia where we arrived a couple of hours later.

No one was at the station to meet us so we set out on foot to my sister's farm. Degina knew we would be joining her on our honeymoon, but communication had been only by mail (there was no phone service in the country, and we had not established the exact time and date). We were used to walking, since that was our main mode of getting around. If we had our bicycles, they would have not done much good on the soft sand roads on which we now traveled. I did, however, know the way. After about an hour, we were relieved to drop our suitcases on the porch as Degina gave us both a hug, gushing to Hattie about how horrid her brother was to make his bride walk through the mud.

The next ten days were a complete vacation. We did not have to worry about making our way through the big cities or running to catch various steamers. After several days of dressing and acting formally, we now wore our old clothes, reveling in just being together. Degina and her husband had only one child at the time, Kendriena. We had fun trying to get her to walk, but she was content to just scoot around on her bottom. The farm wasn't much to look at, but once the weather lifted, I set out with my watercolor kit, sketching the surroundings. Several small lakes punctuated the second-growth forest that made up the place and the fishing was good.

Our new marriage almost ended abruptly. One of my sister's neighbors was a former clergyman. In retirement, he became increasingly unmoored. One morning, he spied me walking about when I was looking for a place to start sketching. Sure that I was an unsavory intruder, he returned to the house for a loaded shotgun. Fortunately, his son was at home to take the gun from him. I blithely started my work, unaware that this was taking place (learning about it years later). If our church was a rather small pool in which to meet one's spouse, the community around this lake was even smaller. The son who restrained his father became Kendriena's husband about twenty years later. I suppose that if his father had taken my life their mutual attraction might have been somewhat diminished. We survived the rest of our honeymoon, taking the 8:49 train back to our lives together in Grand Rapids on the tenth of September.

We had been together for over seven years, so we were quite used to each other. However, living together is entirely different, as we began to adapt to life together. The biggest challenge was not so much adjusting to each other's tics but to living on our own. All of our lives we had lived with our large families in our respective homes. Each of our father's authority was uncontested; they made all of the major decisions including for us. Now, not only was I responsible for my own life, but for Hattie's, too. She made it easy. I realize that she now managed me as easily as she controlled those big horses that terrified me.

As a special treat for her, I purchased a gas stove, so we no longer had to haul in wood to cook. Especially gratifying was not waiting for the kindling to ignite in order to make a cup of tea. Hattie was nervous as I suppose any young bride would be with having to cook, constantly providing meals, but my appetite was ravenous, so I thought she was a pretty good cook. As a grocer's daughter, she was aware of many more food stuffs that my old country mother. Like any prudent couple, we bought a store of potatoes so as not to starve over the winter. Life in the New World was pretty good, but we were not that far removed from the privations of the old.

We settled into the routine of running our house and making a living. Mondays were washday, requiring that we arise at four-thirty in the morning. I am not sure what was worse, the incessant ticking of the Baby Ben alarm clock through the night or its piercing ring in the dark. I stumbled down to the big stove in the living room, shook the grate, opening the vent to invigorate the previous night's coals. Then I carried on to the back room to lift a heavy boiler of water on to the stove, lighting the kindling which I had laid out the night before. Before filling the boiler, I primed the pump with a bucket of water I always kept on hand. In summer, we used the nice soft rainwater captured in the cistern. In winter, we pumped from the deeper well. The sandy Grand Rapids soils assured that we had ample water, even if the arm tired from "shaking hands" with the pump. In the winter, I made sure that the pump lost its prime, so that the column of water in the pump shaft did not freeze overnight. Winter meant that it was also necessary to break the skim of ice on the top of the bucket. We ate while the laundry water warmed on the old wood stove. I got up frequently tending the fire, adding some oak to the blazing pine.

After breakfast, I shaved before helping Hattie with the laundry until it was time to go. Most young fellows with downtown jobs were clean shaven as was now the fashion. The big beards and mutton chops of the last century were now found mostly on the older men and those working in the factories who found the daily routine of stropping a razor to be too much work. I switched to a Gillette "safety razor" a little after this, making the morning routine easier. While I headed to the Dickinson Studio, Hattie stayed home scrubbing the laundry. Washing machines were still not worth buying. Her entire morning was consumed with the back-breaking work of scrubbing our clothes one piece at a time on the washboard. There was still no inside toilet or bath in the Jennette Street house. Evenings before retiring, we visited the privy together (it was two-hole), since Hattie was reluctant to go alone in the dark. We became quite quick in the winter. We took our baths in a big wash tub near the kitchen stove, again after the same laborious process of warming the water. When I wanted to splurge, I took a bath at a downtown barber shop, costing fifteen cents for the hot water, soap and towels.

We bought our supply of winter potatoes from an uncle of my pal Jake Feenstra. We visited their farm with Jake, getting to know the family. The farm was out near Eastmanville. After being invited, we went out on a winter's day. We took the interurban to Coopersville where they met us in their horse-drawn sleigh. There was not much work to do on the farm with snow on the ground, so the farmer and I spent the day hunting rabbits. Though I was too young when we left the Netherlands, I knew that it was popular to supplement the winter diet with small game and fish caught through holes broken into the ice. A little fresh game was an appreciated addition to the bland winter diet.

They were a tight-knit family, but gave up one of their bedrooms so Hattie and I could sleep in privacy. This was a sacrifice, since I recall there were seven or eight kids - all boys except for Jennie, whom I think was the oldest. After an evening of singing and telling jokes, Jennie took us upstairs to the bedroom. For their guests, they stuffed the "tick" with new straw, so we needed a stool to climb into bed. Jennie suggested we get undressed near the chimney in the corner, "As it's a shade warmer." By their standards, this was solid comfort. I guess it actually was not all that more primitive than our drafty home with its store-bought mattress.

The next morning, the two oldest boys took me hunting, but it was so cold that few rabbits were out. The boys claimed that this would not be a problem, pulling a ferret from a grain sack. Coming upon a promising rabbit hole, they dropped the ferret down it to flush out the occupants. No rabbits were at home or they high-tailed it to a different opening out of our sight. The ferret preferred the hole to the sack, not to be seen for the rest of the excursion. We trudged home for a shovel, returning to the hole. Jake became more exercised as, bit-by-bit, he scraped at the frozen soil.

"I'll kill that little monster," he exclaimed after a half-hour's work. Of course, finally grasping his prey, he did not, since a dead ferret would hardly be the point of so much work.

Early the next day, we rode their sleigh to the interurban station in Coopersville. The straw under blankets and the hot water jugs between our feet did little to stem the bitter cold. We said our goodbyes and thank yous while stomping our feet to restore circulation. After maybe fifteen minutes, we saw the head light far off in the woods, the only bright spot in a grey Michigan winter's day. The interurban car was not much warmer, but it was out of the wind. The bonhomie of the small crowd returning to G.R. buoyed everyone's spirits. I put my arm around my sweetheart as we looked over the operator's shoulder down the track towards the future.

We were not in the Jennette Street house for very long. After seven months, father said that he and mother needed to move in. Mother's heart was failing so that the stairs up to their residence above the paint store were becoming too much for her. They could live on one floor in the Jennette Street house. I had thought that maybe Hattie and I might have lived there forever. Little did I know that would be the first of many moves we would make over our lives. I had not yet learned that to be American meant to be on the move, whether for more space for children or for a better opportunity. When our parents uprooted us from Holland, they set us on a course whereby we would cover more territory than they could even dream about. The world expanding with interurbans and steamers was about to explode with an unimagined variety of transportation options.

I did not pay much attention to the first automobiles. They were impractical and expensive, rich men's toys often broken down by the side of the road. I was certain that they would never replace the horse and buggy or especially the street car, which for a nickel or two, took us everywhere we wanted to go.

We regretted leaving the Jennette Street house. It was close to everything important in our world - our parents, the Alpine Avenue church, and my pals from the neighborhood. Our carpets had been cut to fit the rooms. However, we found a place not too far away. Rent was an even better eight dollars per month.

Hattie gave birth to our first baby, a boy, who in the Dutch tradition, we gave the English version of my father's name: Melvin Harold. That day, the first of August, Hattie sent me off to work even though she had slight pains. No sooner had I settled into my first assignment of the day than Mr. Dickenson came to my desk to tell me that he had received a phone call asking me to come home. I flew on my bicycle across the Leonard Street Bridge. After first checking on Hattie, I ran down to the corner grocery to call the doctor, who did not answer, and then called my brother-in-law, John Lindemulder. Mrs. Postma, our midwife, was with John's wife, Louise, taking care of their first-born. We all agreed that our situation was more pressing and Mrs. Postma agreed to come over. I continued calling for doctors until at last Dr. Thompson answered saying that he could come, but not until one-o'clock that afternoon. By the time I was back home, both Hattie and I were panting. Things settled down briefly when the professionals arrived. Dr. Thompson examined Hattie at one o'clock. Sure that the baby would not be born until three, he promptly left.

Fortunately, Mrs. Postma then arrived, calming us down before giving me a list of supplies she needed. Dr. Thompson did not arrive until three-thirty, but that was no problem except to my mental health since Mel was not born until four-thirty. By that time, I was banished to the front room, dreading the horrible sounds coming from my wife in the bedroom. As much as this anguished me, I figured that if the doctor or mid-wife were not raising their voices, things were going relatively well. At last Hattie quieted, and I heard a new squalling voice, so I could enter the bedroom. Our son was a small red mess, but I could not have loved him more. His poor mother was exhausted, but quite pleased with her boy and surviving the ordeal.

The doctor and the mid-wife left, but Mel remained. We confronted the enormity of what we had done. This loud creature was completely dependent on us. We had no idea how to make him happy. We looked at each other, gulped, talking to the little guy, trying to figure out how to communicate. Mrs. Postma's return the next morning was a great help. She knew all about caring for babies, showing two rookies the ropes. I waited for her to arrive before leaving for work. I could get downtown quickly on my bicycle, but Mrs. Postma had to walk from her home a mile away. She chided me that I need not wait, since Hattie would be alone with the baby many times after this day. Mrs. Postma was a blessing for all beginning families. She would eventually help with the birth of all of our children. Because her services were in such high demand, we contacted her as soon as we knew we were expecting. Neither she nor we had a telephone, so we would visit her at night, quelling the rumors of Hattie's expecting until we were ready to announce.

I had other things on my mind, literally. Maybe I was affected by this new responsibility more than I realized. I took the responsibility of starting a family seriously. One afternoon, I left work with a splitting headache. This was rare; I had to be incapacitated to leave my drafting table. I usually became so engrossed in work that the day flew by without my noticing.

Leaving the office, I could not even mount my bike, instead stumbling to the streetcar to get to the doctor as soon as possible to alleviate the blinding pain. Shocked by my high fever, he gave me medicine before sending me home. He came to see me the following morning. I recall very little of that week except that the medicine broke the fever but left me very weak. For the first days, I had double vision, barely able to walk. After a week, I could stagger around the block, but it was a nearly a month before I went back to work.

I learned a valuable lesson from this experience. Walking around the block during my convalescence, I met a couple of men in the neighborhood of whom I had been completely unaware. Both suffered from terminal illnesses. This put my own situation into a better perspective. As a young person, I wondered why God had sent me this trial. From them I learned that we are called to be joyful and uncomplaining under the most trying of circumstances. My perception of the Book of Job changed from being a nice parable to a road map for living. I knew the Lord was asking me to reflect on my life and the success I had enjoyed to date. For faith to be real, it must be unshakeable, built on rock, not on sand. I had no idea how important this lesson would be.

As I grew stronger, I took advantage of this time to fill our wood box. We burned wood to heat water, as did almost everyone else. Wood in Western Michigan was plentiful, growing, well,... on trees. Hattie's father sold quite a bit of it on the side of his grocery store. He traded groceries for it with the surrounding farmers. Without much else to do, the farmers cut wood all winter. Grand Rapids on a cold winter's morning was blanketed with a cloud of smoke. This smell improved the further you walked from town, as more stoves burned wood rather than acrid coal. I do not miss the smell, but I liked the appearance of the low-lying cloud under a leaden winter sky. For now, my gaze was strictly downward as I aimed the maul towards the dead center of the log below me, splitting it so that it would easily burn in the stove. At first I could split only two or three logs, but as my strength returned, I split more than we needed, building up a nice stack by the kitchen door.

Chapter 10

I sacrificed my membership in the YMCA to stay within the household budget. We might have afforded the luxury, but I did not want to spend any more time away from Hattie and the baby than I already did earning a living. I stayed somewhat fit riding my bicycle to and from work and splitting our wood pile. However, I missed the shower baths that I took downtown. None of our rental houses had indoor bathrooms. To bathe, we heated water on the stove. I thought I could rectify this situation. With its wood cooking stove, the kitchen was the warmest room in the house, so it made sense to bath there. I purchased a large oak barrel. After drilling a hole near the bottom, Jake and I carried it upstairs. Into the drilled hole, I jammed a rubber hose, made watertight with a good wad of bitumen. I ran this hose through a small hole in the floor of the bedroom to the kitchen ceiling immediately below. At the other end of the hose, I attached a shower fixture. This fixture was a loop of copper tubing perforated with small holes. Wearing this around your neck would wet the entire body below. Just above the shower fixture, I attached a small valve.

Ready to test this invention, I hauled several buckets of warmed water upstairs to the oak barrel while Hattie pulled the shades before taking off her clothes in the kitchen. Standing in the tub, she put the copper ring around her neck. I usually was the "guinea pig" in my experiments, but not for this one. I could not have served very well since I hauled the water upstairs. Shouting down the stairs, I asked if she was ready. I heard "Yes," and poured the warm water into the barrel. The results were immediate when she shrieked, "It's too hot! IT'S TOO HOT!" I had tested the water with my finger, judging it to be the right temperature, but my finger and her naked body were not of the same sensitivity. Upstairs, there was not a thing that I could do. In the excitement of the experiment, I had forgotten to show her the shutoff valve, so she stood there, gamely taking the heat until I arrived.

Adding to this comedy of errors (Hattie did not think that it was particularly funny), is that the copper ring was designed to be used sitting down in a bath tub. If the water did not hit the body, it splashed against the side of the tub. With no tub, water sprayed all over the floor. I hurriedly shut off the valve, but most of the bucket was now on the floor. A bucket full does not make for much of a shower, but it makes an awful mess on a floor. Neither of us was in a very jovial mood at the time, but my dear bride capitalized on the recollection of this incident for many years in our young marriage.

Fortunately, I was forgiven enough so that early in 1907, our second baby arrived. This time we were blessed by a sweet little girl, Helen. That morning, the ice flows jammed the river, flooding low-lying areas. The boilers at the studio were extinguished, so there was no work. This happened early enough in the day that I was not trapped on the wrong side of the river. I was working at the kitchen table while Hattie bustled around getting the house in order. She mentioned a little cramp, but thought nothing of it, continuing her chores. Perhaps she wanted to put off the ordeal to come, but I immediately telephoned the doctor, Hattie's mother, and Mrs. Postma. Hattie was scrubbing the kitchen floor at three in the afternoon, unaware that in only three hours, a new person would join our family. It was not long before two-year old Melvin understood that things were now very different. As I could not go to work next day, we knew that he would be happier with some undivided attention at his grandmother's house. He soon adjusted. Helen was such a sweet baby that even our rambunctious son could not object. I made a special point of whisking him out of the house after work, mindful of the times I had spent with my father. Together, we inspected the neighborhood. Where else would two boys looking for a little mischief gravitate than towards the tracks and the river? He was as entranced as his dad by the clang, the smoke, and the steam of the towering locomotives. He was experiencing sublime pleasures not available to his baby sister trapped at home with her mother.

Hattie and I always loved the country, spending much of our time courting there. The Briggs Farm, which we knew and loved, was being subdivided, but it was still within walking distance of the street car line, so I could get to work. We bought a five - acre "estate", planning for a family paradise. Here's what the advertisement in Grand Rapids Evening Press said about the transaction: "Kinsey & Wood have sold to Harry Veenstra a five-acre tract on Coit Avenue just north of the city limits for $1,250.00. Mr. Veenstra will improve the holdings next year by the construction of a $2,000.00 residence which he will occupy." The statement about Mr. Veenstra building a $2,000.00 residence within the year was entirely the broker's contribution. We were hard pressed to buy the property, so any so called "improvements" were out of the question in the near term. If we were long on occupants for said improvements, we short on the means for paying for them. We bought the lot at the end of 1904, the year Melvin was born, and did not pay it off until after Helen came along. The price we paid may seem a bargain now, but at that time, it was a goodly sum, especially for two youngsters just starting out.

I tried to secure a loan from the Building and Loan Company, but they would not extend credit to properties outside the city limits. We were beyond the fire protection of the city's professional fire company, relying on the volunteer company of farmers, none of whom had motorized transport. If we were to build a house, it just could not burn. Undeterred, I painted a watercolor of what we wanted to build. My boss, Mr. Dickinson, used his influence to help us secure a loan. In March of 1907, we signed a contract to build our house over the next four months. The same day, Jake Feenstra and his dad began excavating for the foundation. There was no time to lose if the kids were going to play outside during the coming summer.

We had a full basement, furnace heat, a large living room with a fireplace, a large kitchen with separate pantry, and a dining room ready for an expanding family. We entered the house through a hall containing the stairs leading to the second floor with three bedrooms, a den, and a bath. The hall, living room, and dining room were paneled in the Craftsmen Style, which was popular at that time. It certainly was the nicest home in which I had ever lived. Come to think of it, we never owned a house afterwards that we liked as much.

The living room was separated from the entry hall by a large opening that could be closed off by sliding doors, which were concealed in pockets within the walls. These we usually left open, enhancing the space. At the far end of the living room facing the entrance from the hall sat the fireplace flanked on one wall by a bench where one could sit warming oneself while contemplating the sparks flying up the chimney.

With this house, we still used techniques I had learned from my parents: a large "Michigan Cellar" as a cool place to store foods, and a large cistern to capture rainwater. Storm flow from the roof was still the most reliable source of water for cooking and drinking. I had a well dug for water for laundry and indoor plumbing. We still did not have hot running water, but enjoyed the comfort and privacy of being indoors on those cold Michigan mornings. We were willing to sacrifice the camaraderie of our old two-holer for the warmth found inside.

Hattie and I were exceptionally blessed. Of all my siblings, I was the only one building a new house. Only my younger sisters ever finished high school. As I was growing up, our family's finances demanded that we all worked as soon we could. Mother and father did not send me into the furniture factory to build character, but to earn cash. But by indulging in my artistic interest, my parents set me on a course of work that would be the most lucrative of any of my brothers or sisters. I now earned $24.00 per week, which at the beginning of the century allowed us to build a princely house on the northern outskirts of Grand Rapids.

America's industries were booming. With the railroads, the entire continent became a market for enterprising companies. To get distant customers to buy their products, companies relied on advertising in building a brand that consumers could trust. This required artwork, so I was in the right place at the right time. With the demand for art, I could provide my young family with amenities that my parents struggled a lifetime to afford. Of course, they had seven mouths to feed, we had only two. Food was cheaper in America. In the bounty of Western Michigan, we no longer lived as close to the bone as we did in Friesland. Once again, we benefited from the more powerful locomotives pulling the longer trains, carrying more foodstuffs from more places. Naturally, we patronized Hattie's family's store, but cash and carry grocers like Atlantic and Pacific were opening. With them came a need for more national branded packaged products. The expansion of the economy needed an expansion of credit for people to purchase the new available goods. Banks lent mortgages for real estate purchase. I thanked the Almighty for looking over our young family in our new country.

We were building for the future. We thought that this would be the last house we would ever need. It certainly had room for the family we hoped and prayed for. How differently things were to turn out. It was at this time, I became aware of the phrase, "Man proposes, but God disposes." With my success, I did not give it much credibility, but I would soon learn its wisdom.

I had learned the value of real estate from my father. He made sure we lived in comfortable houses, the snow swirls above my early bed notwithstanding. Now that I was building a home of my own, he insisted on varnishing all of the woodwork personally. The results were spectacular. After sanding and filling the wood and concealing any blemishes, he shellacked it to seal the grain before applying several coats of varnish, sanding between each coat. The last coat of the "piano finish" was hand rubbed with oil and pumice stone, just as my father did in the residences of the rich in the Netherlands. He was proud that this was now for his own family instead of just the well off.

I bought shade and fruit trees, berry bushes, and decorative shrubbery; quickly growing sore from the digging. Fortunately, most of Western Michigan is sandy loam, otherwise I would have been in real trouble. I transplanted some mature shade trees, hoping (to paraphrase a biblical expression), to sit under my own "vine and apple tree" in my declining years.

This is when I first met Henry Upholt, who would have a significant influence on my life and vice versa. While we were still living on Alpine Avenue, Hattie and I took turns on Sundays staying home from church to take care of baby Melvin. No one had thought of a nursery in church at the time. It was on one of these Sundays that I was home that Mr. Upholt called on me unannounced. Reflecting on the first time that I met him, it was typical of everything he attempted later in life. He always had good practical plans, but never the sufficient capital or wherewithal to realize them. The man on my doorstep introduced himself as "Henry Upholt", before stating the purpose of his call. He had recently purchased the lot next to ours in North Park. If we combined our lots, we could run a street into our holdings, subdividing into several additional lots that we could sell.

This plan, profitable as it may be, would have defeated our reason for moving to North Park. We wanted the five acres to garden, plant a small orchard, and have plenty of room for any and all children we might have. I did not see Upholt again until we moved to North Park. He never developed his lot, again for lack of funds, living nearby in a rental house. After several years, he despaired of ever building, selling the lot for a small gain.

When the North Park house was finally finished, the four of us moved in the following spring. The house was lovely, fitting our needs with the added custom touches. We thought there would never be a reason for us to leave. Our neighbors were different from those with whom we had grown up. We were no longer in an exclusively Dutch community, and our new neighbors were of a higher social class than those on the West Side. One neighbor was probably Grand Rapid's most prominent architect. Another was a partner in a wholesale grocer who sold goods to Hattie's father. This was all quite different from our old neighborhood, where we attended the same church, so we knew each other's families. Now we lived among strangers; friendly and well paid strangers, but strangers nonetheless. Most were older than Hattie and me, doting on our children as we walked the dirt streets of the neighborhood. Everyone had moved there for the same reason, to get out of the city, enjoying the privacy and the opportunity to grow fruits and vegetables. We had no idea that we were in the vanguard of the exodus from the city that would be a pattern for the rest of the century. When we moved, we still depended on the streetcar to get to town and to run our errands.

Getting to the streetcar could sometimes be quite trying. In the city, I did not pay much attention to the phase of the moon, because streetlights, now electric, dimly illuminated each block. In North Park, if the moon were not out, I stumbled down the road in the dark. The scattered houses gave a faint outline of the street, but that was not enough as sometimes I tripped into the ditch alongside the road. Winter was worse. No one plowed the street. After a deep snow, I post-holed my way across the frozen expanse to get to work. Hattie and the children were trapped. On a snowy day, there was no way to get to town unless Hattie and I carried or cajoled the kids to the streetcar line. I now appreciated why I could buy so much land at such a bargain price.

Because everyone in the neighborhood experienced the same travails, we bonded in mutual aid. We started to appreciate that the norms of polite society in greater Grand Rapids were subtly different than in our previously strictly Dutch community. This new crowd did not go on and on about who was related to whom, since our own familial connections to them were irrelevant. People were more interested in places they had traveled or entertainments that they had enjoyed. As young Dutch people, we had not traveled much (Chicago did count as traveling among our North Park neighbors) and we certainly did not take in many "shows" or concerts. Instead, we quietly observed, learning more about America than we had in our previously sheltered existence. Because of our youth, our neighbors forgave our lack of experience, adopting our young family as an exotic addition to neighborhood, polishing their bona fides as not being snobs, willing to accept the Dutch, if not as members of polite society, at least as potential candidates.

Street lighting was not the only under-developed aspect of our new neighborhood. Children transform from toddlers into youngsters in a nonce. Education becomes a new priority. I knew why I never completed my formal education, but was determined that our children would have better advantages. Our children could not rely on the quite fortuitous arc of my young life. I certainly worked hard, but no harder than most people that I knew, and certainly not as hard as my parents. I had matured enough to understand that America provided opportunities far beyond those of rural Friesland. Judging by the backgrounds of my new neighbors, education facilitated taking advantage of all that America offered.

When we moved to North Park, the farm families there were served by a one-room framed white schoolhouse. The new families moving in overran this humble building with its one schoolmarm. Getting to the school was impossible in the winter. The school board, comprised of old settlers, was not about to raise taxes to pay for a new schoolhouse benefiting the newcomers. They thought that if their own farm could not be subdivided, the newcomers should just move back into Grand Rapids. At the annual meeting of the school board, we newcomers organized, achieved critical mass, and overturned the board. Our new board voted to build a new school closer to the south end of the district where the population was growing. The old timers were not deterred, securing court injunction to prevent the building of the new school. While the farmers pursued the rear guard action in the courts, the rest of us organized, holding countless neighborhood meetings, informing the voters of the problems facing the new board.

The newcomers also voted with their pocket books. Several of the new residents formed a corporation to build the school, confident that we would prevail in the courts. This group was well connected, including Congressman Huntley Russell. He was not intimidated by a few farmers who did not support education. Though not exactly a house-a-fire, the honorable Mr. Russell had enough wherewithal to marry into the Comstock family who came into Grand Rapids soon after the Pottawatomie had vacated the premises, doing very well for themselves selling the environs to those of us who arrived later. Their latest license to print money, Comstock Park, was situated across the river from our North Park home. A new school would make this property all the more valuable.

Mr. Russell was disposed to have a good opinion of himself and was not above singing, in a rather good tenor, "The Sword of Bunker Hill" at meetings to rally the troops. Our actions seemed revolutionary, but probably were not on par with the brave patriots who surrendered their lives on Breed's Hill overlooking Boston Harbor. If he was singing, he was not speaking, so the audience was satisfied with his stirring rendition, if not his rhetoric. The farmers had their day in court, but the injunction was vacated. The board promptly met, authorizing the bonds and property tax to pay for the purchase of the school. I was the youngest man actively interested in all of these doings. With my energy and my bicycle, I attended all of the meetings. I was there just to make sure my children had a place to go to school. I did not think that I played a very active role, but kept track of what was happening, reporting it throughout the community.

So I was quite surprised to be elected to the board and appointed as the treasurer. I certainly was honest enough; that everyone recognized, but I would need to bone up on my math skills. When were these people going to realize that I was just a poor artist without a high school education trying to help his family? In America, it did not matter who you were or where you came from; as long as you were willing to slip into the harness and pull the plow, good things happened. My father worked long and hard in Netherlands, but because of his station in life, never would have been elected to a school board or the church consistory.

Now because of good ears, fast note taking, and a bicycle, I was a leader in our young community. One of my first duties as treasurer was to write a check for $10,000. This responsibility was reward enough for all of the miles I had logged on my bicycle. This was the largest check I had ever written (or would) in my entire life.

When you own a "country estate", you might envision livestock contentedly grazing on the green sward. However, once you price four-legged livestock, you readily consider the two-legged variety. Chickens eat table scraps, need a small roost, but can provide ample eggs and the occasional chicken dinner. I calculated the profits from providing the bounty from our estate to the hungry masses in the city.

Chickens, like any living creature, require an adequate amount of space. As a humane chicken owner, I read up on what my flock needed, setting about building a coop and scratching yard to satisfy the most discriminating of fowl. In truth, this was like building an addition on to your house. After a month of construction, the architectural requirements of our new avian friends were met. Building anything out of wood is easy. It is the finishing and painting that takes time. That's me carrying the four rolls of chicken wire on the streetcar. Urban passengers did not take kindly to a country cousin taking up a row and much of an aisle. Their inconvenience was matched by my plight carrying eighty-five pounds of bulky chicken wire from the streetcar stop to our home.

I selected "Plymouth Rocks", promised in the catalog as a "Handsome Large Meaty Bird." I wanted an all-purpose fowl that laid plentiful eggs and turned table scraps into fat thighs and breasts. My neighbor opted for Leghorns, thinking their white plumage contrasted nicely with his groomed lawn.

Possibly I could have fed one of our birds on table scraps, but we were thrifty, eating most of what we cooked rather than sharing it with our avian friends. See me now on the streetcar now carrying twenty-pound bags of feed from town. I did not stop to calculate what I was paying for a chicken dinner that I could easily purchase from the butcher for fifty cents. Chickens live essentially outside, so during the winter, you have to buy enough feed to fuel them as surely as you need coal for the house. The feed store had "special mixtures" promising more egg production, but I am sure they were actually designed to elicit the last dollar out of the poultry grower's pocket.

At last my flock began laying eggs. I brought the first dozen to work, sure that this was the start of a thriving business. It was the last dozen I sold. There was no question regarding their freshness, but my eggs were smaller than those sold in the stores. I felt betrayed by my co-worker's failure in accepting my smaller product. Could they not just crack open two for breakfast? I guess not. Later, my pullets laid larger eggs as they aged.

If they did not lay, at least they could be eaten, right? Following the instructions in "Modern Poultry Raiser", I selected the bird that I thought was the poorest performer on the nest. Removing her young head was easy enough, surrendering to the inevitable with a good sound whack. The dinner portion of her anatomy had not been consulted on the docility of her demise, and promptly ran aimlessly about the yard. Appalled by the spectacle of a headless creature squirting blood, I was confident she would not go far. My appetite for the anticipated chicken dinner became somewhat subdued. Fifty cents at the butcher never seemed to be more of a bargain than that afternoon.

Following the instructions in "MPR", I took the finally quiescent dinner candidate to the cellar, dunking the carcass in a pail of scalding water. The odor released from the offal and soggy feathers was immediate and overpowering. By now, even buying a chicken for fifty cents seemed like a bad idea. I faced a dilemma. Any profit from my chicken raising was in the basement, daring me to return. I am nothing if not creative. Dabbing a little of Hattie's perfume onto a bandana wrapped across my nose, I returned to the netherworld. Taking frequent breaks, I produced something that might be oven ready. Oh, and the chicken I selected was full of embryo eggs. I never again read "MPR", nor slaughtered another bird. Chickens do not have the good sense to feed themselves, so we were tethered to the chicken coop. The birds were now my complete master. The greatest joy I derived from owning them was watching them scratch about the coop without a care in the world. They knew that they were among the luckiest creatures ever hatched.

Melvin was ready for kindergarten. I can still see the sturdy little fellow with his father's round head holding on to my hand as we climbed the stairs at the neighborhood school. I had a lump in my throat as I waved good bye, his red vest disappearing into the whirl of the classroom. Though I never was at a loss for my parents' affection, I knew that my children would have better educational opportunities than I did. Even in kindergarten, this school had far more resources than our one - room school in Stroobos. I hardly ever think about those days in the Netherlands. My life in America, now as adult, was so very different. The only thing that seemed unchanged was our bed-rock faith. I walked to the interurban, thankful for the opportunities, my family, and my faith. I could hardly wait to see what was next, as long as it did not involve poultry.

Chapter 11

In the summer of 1910, Hattie and I took a trip to Niagara Falls. This was our first trip away from the children since they were born. Niagara Falls was the greatest tourist destination in the United States. Visiting the natural wonders in the Western US was still very difficult, requiring weeks of time and multiple train transfers. Getting to Buffalo, New York, from Grand Rapids was easy. The trip to Detroit took about three hours. There we boarded a steamer that sailed the length of Lake Erie to Buffalo. We transferred to electric rail cars for the short trip to the falls. Stepping off the car, we heard the roar over the billowing mist. This still did not prepare us for the impact of seeing the cascade for the first time. The ongoing power of the rush never paused for a moment. One cannot see and feel this torrent without feeling the power and glory of the Creator and appreciate that this mighty spectacle is but a thimble in his oeuvre. As we stood there, I put my arm around my best friend (and my wife), looking at the falls, then at her, and then back at the falls. We stood speechless and humbled, so glad to share this experience together. As we walked away from the din, we would join our friends who had raved about their honeymoon trips to this natural spectacle.

We stayed overnight at the falls before taking the electric car back to the steamer dock in Buffalo. Back in Detroit, we took the interurban to visit the Upholts, now living in Plymouth, a small city to the west of Detroit. As a metallurgist, Upholt had moved to Plymouth as the superintendent of the Diamond Brass Company. He had found conditions there intolerable before he entered into business for himself. When I had last seen him, he had invented a cheap way to manufacture a small plumbing fixture. Indoor plumbing was becoming commonplace so there was a huge a demand. Upholt's design for this common part was cheaper than anybody else's, so he had no problem raising the capital from wealthy Plymouth industrialists to build a small shop. Most of their fortunes were derived from similar innovations, so they appreciated the efficiencies that Upholt proposed.

There wasn't a single brass company that could compete with Upholt and his sales increased rapidly. However, once they realized that they were losing market share to Upholt, they undercut his prices. Upholt's sales dried up. The larger firms might lose money on the sale of this one fixture, but they made up for it with the rest of their line. Relying on one product, Upholt was at their mercy. Upholt's small company was soon out of business, vaporizing his savings and the initial shares of his investors. Upholt received a hard lesson in the hurly-burly world of Michigan capitalism. There were fortunes to be made, but the successful combined both manufacturing and business savvy. A clever idea could be subsumed by the demands of the market and the tough operators guarding its portals. Upholt was a good engineer, but unfortunately, not a very good businessman.

My career at Dickenson's had stalled. When in doubt, I reached for the next rung on the ladder. In my case, this was the Bartlett-Orr Company. If I competed successfully in Chicago, I figured why not try for top, which then, as now, meant New York City. The Bartlett-Orr Company was, in my opinion, the best commercial art studio in the country. I sent a portfolio of my automobile illustrations, and to my surprise, I received a letter offering me a position.

In late fall, I set out for New York, arriving at the Pere Marquette Train Station in Detroit. Now, as a big-time New York artist, I walked to the taxi queue, directing the driver to take me to the "Detroit and Cleveland Boat Dock." The cabbie pulled away from the curb, made a quick a U-turn, stopping at the curb across the street from the train station. "There you go," he remarked, gladly accepting the fee for pulling down his meter flag. "Thanks for the trip, keep the change," the chastened big-time New York artist told him stepping out. At least I was not run over crossing the street. What a rube! New York would be very interesting, if I survived.

Life Before Heaven

The evening cruise to Buffalo made up for my humiliation. Then as now, life on the water was quasi-legal compared to on land. I guess the steamship operators felt that if they went between Michigan and New York State, they need not comply with the laws of either. I hazarded a nickel to the on board slot machine. In one miraculous pull, my nickel was multiplied by forty-fold. A two-dollar jackpot in nickels feels certainly more substantial than two bills in the pocket. At least I had re-paid my cab fare from the afternoon.

Once again I was in Buffalo, the site of my adventure with the mountebanks when I came west as a young Dutch boy. Now, back on the New York Central, I was a thoroughly American young man. I made my way into the crowded car finding a seat next to another passenger about my age. His name was Schmidt, a bookkeeper. Like me, he was heading to New York for a better opportunity. We hit it off, agreeing to stay in touch in our new city. Further along, probably near Schenectady, I looked out the window to contemplate what my life would have been like had I not been on that train to Michigan, more than twenty years before. Certainly I would not be an artist, nor would I have had so much material success. And I would not have met Hattie. Life would have probably been just fine, but not as exciting. What would New York hold in store?

New York had changed in the twenty-three years since our family had traveled through there. I stepped off the train onto a dark platform, making our way to the gate. I could not have been more surprised by the spectacle awaiting me. I arrived in the newly constructed Grand Central terminal. I found myself in the grandest interior space I had ever been in. Light streamed in from the soaring windows. Above, the graceful curving ceiling demarked the heavens. Like the rest of the crowd, I stayed not long to marvel at this testament to American ingenuity, but quickly followed them up the stairs to the street.

Chastened by my experience in Detroit, I walked to the YMCA to check in, taking their list of acceptable rooming houses.

I bunked next to Schmidt in the dormitory. As night fell, I hesitantly got to my knees for my prayers. Standing up, I saw with great joy that my friend Schmidt had joined me. I knew that I had found a true friend. During the short time we were together in New York, I discovered an intelligent and likable man. As you might have guessed from his surname, he was Lutheran.

We found a suitable brownstone on the far Upper West Side. The screech of the "el" outside our window meant easy access to my art studio in Midtown. Schmidt did not have a position when he came. After several weeks of looking, he ran out of money before returning to Buffalo. I missed him. When things were rough at the studio in the beginning, I missed confiding in him after a hard day.

The following morning, I had an appointment with the Bartlett-Orr studio head at nine o'clock. I left our rooms in plenty of time, arriving on the street in front of the studio long before my meeting. I sat down on a bench near the exit of the subway exit. Watching the people emerge from the subway, I noticed a man who reminded me of a colleague from Dickinson's. I whistled towards him with the four-notes that identified us as Dickinson artists. He lifted his head momentarily. Thinking better of it, he continued on his way before I whistled again. This brought him to a complete stop, turning with an expression of utter disbelief as he walked over to where I sat. "What on earth brings you here, Harry?" were the first words out of his mouth. I told him that I was heading to start work at Bartlett-Orr. Why this would shock him, I do not know, but he took me in arm, saying "That's where I work. Before we go in, let me tip you off on a few things."

We sat on the bench where he described the pitfalls awaiting me. Without his helpful revelations, I doubt if I would have survived. The challenges were not technical; I was good enough to do the work, but psychological.

Mr. Williams, my new boss, had gathered around him a group of men that were at the top of their profession. He was satisfied with nothing short of perfection. The shop was run in a manner conducive to great individual expression. This contrasted to the tight regulation of the Midwest. Here, there was no time clock, no definite hours. Each man set his price for a job, obligated to deliver on it. A good man could earn up to a dollar per hour, an unheard wage at the time. This was all a fringe benefit for me. I had never planned to stay in New York permanently, hoping only to gain valuable experience, as I had in Chicago. This led to a very competitive atmosphere in the studio. The horseplay among the artists that was the norm at Dickenson's was not the case here. As the most junior member, I was given the worst desk at the front of the room, with the poorest light and everyone looking at my back. I wondered if I had made a huge mistake in the service of my ambition. My wife and children were without me, over 800 miles away. I was away from my friends and church. Now I had signed on to work in the greatest snake pit in the country. I wonder what my father would have thought. Sure, he took a big risk in moving his family to a new country, but I placed a similar bet every other year. So far it had paid off. I was at the top of my profession, but at what cost?

The Lord gave me strength for what was to be one of the most challenging times of my life. Looking out at the drafting room, there seemed to be group of normal, friendly men. Most probably were. But, no sooner had I become absorbed in my work, than I heard the comment, "That new fellow sure has big ears." Well, no argument from me on that part, or "Can you believe that haircut?" This one hurt, because I thought I did not look too bad or too provincial. I kept still, not turning around, because once I did, all I would see a sea of artists concentrating on their work as if nothing had happened. At Dickinson's we also hazed new men, but never in such a mean-spirited fashion. I suppose this was the way for the more insecure men to prove some supposed New York superiority.

Mr. William's desk was in the senior position at the rear of the room, taking all of this in. He never interfered, so it was obviously part of the corporate culture. I thought it was as a dumb way to foster the supposed excellence of the shop, but it focused my concentration. Some men could not bear this torment before soon departing, but I was made of sterner stuff. Finally, I was accepted. Like most, I chose not to participate in this puerile nonsense, associating with the few other Christians in the shop. Fortunately, I had been warned by my friend Allie Berg that morning when I emerged from the subway on my first day. This was part of God's plan giving me the strength to weather this challenge. I hoped that the example of my reaction, with that of the other Christians in the shop, would lead to a more tolerant workplace. I prayed for strength, and God helped me to "turn the other cheek." I began to understand that my leaving the friendly confines of Dutch Western Grand Rapids was another part of God's plan for me. I re-committed to do my best, ignore the buffoons and eventually be reunited with my family.

Columbus Day is a legal holiday in New York. I chose it to look for a new home so that Hattie, Melvin, and Helen could join me. Across the Hudson from Manhattan there was a Christian Reformed Church in the small town of Englewood, ministering to the Dutch immigrants who stayed in the Hudson Valley with its familiar names, rather than head for the larger "kolonies" in Michigan and Iowa. Allie Berg accompanied me on the subway to the northern Manhattan ferry terminal, before pointing the way across the broad river. Within twenty minutes, I was across, walking up the one road between the terminal and the town, perched up on the palisade above. There I located a tidy rental home that was close to the church, the ferry, and a park with a tennis court. Tennis was no longer confined to the country clubs, and I had embraced this game of stamina, co-ordination, and guile. I entered into a lease before finding a Western Union office to wire Hattie the news. I then hurried home to compose a more thorough letter.

While this letter headed west to Michigan, a different disturbing letter came my way. Hattie's parents wrote that she was ill, suggesting that I return immediately. Mr. Williams granted me a leave of absence, and Allie loaned me the cost of a train ticket, since my cash was either tied up with Hattie, loans to my family, or the new lease. Service on the New York Central was now faster than ever as I traveled west, but this trip seemed as slow as my first trip west as a boy. Gathered in my arms in Grand Rapids, she tearfully gave me the news that she had contracted tuberculosis. If her parents had told me this news before I left New York, I would have resigned my position, returning to Michigan for good. Fortunately, as it turned out (God's plan again), they did not, so I did not.

Her doctor said that she could recuperate in New Jersey as well as Michigan, providing we arranged for someone to help with the housework so she could get plenty of rest. Sunshine, rest, fresh air, and plenty of good food was all that she needed to fully recover. This was good news. I persuaded my young sister Minnie to come and help out around the house until Hattie was well.

For Hattie's sake, I booked a private Pullman rail compartment. Usually these needed to be reserved well advance, but, providentially, one remained available on our date. Only one car going to New York was attached on the Chicago train, but this allowed us to make the whole trip without stepping from train. In Chicago, we connected to the Wolverine Express, continuing to New York through Ontario, Canada, the most direct route.

I ignored the expense. I would never enjoy such luxury again. We had a compartment with berths for five people and a private bath. The porters catered to our every whim. However, I still must have looked the imposter. While sitting in the first-class lounge, the Pullman conductor demanded to see my ticket. He was quite chagrined that not only was I one of his passengers, but occupied one of the better state rooms.

Hattie loved our new house, thrilled to be together again "en famille". The breeze coming off of the Atlantic Ocean did a world of good for Hattie's lungs as she began to feel stronger. Minnie did not have to stay long. Melvin became interested in a new form of transportation under his purview, the multitude of steamships plying the Hudson River under our gaze from the top of the Palisades.

Our new home was charming, but older than the "dream home" that we built in North Park. While our North Park home was built in the latest "bungalow" style, low slung with many carpenter details and deep eaves, the Englewood house was a proper upright lady with a large porch bracketed with ornate white Victorian trim. Hattie looked great sitting on this porch in her stylish white shirtwaist that was coming into style. The detailing of the porch perfectly framed the frills of her blouse.

With a membership of only 30 families, our Englewood Christian Reformed Church had not grown appreciably. This contrasted to the West Side power congregations where Hattie and I worshiped before this. The Dutch were now a small minority in New Jersey. I was delighted to be reunited with my Christian School friend, Lee Huizinga. He served as the pastor while attending medical school at Columbia University across the river. Lee would go on to be one of the giants of our denomination. He was studying medicine in preparation for entering the mission field, becoming a nationally known authority on leprosy. With this knowledge, he traveled to China to spread the gospel and minister there. He was there when the Japanese overran the country at the beginning of World War II. Refusing to abandon his flock, he was confined to a concentration camp. There he would die before his heavenly reward.

That misery was still in the future. We made friends easily in the small congregation. Friends from Michigan took advantage of our location to visit New York City. Many of these families had earlier scurried through this entry port. We now wanted to return to see what we had missed. New York was now the most modern and dynamic city in the world. Hattie's parents joined us for a visit, relieved that their daughter had fully recovered. When she was ill, she had consulted with the best doctor in Grand Rapids, but I was not entirely convinced of the diagnosis of tuberculosis. My mother-in-law liked our picturesque church as much as the grander sites in the city. She exclaimed, "Het is zoo kerks. – This is so churchy." From a pious Dutch woman, this was high praise indeed.

We spent most Saturdays sightseeing with our visitors. This was an opportunity for me to study the old masters at the Metropolitan Museum of Art. We loved the vistas of seeing the city from the river taking the Circle Line around Manhattan or the Staten Island Ferry near the Statue of Liberty.

When I returned to work on Mondays, I described the wonders we had seen over the weekend. My fellow artists stared at me blankly. Most had spent most of their lives there. Showing any appreciation for the riches of their city would mark them as rubes. They maintained their steely urban resolve rather than display any appreciation for the city. Their loss was my gain as Hattie and I jumped at the chance to do things we could not do in Michigan.

The annual Bartlett-Orr picnic cemented my acceptance in the studio, though almost a full year after I had arrived. We ferried over to Staten Island, settling into a baseball game, pitting the artists against the engravers. This rivalry defined the firm, since each of the principals led one of the groups. In my final at-bat, a juicy pitch crossed the plate, as fast as the engraver's pitcher could throw it. He thought he had thrown a fastball strike. Lunging, I heard a satisfying crack. My hands stung as I ran for first base. Rounding first, I slowed down. The ball was long past the outfielder, so I marshaled my speed to stretch the run. As I rounded third, Mr. Williams whirled his arms for me to race towards home. I scored easily. This winning run was probably more important to Williams than all of my good work during the year. After this, there were no more comments about my ears (which were still large), or my haircut (which had improved in a more urbane style).

That fall held greater changes. Dickinson's in Grand Rapids finally offered me the position as head artist. Through a series of letters, I negotiated my acceptance. I would not return unless I had authority to hire and fire the artists working under me. I could not tolerate any dead wood or interference if I was to be responsible for our output. Dickinson's had never granted this authority to any previous head artist, but I was a known quantity, so they acquiesced. I would return at a salary twice that of when I left. Negotiating with Dickinson's was the easy part; leaving Bartlett-Orr was harder. It was with some trepidation that I asked Mr. Williams if I could meet with him in private. Mr. Orr's office was available, so we both stood briefly in there.

"Mr. Williams, I appreciate the marvelous opportunity I have had here, but I am returning to Grand Rapids. I have been offered the position of head artist at my own studio," I stammered.

"You have now, have you? Get out, you ungrateful wretch. I took a gamble hiring you. Now, I will never hire another man from the West. Get your pens and tools and leave. Now!"

That went well. I probably should not ask him for a recommendation any time soon. Williams realized that many of us came to garner some experience with the best, using it to enhance our careers back home. A colleague was hired as the head of the art department at the Packard Motor Car Company in Detroit based on his Bartlett-Orr experience.

We made good friends during our two years in Englewood, appreciating the easygoing life we lived. Some, including Rev. Huizinga saw us off at the train. This would be the last time I saw him. He graduated from medical school to begin his work in the mission field. Of course, on the day he saw us off, the future trials were unknown and our tears were of a less serious sort.

Sitting on the train as it pulled out of the small Englewood station, I reflected on what had happened in the three years since we had left Grand Rapids. For one, our children had grown. The little guy whom I had taken to kindergarten now came home, proudly declaring, "I made the team." When asked what position he played, he replied, "I take care of the bats." Helen now walked up and down the aisle of the train. Before long, we were in Jersey City, transferring to the subway to go under the Hudson River to the docks. We had tickets for the steamer to Albany where we would catch the train west. Hattie asked me to go to a nearby fruit stand to pick up some provisions for our trip.

The stand was open on all four sides, where I reveled in the selection. After paying, I walked back to the gangplank of the boat where Hattie and the children waited. Reaching into my pocket for the tickets, my wallet was missing! It contained the tickets for our trip and all of the money just drawn from the Englewood bank. I rushed back to the fruit stand. I had put my wallet down to purchase the fruit. Milling around the stand were a score of customers, any of which could have casually picked it up without any attention. Apparently, like me, they were so taken by the riot of colors of the huge selection that a drab brown wallet went unnoticed. It was right where I had left it. After the momentary panic, time started to unfold again. I doubt that an apple ever tasted as sweet as I watched the beautiful Hudson River Valley open before us.

Chapter 12

Without further mishap, we wended our way across the northern tier of the country, first by the New York Central from Albany to Buffalo and then by steamer across Lake Erie to Detroit. Hattie and I prefer traveling by boat than by train. As an artist, I definitely prefer the light, even on an inland lake like Lake Erie, over being on land, where the trees absorb so much sunlight, casting shadows. In Detroit, we boarded a small steam launch to visit the pleasuring grounds of Belle Isle. This "beautiful island" is a Detroit city park, featuring many interesting attractions as we perambulated the wide walk around the island. The children ran on ahead, looking for the next ice cream stand or carousel. Our day there was a nice break from the stress of travel and work. We enjoyed New York, but were happy to be returning to the city where we grew up. We were sure that we had not become so jaded that Grand Rapids would seem like small potatoes. We were anxious to return to our families and summers by a lake. I now knew that my work was equal to anybody's in the country, proud to be the top man at Dickinson's.

In Grand Rapids, we took a horse drawn cab to the Lindemulder store on the West Side. Hattie's dad had built a two-story house next to his store, so they no longer lived above the store. There was now plenty of room for guests. Our furniture was coming by rail from New York, so we thought we would have a week to find a place to rent. The one week we had planned on staying with Hattie's parents stretched into seven! Each day dragged by, but our furniture did not arrive. The house we rented at the corner of Tamarack and Tenth continued costing us rent, with little in the way of benefit. Every day on the way to work, I stopped by the offices of the railroad that carried our furniture to hear the same sorry refrain. In frustration, I turned to a young station agent from another railroad who attended the Broadway Christian Reformed Church. Through perseverance, he tracked down our goods. They were stashed in a railroad warehouse in

Indiana. The bill-of-lading was filed under the letter "B", a common confusion with the letter "V". How they got "Terre Haute" confused with "Grand Rapids" is beyond me. Our furniture arrived a few days later and we moved into our house. The furniture looked awful, my heart sinking "straight to my boots", as Hattie would say. I thought it would cost a fortune to repair, but in Grand Rapids, there were plenty of experienced craftsmen. Our furniture was soon returned to its original luster. I called the railroad, where the freight agent confessed, "Submit a claim for less than the freight bill, and it will probably be honored." I followed his advice. The claim was allowed without protest. The check covered all of the repairs. We settled into our new home as I concentrated on the challenges of managing an active art studio.

Our landlord offered us a discounted rent of $15 per month if I signed a six-month lease, but we planned to move back to North Park, so I demurred. I soon found a wreck of a house in the country, but Hattie would have none of it. She had grown accustomed to the convenience of our newer house on Tamarack Avenue. Before, we had enjoyed houses with indoor plumbing, electricity, and central heat, but never all in the same house. These once luxuries were now necessities as our "temporary" stay lasted for seven more years.

The longer I live, the more I marvel at the plan that the Lord lays out for us. Of course, blundering through life, we lurch from event to event in confusion. When we prayerfully reflect back, we see His hand at work, even as we are unaware. Now was such a time.

On the evening of April 13th, 1913, Hattie and I enjoyed a fine evening with her parents visiting friends. We all had so much fun that we stayed longer than was prudent. It was dark when we left together to walk to our respective homes. My mother-in-law was in fine spirits and the stroll home posed no unusual challenge. We bid Hattie's parents good night under the streetlight at the corner of Eighth and Tamarack.

We walked the short distance to our home, where I paid the babysitter after looking in at our two children sleeping peacefully. As we got ready for bed, I reached over, patting Hattie's mounding belly that she was now sharing with our third child. We had not yet fallen asleep when I heard a loud knock at the front door. Opening the door, I found a distraught Andy Lindemulder, Hattie's younger brother. He breathlessly explained that their mother had suffered a heart attack. Since Hattie was pregnant and our two children were fast asleep, I alone followed Andy back to their parents' home next to the store. When I arrived, "Ma" Lindemulder had already passed. I rushed back to tell Hattie. Losing a mother is a grievous loss for any family, but this was especially so for the Lindemulders since she was the family's spiritual rock. Just as Jesus commissioned Peter to lead his church, He had commissioned "Ma" to minister to her family. As we sadly sat around the Lindemulder house the next day, I said a silent prayer, thanking God for bringing us home from New York to be together in this time of trial.

About a month after the death of her mother, Hattie complained of pain so I walked to get Mrs. Postma again. When I quickly returned, Hattie assured me that there was no rush. Waiting, I did not walk over to the Lindemulder store to call the doctor until directed by Hattie through clenched teeth. This lack of urgency meant that our third child, Rolf, arrived before the doctor did. Mrs. Postma and I did the best we could, but the doctor scolded us for the extra pain my darling wife had to endure. Our postponement cost Hattie a few stitches to repair the damage. This was minor in the great procession of the heavens. Our family had lost one saint, but gained another. The small squalling baby in my arms, Rolf, would go on to be a minister of the gospel and a missionary for our faith. Knowing none of this, I thanked God for a healthy baby and a recuperating mother.

Around this time, the Upholts paid us a visit. Once again, I loved seeing Henry, but with him, things were always "a half bubble off of plumb". This time it was the kids. The Upholts had a son they called Henry Junior, who was about the same age as our Mel. Unfortunately, Mel liked to tease Henry Junior. Junior pronounced his words with a bit of a lisp, so that his own name came out as "Chunior". Of course, an anomaly like this is fodder for another five year old. Children can be some of the cruelest creatures you will ever encounter.

The Upholts spent the evening with us while the boys were in Mel's bedroom upstairs. There was no bathroom upstairs so we left a small pot with them in case they needed to relieve themselves. After a while, poor "Chunior" trundled down the stairs with one pajama leg soaking wet to a horrified expression on Mrs. Upholt's face. "Melfin pushed me in the char". It was all I could do to keep from bursting out laughing. I rushed up the stairs to punish "Melfin". I was happy that "Chunior" had not put up a fight, tipping the chamber pot over and the contents onto the floor.

The following day, Mr. Upholt asked me to attend church services with him. In cities other than Grand Rapids, a Christian Reformed Church was not always available, so I had attended churches of different denominations over the years. I have felt at home in Presbyterian churches, since our faiths spring from the same Calvinistic doctrine. None of this prepared me for my first time in a Unitarian church; this one incongruously named "All Souls". At least that did not presume upon "All Saints". I was curious as to what kind of sermon I would hear, but never dreamed that a self-described "man of God" would mount the pulpit to speak such blasphemy. At the close of his sermon, he recited a poem about our Lord's life which suggested that He had love affairs like any normal man, before closing with these two lines,

"And then came a man named Paul,
Who spoiled it all."

I was never happier to say the "amen" at the end of a service than then.

My father's business was one of the more advanced in adopting new technology. This was not my father's doing, but his junior partner, brother Gerrit, who had a mechanical bent. He was the first of the brothers to ride a bicycle, and then he convinced the old man and my other brothers to invest in a telephone, and now an automobile. The vehicle they purchased was more a "horseless carriage" than an automobile. The front was graced by long rounded dash, built by a carriage-maker, no doubt. This left no room for a windshield. However, it motored so slowly that this was rarely a problem. The lack of speed was a blessing since the wheels were tall and skinny, inflated to very high pressures. Any trip was a jarring, noisy adventure on a primitive suspension. I personally did not see much of a future for these contraptions, since they seemed to be broken down as often as they were running. But there was great enthusiasm for them in Michigan because people from all over the country were buying them and we were making them. I thought that as long as they did not break down on my street, but somewhere in, say, Detroit, everything would be fine. Things changed quickly. Soon, we would all be driving. The challenge would not be in navigating the rutted roads, but in avoiding the plague of other newly minted drivers. Now in addition to cancer and stroke, there would be an entirely new way to die.

My brothers purchased a Chalmers which was popular with many businessmen because the rear seating area could be converted to a compartment for the delivery of goods. You started it with a hand crank, requiring the spark advance to be set "just so" as not to backfire, breaking your arm. This was desirable transportation? If a tire blew out, which was often, you laboriously wrestled on the spare tire pumping it up by hand to the required sixty pounds of inflation - fifteen minutes of grueling labor. Even if I liked horses, which I did not, with Dobbin, I would have been at my appointment half an hour ago without soiling my clothes with sweat and mud.

Our brother Charly, inheriting father's willingness to take a big geographic risk, purchased a farm in Wisconsin, all the way around the large intervening lake known as Michigan. The land was dirt cheap because you could not get to it; about as far from civilization as anything could be. However, in our possession was now a vehicle that could go anywhere. Charly's letter proposed that his younger brothers, Nick, Gerrit, and I visit his western holdings across the lake. I am sure this was not the enterprise my poor father had in mind when consenting to the purchase of the used vehicle in the first place. However, an automobile might be of limited value. You certainly could not undertake this trip by horse and buggy. I was not sure that you could do it by car, either, but was willing to trust in Gerrit's mechanical acumen to overcome the inevitable breakdowns.

The hearty adventurers gathered in front of our parents' house. We snapped a picture with our new "Brownie" camera, which made memorializing momentous family moments like this a "snap". Until now, any likeness that you wanted required going to a photographer's studio, holding still while the flash powder exploded. The snapshot pictures were tiny, not matching the studio's quality, but it was fun to have a record of the less formal parts of your life. You certainly got a much better sense of who a person was from these quick photos than from a studio portrait. As an artist, I wish I could capture instantaneous images instead of laboring for an hour on an outdoor sketch, capturing the fleeting light and clouds.

On a Monday morning in the summer of 1914, we set out. Our first objective was Nick's in-laws in the tiny ville of Watervliet, Michigan. In those days, you were sure everyone would be home, since, without automobiles, it was hard to leave the farm. There was no need to call ahead, because they had no phone to call. After a brief chat with them over dreadful coffee, we were again on our way, negotiating the spider web of roads southwards towards Indiana. Roadmaps would not come into existence for maybe another decade. We knew, however, that if we kept the lake to our right, driving towards the sun, we would soon hit Indiana. Apparently, the farmers tired of giving out directions nailing up arrowed signs suggesting, "Kalamazoo, 26" or "Benton Harbor, 13". Our navigation succeeded as we pulled into South Bend, Indiana. I took a picture at Notre Dame University of the statue of Christ that would go on to be known as scurrilously "Touchdown Jesus" as it was bathed in the glow of sunset. Catholics fancied religious symbolism and art, but those who thought more about these things in our church thought it tread too close to "graven images". However, on that summer's afternoon the image was all quite sublime.

We exchanged the Catholic erudition of South Bend for the hotbed of mammon that is Chicago. After a lovely morning motoring through the Hoosier countryside, we were tripped up by the countless suburbs protecting Chicago's southern flank. Even then, Gary, Indiana, was hotly (literally) engaged in the making of steel. The sunny morning dimmed under the perpetual cloud above the steel mills. These factories held us in their thrall. They were much larger and formidable than the benign furniture makers that we knew. Gerrit, our sole driver, dared not glance from the road clogged with more automobiles, buggies, and dray wagons. Nick was a novice, never having driven on the open road. Chicago roads did not seem like a particularly opportune place to learn. None of the aids to driving that we expect today, like signs, lanes, or even pavement, were in place. We entered Chicago in the afternoon. Intersections were mayhem, with the traffic sorting itself out to prevent collisions. We confined ourselves to State Street, plunging our way northward. The steady stream of traffic accompanying us gave us a priori rights at the minor corners, but when crossing another arterial, it was every vehicle for itself. In the Loop, a policeman directed who could go and who must stop. Gerrit, not familiar with this convention, nearly drove through an intersection if not for the whistling insistence of one of Chicago's finest, who at about five and a half feet in stature brooked no challenge to his authority. Poor Gerrit was a complete wreck when we pulled into Evanston, Illinois, for the night. He complained mightily about my pointing out of the many sights that I recognized from my earlier trips to Chicago, none of which he dared notice while delivering us in one piece to the northern side of the metropolis. We thanked him before telling him he was being a baby and walked over to the lake front.

Our hotel did not have parking. Looking for a place sympathetic to us of the motoring set, we found a large barn converted to the sales of Cadillacs. The dealer-mechanic offered our Chalmers berth for the night, exclaiming, "Packard will offer an electric starter on their automobiles. You strapping lads know how hard it is to start an auto. How are they going to accomplish that? I sure would like to know. It will never work!"

I hoped he wasn't correct. I dreaded starting the Chalmers. Buying a Packard was out of the question. Perhaps the best course of action for me was not to learn to drive.

Our good progress through Michigan, Indiana, and Illinois came to an end in Wisconsin. The fine sandy soils of the previous three states gave way to a tenacious mud which tore at our tires as they sunk into the roadway. We faced the inevitable blowout. Carrying no spares, we fashioned a repair on the spot. Fortunately, my brothers had brought their paper hanging overalls to protect their clothes. The only protection from my work world, if I had bothered to bring them, were my sleeve guards and eye shades, which I wore at the drafting board, so I was not much help. After pushing the car to a spot where the ground was firm enough to support the jack, we lifted the car to remove the wheel. Peeling the tire off the rim to access the inner tube was difficult. Once the inner tube was in hand, we had to find the leak; not always easy.

Patching what we were sure was the leak, we then stretched the tire back onto the wheel which we bolted back to the hub. We took turns pumping the completely flat tire up to the required 60 or 70 pounds of pressure. This might be repeated as often as two times per day, so that our time by the side of the road might equal our time on it. These early tires with their high pressures and small road contact patches did not last very long. When I bought my own car two years later, I replaced a tire after 1,299 miles.

The roads were so deleterious that we purchased a guide log promising "The Most Felicitous Route for Motorists between Chicago, Madison, Eau Clair and Other Cities of Wisconsin". If it saved us one flat tire, we thought it would well be worth the exorbitant price of twenty cents. It did not. The directions given, "Proceed seven and one-quarter miles until you see a red barn on the right; turn right to Robinson Road, mileage twenty-two and one-half; turn left and follow the phone poles with red and blue bands," were unreliable. We suspected that there was no red barn or red and blue telephone poles. The next day, through dead reckoning and roadside signs, we arrived in Appleton, Wisconsin. We drove by a hotel, but Nick insisted that we not stop. "Pull around the block. They will charge us more if they see we are wealthy enough to own a car." Looking at our bedraggled Chalmers, I cannot believe it met anybody's expectation of luxury travel. It was on this day that we experienced our first concrete paving. It was only a few miles long and one car wide, but while we were on it, all of our troubles floated away. We resolutely stared ahead, hoping it would never end. We had no idea who had built it or why, but to us it was an artifact from a particularly beneficent civilization. It went a long way to improving our poor opinion of Wisconsin roads.

We had been on the road for four days. Leaving Appleton on Friday morning, we at last came near Charly's farm, close to the small town of Birnamwood. We were far enough from Chicago that Nick could try his hand at driving. Nick got behind the wheel. Everything went well until we crested a hill. Below us we saw a load of hay, now approaching very quickly as our car picked up speed rolling down the hill. Nick had no experience driving a car down a hill, so the concept of a brake was still alien to him. Rushing to the load, he quickly swerved around it. Fortunately, no one was in the other lane. I think the farmer was as scared as we were. After this incident, Gerrit resumed the driving duties.

We shared all of our expenses, including the purchase of cigars. While our church discouraged cigarettes, tobacco was too engrained in Dutch culture to avoid entirely. Cigars and pipes were tolerated. I was never much of a smoker', certainly not then. Chalmers of this vintage had no windshields. This was not too much of a problem, except when I sat in the back seat. Gerrit and Nick were in the front, smoking away, oblivious to the fact that the air "rushing" by rapidly burned their cigars. Did they not have any sensitivity to the fact that their racing burned through my share in the tobacco fund? It was bad enough to support their habit, but now they did not have the courtesy to protect this precious resource. Brothers are like that.

There were no filling stations conveniently spaced along our route, so we carried five-gallon cans on our running boards that we filled wherever we found petrol. Looking back, I shudder to think of what could have happened from an errant live ash from a cigar or a crash with an overly-wide hay wagon. Our Chalmers had no gas gauge, so after a couple of hours of driving, we pulled over to measure the depth of fuel in the tank with the dipstick attached to the cap.

Charly was happy to see us. His life was quite lonely in his neck of the woods. He opened his cigar humidor to us before leading us about his barn, proudly showing the implements and how he used them. He looked with envy at the Chalmers, because he was saving to buy a tractor that would greatly improve his ability to farm.

Despite the profligacy with the cigars, our trip was economical enough that we could afford to take the car ferry from Manitowoc, Wisconsin to Ludington, Michigan. The trip from Ludington to Grand Rapids, back on Michigan's sandy roads went without a hitch. However, we were all shaken and road weary from our adventure motoring. Though I had fun hooting and hollering with my brothers, I suggested if we were to spend a week together, we should do it in something other than an automobile. It was especially good to see Charly again. I had forgotten how much I missed him. It is funny how you lose touch with your own nuclear family when you start raising one of your own. I would not trade time with Hattie and the children for anything, but for a few brief days it was fun to revert to the hi-jinx of when we boys ran wild along the canals of Friesland and the Grand River.

Whenever I returned to Grand Rapids, the Grand River was never far from my life. Though it is not much of a river when compared to the Hudson, it is substantial enough to pull along snags in unhurried majesty. I never lived more than a half mile from it, usually crossing it twice a day. I always like messing around in the small boats and canoes for rent at the various liveries on the bank. If Hattie was not as keen as when she was younger, I could always find a willing mate in Melvin or Helen.

I am to be forgiven if I let my love of the river cloud my better judgment. I knew Henry Upholt as a good friend, but as a dreamer, who never seemed to get across the finish line on any of his projects. Like most dreamers, he was a good talker. I too, was spun along with his stories. Like us, the Upholts had returned to Grand Rapids. He was running a small factory in the small town of Belden, working on an invention for a farm tractor that he had tried to sell unsuccessfully to the Ford Motor Company. Additionally, he had set up an office in Grand Rapids billing himself as an "efficiency expert". Henry was anything but efficient, but I bit my tongue. With all the things now made in Michigan, there was great interest in how to extract more profit from the factory floor. If you paid attention, there were always efficiencies to be gained. Even in our art studio, I implemented new procedures for cleaning brushes and pens which not only saved time, but the Dickinson's precious rags. Now as part of management, I appreciated how much clean rags cost us.

Upholt's office was near mine so we lunched together frequently. Over one of these lunches, I mentioned how much we had enjoyed North Park, regretting not keeping our custom-built house there. The prices in that neighborhood were now more than we could afford. On one of these days, as I put the napkin on my lap, Upholt told me that he had a found a farm for sale just up the river from North Park. He envisioned that we would buy it together, sharing the farmhouse. I knew that Hattie and the rest of our young family would have no interest in sharing a house with the Upholts, especially after the "Chunior" incident, but I said I would look at the property with him.

The following Saturday, we made an appointment with the real estate agent, driving up to see the property, 80 acres fronting on the river. The property was certainly not worth more than what was being asked, but the river frontage intrigued me. I loved the river; did not other people? There were few trees along the bank, perhaps because the bottom land there partially flooded in the spring. To the north of this low area was a somewhat higher bench perched above flood stage, graced with many stately trees. I believed that there was development potential for "water front" lots in this area. Upholt was not convinced, but asked the farmer not to do any timbering in this area until we made our decision as whether to make an offer.

Upholt and I talked it over. Like anything else in his life, he needed someone else to finance the deal. Any money he had ever made was tied up in his numerous entrepreneurial ventures. Hattie and I were not interested in the farmhouse, so I proposed to Upholt that he move into it, but we would take the northern forty acres. He could keep the farm house and the forty acres that were being farmed. He was getting the better part of the deal, so I insisted on free passage across his land and that he build a bridge for me across a small creek that bisected the property. Since he intended to farm, he readily agreed to the deal.

We bought the farm for $3,950. My half was $1,975, then a considerable sum. I paid cash, receiving clear title to 40 acres. Upholt could only raise a small down payment on his parcel, so he could not join me in the platting of my property. Upholt could not borrow any more money. I think the banks were aware of his spotty record. This was too bad, because the subdivision proved to be quite successful. Nonetheless, the Upholts enthusiastically supported my project. I suppose my dream was contagious. They suggested the Indian name of "O-Wang-Ta-Nong Park". This supposedly was the native Pottawatomie tribe's name for the Grand River. We laid out lots along Abrigador Trail and Mayawang Avenue. They are still there.

There were two ways to access my property, one from the river, the other across the Upholts' property. We had a verbal agreement that I could cross his property after he built the small bridge across the stream dividing our properties. Why I trusted Upholt to build this bridge escapes me. I guess we always think the best of our friends.

Hattie and I contracted with a carpenter to build a small cottage for us so we could take the children up for the summer. I borrowed my father's wagon to haul some old furniture up to this cottage. This was with a new horse, but she responded well to my inexpert driving. I could no longer rely on Hattie taking the reins, because she was home with the children. My trip north was slow, but uneventful, as I was perfectly willing to let the horse set the pace. Everything went well until we came to our land. Upholt had not built the bridge. The creek separating our parcels was not flowing swiftly, but was close to the top of its banks. The banks were broken down where the farm track crossed the creek. I came up to the crossing, urging the horse forward. She gamely entered the water, plunging up to her knees. We kept moving until the skinny wheels of the loaded wagon stopped dead in the soft bottom of the creek. I tried a little tap with the whip to no avail. Fortunately, Upholt was home. After eliciting the help of another neighbor, we extricated the wagon and the load. Upholt finally built the bridge after that. Upholt and his wife liked farm life, eking out a meager income from farming. Since Western Michigan is so fertile, vegetables were readily available so that prices were low. Mrs. Upholt would take her wagon around North Park, selling their produce door to door, quite remarkable for a woman of her background and education.

The township board approved the plat before I recorded it with the Kent County register of deeds in July, 1914. After our cottage was built, I constructed a boat dock on the river, to which I moored a small motor launch. It was a temperamental craft, but when running, it made getting to town easy and fun. It was faster than the rowboats to which I was accustomed, so I was willing to fuss with the engine.

My realtor, J.J Wood, opened for business on Memorial Day, 1915. I had appreciated Mr. Wood acumen since purchasing our North Park lot from him. Good business follows good businessmen. Mr. Wood's magic continued as we sold five lots on the opening day. The purchaser, Mr. Hodge, planned to build a small pavilion among the trees. His son later purchased three more lots, resulting in a nice shady family compound. He and his wife sold refreshments to the canoeists and other boaters on the river. I flew a large American flag from the end of our dock. Our home became a favorite with my family and Hattie's, coming on weekends to swim or row our flat-bottom boat.

During the workweek, I took the motor launch to the North Park Pavilion, picking up passengers from the streetcar terminus. I also shuttled prospects to the property in the launch. More than one sale came about from the romance of approaching the property from the water.

I encouraged people to picnic on the property, so they could envision building their dream home. This attracted more than potential buyers, so every Sunday morning I made an inspection tour, rousting out undesirables. Inevitably these folks arrived by motorboat with a keg of beer. The liquor led to carousing and fights, so I started my rounds early before they had time to drink much. I marvel that I never had much trouble, because occasionally I encountered a drunk, even early in a morning. In the days before Prohibition, drunkenness was pervasive since there was a saloon on every corner. Each one had five or ten men who were permanent residents except when they stumbled out in the daylight to raise enough funds to return. When the time came, I saw no other solution than to become a Temperance man through and through. Meanwhile, I asked the picnickers who were drinking to leave. They would return to their boats to find a more accommodating shore. I always counted my blessings, because I was one, but they were many, possibly making my life difficult. However, if I ever needed the sheriff, he would have readily conducted interrogations with his billy club, receiving a few bloody heads in reply. Law and order were a way of life then, not just a phrase.

Although approaching by boat was a more pleasant way to access our land than crossing Upholt's property, I could not rely on it, especially when the river froze over the winter. Even in October, people do not go out of their way to ride in small watercraft. I now had made enough income from the sale of lots that I could build a proper road across the swampy area upstream from the brook crossing. I could afford to have needed fill imported, but a more formidable obstacle presented itself in the form of the Grand Rapids and Indiana Railroad, perhaps remembering me from when I was kid throwing rocks at their rolling stock. In any event, the railroad had no interest in granting any passage across their right-of-way. I was to find that a railroad is the most intractable entity ever placed on God's green earth. They answer to no one, and their idea of negotiation is for you to stand on the track until a locomotive comes. I wrote letters, made phone calls, and visited offices - all to no avail.

While sitting one afternoon with Mr. Hodges in his pavilion, we discussed the matter. He, of course, was as interested as I in securing better access. He was an endless talker, calling me day and night with suggestions he had literally dreamed up. Whenever the children heard that Mr. Hodges was on the phone, they pulled up a stool for me; I would be there for a while. The first telephone in our home was attached to the wall, about five feet off of the floor. On this day, Hodges had a very practical suggestion that at first I resisted. He said I was starting at the wrong end of the railroad. He suggested sending a gift to someone lower, but still influential.

I was surprised to receive a suggestion from a Knight Templar and man of considerable probity.

I exclaimed, "I have never bribed anyone, and do not intend to start now."

"I don't intend that you should. Haven't you ever sent Hattie a box of chocolates or flowers? She would be insulted if you thought that was bribe."

"Send a box of cigars to the section foreman and see what happens. I notice that he enjoys them when rolling by on his handcar."

I did not see the harm in this, giving it a try. I could hardly believe my eyes when a week later, a gondola loaded with men and materials stopped at the crossing, pushed by a single engine. The crew fell to work. By sundown they had installed the crossing across the tracks.

I did not ponder this miracle for very long. I trust that my pestering of management got them to finally move at about the same time my cigars arrived. I found it hard to believe that a section foreman would undertake to build a crossing on his own. Stranger things have happened, and I was not one to questions how the wide world operates.

Chapter 13

From then on, I stopped bringing people by boat. Instead, I met them at the end of the streetcar line. Eventually, I paid for a taxi to take men from our little community to the train, once in the morning, and once at night. I did not charge for this; including it in the price of buying a lot.

About this time, I subdivided the land at the rear of the farm along the Plainfield Road into one-acre lots. These also sold well, especially since I was willing to accept land contracts with a small down payment. These properties would produce income for years to come. Mr. Hodge even bought one to build a permanent residence; the pavilion was strictly a summer residence.

In the meantime, Upholt's affairs were not going well, forcing him to sell the farm. I was relieved that the new road was finished so we did not need to rely on the new owner for access. A certain coolness developed between Upholt and me. I had offered him partnership every step of the way, but he was never in a financial position to participate. He realized that I had been thrifty in my affairs, frustrating him that he was not, in spite of his efforts to invent or start new businesses. Upholt never spoke ill of me or anyone else, but I am sure that my relative success weighed on him. This was a bittersweet part of the success in selling the lots.

A key part of life on the river was our motor launch, a commodious watercraft capable of carrying up to twenty passengers. It was built for comfort, not for speed, but none of the distances involved was too great, so the passengers never seemed to mind as they took in the sights along the river. A wheezy two-cylinder motor spun the propeller. This power plant was as good as any on the market, which meant that it demanded constant attention to keep running. In the early days of the motor age, no vehicle was very reliable. Things would eventually improve, but this was not the case at the beginning of the century. The engine sputtered to a stop at the most inopportune times. At the end of one of our summers on the river, I loaded furniture that we wanted back at the in-town house into a rowboat to tow behind the motor launch. In addition to the rowboat, I had a full load of passengers to take to town. We were about halfway when the motor "conked out". Perhaps we overtaxed it or more likely, the gasoline had picked up some water. Anything could go wrong and did. I hailed a tow from another passing motorboat. Boaters were willing to help, knowing that they would likely need help next. They towed this unwieldy flotilla to the North Park dock where I discharged the passengers to catch the streetcar back to Grand Rapids. I spent the evening alone at the cottage, where I transferred the furniture from the rowboat into the motor launch. In the dark, I fell into the river. Since it was August, I was not too cold, but was still shivering after a few minutes. I took off my clothes, laying them out to dry, crawling under a canvas sail to sleep. After a fitful night, I woke early to put on my clothes, which if not soggy, were not very dry. Under the sunlight streaking through the trees, I laid my stiff back into the oars, straining to get the motor launch to follow the little rowboat. Fortunately, my efforts were with the current. If I rowed against the current, I would have drifted backwards downstream. I pulled up to the dock a little before nine - tired, hot, and bedraggled. After explaining to the canoe livery that I would return later in the day, I hurriedly set out for the office, certainly the worse for wear. I survived the day chafing in my damp wrinkled suit. In the evening, I used my brother's wagon from the paint store to cart the furniture. A boat mechanic on the river drained the fuel line, resurrecting the launch. I had envisioned our life on the river as a time of recreation and refreshment, but that was not always the case.

That fall, Hattie gave birth to our fourth child; this time a girl. We named her Alta, after my mother. Getting better at it, we managed the birth without our usual drama. When I arrived home from work, Mrs. Postma and the doctor were there in ample time. The doctor, seeing everything was in order, left for a bit. Hattie responded by getting up and ironing while she counted the time between her contractions. We were getting better at this; at least we were not as nervous.

Our new girl was a little chatterbox – making her presence known in our growing brood. The other children were now old enough that they did not see her as a rival or a threat and immediately adopted her. Her aunts and uncles, adapted the song that they had originally sung for Alta's mother,

"And Hattie sly as a fox,
Mouth keeps going like a chatterbox".

If this described Hattie as a girl, it now certainly described her baby daughter.

Until this time, just before the Great War, most Grand Rapids art studios were allied with a printing press. The new success of independent art studios eroded this system. Artists on their own with shoestring budgets underbid the more established houses allied with the presses. Dickinson Bros. was not immune to this trend. For the first time since I started working for them, they experienced a fall-off in business. They thought I could promote business, so they asked that I go on the road to the southeastern part of the state to meet potential clients. Being away from home, especially with a new baby, was not very appealing to me. I uncovered some business that my predecessor had overlooked, because the accounts required walking some distance from downtown. But there was not enough business to be found by shoe leather alone.

I made a deal with Dickenson's to start an independent studio. I would bring my printing work to them; they would bring their art work to me. Additionally, I could secure business from the other presses in town. I rented space in the Association of Commerce building, hiring the best Dickinson artists. With a burgeoning family, I was motivated to make my new venture a success. I had saved enough to run the business for several months. If I did not make it, I would look for work.

With my own office, I could sell real estate too, forgoing the commission I paid to the realtor. Learning the hard way on what it was to solicit business by foot and streetcar, I broke down to buy my first automobile, a six-cylinder Studebaker. I only wished that it would prove marginally more reliable than my motor launch or my brothers' Chalmers. If not, my little company, Central Studios, would not be long lived. Hattie's family thought that I was "sticking my neck out too far," especially with the purchase of the car. They always bore a mix of fear and envy with how I made a living, whether by real estate speculation or something as ephemeral as drawing pictures. They were literally "meat and potatoes" people, making their living selling those substantial commodities. But, I had never gone to them for a hand-out or a loan and they respected that. They sure liked spending Saturday afternoons at our cottage on the river. Hattie's brother John tried to dissuade me from the car purchase. Maybe he remembered my inexperience with horses. After I explained the business reasons for the purchase, he agreed to give me driving lessons. I did not ask him why he was dead set against the car when he had one mostly for pleasure. I imagine that he thought it was an expensive luxury that I should not purchase until the business was well established. From my perspective, the pace of business had picked up. I needed to compete at this new speed for my new business to survive.

My bank account was almost exhausted and I was pretty discouraged. I did not admit to John that he was right, though I did get the hang of starting the car, keeping it running with the elaborate set of levers for throttle and spark advance. Most days, I did not scare myself, other drivers, or the horses and wagons sharing the road. At last, the work came in, first as a trickle, then as a torrent. In three months, we went from not having enough work to having too much. In this business, you never turn down work, so my dream of spending more time with my family vanished as I now worked over twelve hours per day, six days a week. The only time that I saw my family is when we walked to church.

In 1918, our hearts were gladdened by the birth of our fifth and final baby, Virginia Lois, the only one of our children not named for a relative. Unlike Alta, Virginia was born during hard times. During the Great War, coal was in short supply, so we limited the rooms that were heated. I thought of the cold nights I endured as a boy when we had first moved here, so I knew these restrictions would not last and tried to make the best of them. Suspicious of the Germans, I was happy to do my part in defeating them. In Friesland, we lived harmoniously with our neighbors across the border, so I was stunned at how treacherously they crossed the Belgian frontier. When Virginia arrived, I purchased a small coal heater for the room where Hattie and the baby spent most of their time, but we economized further until the poor baby girl contracted pneumonia. My mind raced back to my family's losing battle with diphtheria. Virginia's battle was just as dire, but she pulled through. I believed her condition was caused by the lack of heat in her room.

That winter was one of the most severe in Grand Rapids' history, snowing almost every day. The drifts grew so deep that there was no longer any attempt to keep the streets clear. Only strategic arterials were kept open. The side streets consisted of two thin trod paths of the sidewalks; the traffic lanes drifted over. The older children and I struggled keeping this lifeline open. Dr. Thompson drove his car as far as possible to walk the rest of the way. He would have had better luck if he had kept his horse and sleigh. The farmers around Grand Rapids, used to unplowed roads, had not abandoned their sleighs, so their lives proceeded uninterrupted. While many things were so different from life of when I had grown up in the Netherlands, when the Creator decreed, we returned to a more primitive era, even here in America.

As the war wound down, the Michigan economy picked up. A 96-acre farm came on the market, not far from our lots along the river. This farm fronted the river for a half-mile. I thought that families like mine might enjoy it as a haven from the cares of the city. Most of it was out of the floodplain, covered with beautiful shade trees, giving it a stately, park-like appearance. The property came on the market due to the death of the owner. The trust company administering the estate had offices across the street from my studio. A few mornings after visiting the property, I walked over, making an offer, which the widow accepted.

I had picnicked on these banks before. I knew that it was poor farm land, but ideal for my purposes. After selling our North Park home, we wanted to build another residence in the suburbs. We did not build another home, but in nearby Comstock Park, found a commodious two-year old farm house. The owner had run out of money before finishing it. This was ideal, because we put in our own finishing touches.

A basement ran under the entire house, a new "luxury" for us. I contracted for a concrete floor to be poured, so that we would have another floor for minimal cost. I started on a plumbing system by digging a well that fed a pressurized tank. We would now have a modern bathroom with running water to a tub, toilet, and sink. I had hoped to run the pump and pressurize the water tank with electricity, but Consumers Power would not run a line to our house. Similarly, Grand Rapids Gas would not extend a line. I needed to improvise. It was easy enough to install a small gasoline motor to pump the well, pressurizing the water system. I would fire it up for a short time when I came home from work at night.

Gas for lighting was more of a problem. I adopted technology from one of my neighbors. This solution was short lived, because I never have seen anything like it since. It consisted of a large flat metal tank called the carburetor (but very unlike an automobile carburetor). Into this tank, we poured a special high-test gasoline shipped from Toledo, Ohio. It was so volatile that the company claimed that a drop from the second floor would not reach the ground. This miraculous material was too expensive to waste on this experiment. However, I can vouch for its volatility. When I poured the liquid from the shipping barrel into the carburetor, a thick layer of frost formed around the spout. We placed the carburetor in a three by five foot pit in the basement. The carburetor was connected to gas lines running throughout the house, pressurized by a small pump that I wound by hand.

Whenever we turned on a gas valve, whether for lighting or for the stove, this pump blew air across the fuel in the carburetor. The vapor wafting off the liquid in the carburetor then flowed up through the pipes into the house. The system had a few drawbacks. For one, a person should never go into the basement to inspect the system alone. A gas leak from the carburetor could block off air. Our neighbor with the same system fainted from not following this precaution, nearly dying. Second, you had to stay on top of it if the system needed fuel or winding. Inevitably, we would be sitting down for supper when the lights would flicker. I bolted downstairs, with Mel close behind, to wind up the blower. Perhaps it was dangerous, but for us it was very important. The system worked as well as city gas. I was grateful that we could have modern lighting in the "country". Without it, our new house would have been a bad investment.

I remember this system for a very different reason than the comfort it provided us. I enlisted my father-in-law, "Pa" Lindemulder to help build the concrete well that contained the carburetor. I contracted for the excavation, but Pa built the forms for the walls. I ferried the concrete down a ramp set on top of the cellar stairs. Filling the wheelbarrow as full as I could manage, I lurched down the ramp, holding on for dear life. I was wheezing pretty hard so he encouraged me to carry smaller loads.

"We have plenty of time," he calmly noted.

We did indeed have plenty of time that day, but my own life accelerated in an unanticipated way. Near the end of the day, I burped loudly. I thought it was indigestion from the large lunch of liverwurst sandwiches and homemade apple pie that Hattie had made for us, but there was something else in my mouth. I coughed up blood! This was disconcerting, but I thought that maybe I had exerted myself too hard. I should have been resting on this Saturday, instead of embracing heavy labor, but I figured that if the old man could to do it, so could I. However, I had been running flat out for the past ten years, earning a livelihood for my now large family. I managed the art studio, always worried about paying the staff or finding more work. The land business was successful, but weeks would go by without our making a sale. Little by little, I was running myself into the ground. That little spot of blood was the sign of much bigger issues than a little exhaustion on a Saturday afternoon. Soon, our cozy life along the banks of the Grand River would be ripped apart. God had a new plan for me and my family rather than a comfortable life among the newly affluent Dutch in Western Michigan. When my family arrived here over thirty years ago, we scrambled to find work and make ends meet. The Dutch were the labor that made the primitive factories hum. Now many of us owned small businesses of our own. Through hard work and initiative, we climbed the economic ladder; no longer stuck at the bottom. But the road upward is never direct as I soon would learn. Man proposes, God disposes.

No sanitary sewer main ran by our new house, so we managed all of our waste on the property. Like our gas pipes, the new system was cutting edge. Until now, most houses in the neighborhood relied on noxious cesspools. We installed a septic system that could function for years without maintenance. Two concrete tanks were installed in a series behind our house. The first tank gradually filled with the sludge digested by biologic action. Water from this tank, after the solids dropped out, overflowed into the next tank. The effluent was further purified in the second tank, slowly leaching into the surrounding acreage through branching pipes.

The first tank had a small manhole for access for the required periodic cleaning. This access was to lead to a near tragedy. The rear of our lot was located quite a bit higher than where the home was located. During periods of heavy rain, flows from this area would run across the lawn. During one of the cloudbursts that occur during the Michigan summer, we were sitting on our porch marveling at the power of the Creator, enjoying the cooling rain. Our peaceful interlude was interrupted by a very unpleasant odor followed by Melvin running out from the house exclaiming, "The sewer is backing up in the basement!"

I could not imagine how this could happen until I recalled that the lid to the septic tank had been recently removed. Maybe it had not been replaced. A torrent of water poured across the opening. This was more than the system could accommodate through normal action. At least it was getting a good flushing. Mel and I ran across the lawn toward the tanks. We could not find the access since the sheet of water flowed right across it. Looking for the opening, I stepped into it, falling up to my arms before almost disappearing. This story might have ended right there in ignominy of my drowning in a septic tank if not for the grace of God. Mel helped me out. At least we now knew where the opening was located, securing the lid in place. Returning to the house, we assessed the damage in the basement. There was over a foot of standing water that fortunately drained over the next several days as the septic field dried out. The basement was a mess. Mel and I worked on cleaning it up. It was great to have one of the children who could now help with these chores. He was a great help. Scrubbing the mud off the surfaces took a lot of elbow grease, which he applied daily.

Living out of town posed other challenges. We needed to go to Grand Rapids, nearly five miles away, every day. Later in the twentieth century, a commute like this would not faze anyone, but with our primitive automobiles or the long walk to the end of the streetcar line, we were challenged daily to get to school and work. Mel was now in high school, needing to go to town, as did I, daily. Hattie stayed in Comstock Park with the other children, but the distances made it a challenge for her to visit other women. We had only one car which Mel and I drove on weekdays. Church attendance was another challenge. We could manage the five miles to Broadway Christian Reformed Church as a family on Sundays, but we still had to figure how to get one or the other of us to circle, prayer meetings, and catechism. The automobile that once seemed such a luxury was now a necessity. We loved our life outside of town but it came at a price.

Our busy life continued on its upward trajectory. While we were preparing the house so that we could move in, the Great War came mercifully to an end. Our sacrifices paid off with the victory by the Allies. During the war, "heatless days" were enforced. This made the work in the studio very difficult. Art is a sedentary occupation. Even wearing an overcoat was not enough to overcome the discomfort of watching the frost build up on windows. The ink did not freeze, but did thicken in the bottle into a black sludge. One cannot draw a very straight or precise line if your fingers are shaking and your teeth are chattering. Some days we just had to chalk one up to the Hun, going home. It might have been on one of these days when outside, I heard whistles and sirens from all over town. Cars roared about town with junk attached to the bumpers, adding to the racket. It did not take long to understand that the noise meant the signing of the Armistice. I was relieved that the Bosch were defeated and that our days of privation were coming to an end.

I was counting on platting and selling my new land on the river front. I needed a loan to pay for the cost of bringing a road into the property so that I could market the lots. In spite of the success that I had with the previous parcel, the bankers who walked the property turned me down. They could see that the farm was a marginal proposition at best. However, funding a project for lots for second homes did not seem prudent, either. The rampant speculation and easy money of the Roaring Twenties had not yet started. If I had approached them five years later, they probably would have lent the money and then speculated and bought the lots for themselves. I approached my brothers to see if they could help with the monthly stipend I was remitting to my parents. They scrambled, refunding the money I had "loaned" my parents. A friend loaned me the rest. With a road and clear title, I could once again, sell lots. I needed money for marketing, too, since I decided to sell the property directly, keeping the real estate commission for myself. But this meant that I had to pay for advertising, instead of it coming out of the broker's pocket.

During the summer of 1919, I surveyed property into platted lots, so the township board could approve it the following January. We were in business the following spring. Once again, the property sold well. I did not do business on Sunday. However, many people visited the subdivision on Sunday, coming by the office the following Monday to sign a contract with a check for the down payment. This was an interruption to my artwork that I always welcomed, since I had a lot of money tied up in the land.

Other sources of income popped up. Near the far edge of the property, a Grand Rapids advertising company erected a billboard. Someone finally figured out that if motorists could afford a car, they could afford other things, too. Signs popped up along the roads like mushrooms after rain. The advertisers were paying my neighbor a small rental for this sign. From the recent land survey, I knew the sign was on my property, so I rectified the mistake. As much as I appreciated the modest income, this was not my main reason for correcting the misunderstanding. This part of the property was formed by the crossing of two roads, a good place for a gas station. Some years later, I sold it for that very purpose.

There were more blessings. The county road commission tested the far corner of my property, determining it contained gravel ideal for road construction. Soon they were sending me checks for each load that they trucked out.

I mention these last two items to show how much of what happens in life is not planned, but driven by God's will. If one concentrates on God's message to us, we are not overwhelmed by the good and bad that we encounter proceeding through life. These examples also illustrate the impact that automobiles were having on the Michigan economy. I was now getting commissions to illustrate car parts that were made in our part of the state. The billboard, gas station, and gravel pit were all driven by more cars taking to the road. The better cars and roads made our daily commute into town easier, too.

We loved Comstock Park and our happy life there. It was the beginning of a new era. America was becoming mechanical and modern. Our life was to radically change. Looking back at Comstock Park, I see lazy days on the porch in a straw boater, the girls in pinafore dresses tumbling across the large lawn. The boys in their knickers are sailing model boats on the pond. Our family was healthy; business was good. My opening of an independent art studio was a success. I was tired, but it all seemed worthwhile.

There was an enormous barn on the place, which was popular with the children, frolicking in the hayloft. We bought a bunny who had the run of the place, but could always be induced from hiding with a well-timed carrot. Rabbits never exist individually. Although we bought just one, little ones followed. Never one to look a gift horse in the mouth, I butchered one, making a mess of cleaning it. The gamey taste and resulting mess disabused me of any more pretensions of raising livestock. Chickens, rabbits; it did not matter. They were all safe from my hatchet, though it hurt my country Friesian soul to let such a readily available source of protein move about unmolested.

By now I had platted and sold parts of two farms, so I am sure that my neighbors had an inflated sense of my net worth. However, the development of land can easily devour any money you make from the sale of it. I was ahead on these ventures, but barely. The son of the local butcher opened an automobile agency, coming by frequently, hoping to tempt me with a new model to replace the Studebaker. By now I knew the idiosyncrasies of the beast, where to buy good gasoline, and always carried two spares. Mel, happy to have a daily ride, patched the spares that punctured, so now we had somewhat reliable transportation. My faith in the Studebaker would not be misplaced.

New cars were not much of a temptation. Thrift ran through my family. We had seen too many hard times not to save. Whatever pleasure I would have from driving a new car would be balanced against the approbation of my brothers. We lent each other money because we knew it would not be frivolously squandered.

We lived within walking distance of the fairgrounds for the West Michigan Fair. Since it was so close, Hattie and I walked over for old time's sake. We had not been back since I had won three second prizes as a young man. When we were ready to return home, we could not find Mel. As a young man in his own right, he walked over on his own, but we had planned to walk home together. After a quick circuit of the fairgrounds, we left without him. He could walk the mile back home on his own when he was ready. Still, I thought it was strange that we did not see him since the fair grounds were quite small.

We had just set out for home when we heard rapid footsteps behind us. Turning, we saw Mel running towards us. When he caught up, we noticed that he was carrying a box of California grapes, Hattie's favorite fruit. With the improved rail service, California grapes were not a rarity, but were still a luxury.

"Mel, where did you get the money to buy those grapes?" I asked.

"Dad," he replied, "Did you see the tent with the Wild Man?"

"Of course, it was hard to miss. You could not avoid hearing the moans and growls."

Inside the tent, a cage prevented the "Wild Man from Africa" from wreaking havoc on the good citizens of Kent County. You could view this aboriginal curiosity for a dime. Hattie and I had enough experience with fairs to keep our money in our purse and pocket. But Mel was curious, falling into a conversation with the barker at the tent's entrance. When the crowd thinned out, the barker said that the wild man's throat was sore from all of the growling and asked Mel if he could duplicate the sound by rubbing resin across the string. Mel, like his father, was nothing if not enterprising, accepted the offer, especially since the payment of fifty cents was involved. No doubt for this amount, Mel added a few moans of his own. I thought back to when we walked by the tent when looking for Mel, trying to recollect the vocal stylings of my boy. He certainly did have a way with the rosin and string.

With his earnings he bought his mother her favorite, grapes, which we thought was pretty nice.

Chapter 14

Life was good. We loved our Comstock Park house. My business was growing. Our children were growing and loved life on our "estate". I was forty years old and in the prime of life. I worked hard, but enjoyed life so much that it was not a burden. God had blessed my endeavors. Michigan was booming - my risk had been rewarded. I could not ask for a better wife. We had shared so much together, now having lived together for as long as when we were apart growing up.

But we are well served to remember that our lives and all we have are but gifts from God. We had always believed this, trying to practice it daily, but we were to learn it in a much more fundamental way. God challenges us only with trials that we can bear through faith in Him. Through faith, we can endure all things.

My father had been failing mentally for some time. He recognized me and the other siblings, but his conversation became increasingly limited. We spoke now entirely in Dutch, he fluently as I struggled, now so accustomed to English. I smile at my parents' final years together. Mother became profoundly blind, so she did not bother switching on the lights. They now had electricity, but it did them little good except for preventing them from burning down the house by knocking over a kerosene lamp. The old man did not mind the dark, either, as he was usually fast asleep when the sun went down.

Father (I would never dream of calling him "Dad", like my children did me) had a hard time moving. This was actually a blessing, because he became confused when outside on his own. I don't know if he minded living in a darkened house, since we always turned on the lights when we arrived. Many a time I came up on the house where not a single light would be on. I knew they were home since they were past the age of going out. Mom knew her way around her own house, needing one of her children only to guide her once out on the street. I would come in and mother would be washing dishes in the dark. She knew every inch of the house, so it mattered not to her if the lights were on or off. Maybe father found comfort being there in the dark with her. One time when I came in she was leading him by the hand to go to the bathroom as you would a child. I realized that they had gone through so much change together that the presence of the other was the only constant in their lives.

My mother was to be denied this comfort when our Lord took father to his reward in the summer of 1919. After my brothers called me, I found him in bed as if asleep. He had lived a life of great dignity and probity. I thank God for all the gifts he gave me - honesty, a willingness to work, a sense of adventure, and the value of a strong faith. I hope that a small part of his strength resided in me. Everything he did was to make his family stronger and full of grace. By now, I was fully launched, a man in full, no longer the baby brother, but I missed the protection that exuded from his quiet strength. He was never a rich man by any means, but I knew I would be safe as long as he lived. He died just short of his eighty-first birthday. I always thought of him as a conservative man, but I realize that pulling his family out of Holland to move to America was a colossal risk. Life had worked out well, especially for me, but who could know this from the limited flat perspective of Friesland?

Father's death was not the only tragedy that befell us. Hattie's father passed away less than four months later. A very different man than my father, he was, none-the-less, the rock of his family. He was outgoing and his grocery was the center of their neighborhood. No one in the blocks around the Lindemulder Grocery Store ever went hungry, even when behind on their bill. His entrepreneurial zeal was a role model to me. I am sure that he questioned my judgment in hauling his daughter all over the country or my jumping from job to job. But if he did, he never said anything about it. He always took care of us and his gentle bonhomie rubbed off on his children. I could not have had a better father-in-law. I recommend marrying the daughter of a grocer. You certainly get your choice of produce.

These challenges, if hard blows, were expected. Death is a part of life as surely as birth. Both of our fathers lived their lives with a goal beyond. Now, without them, I was to face harder, unexpected trials. I had been working very hard. Work was good, but I had experienced too many slowdowns to ever turn down a job. Having too much work can be just as difficult as not having enough. I scrambled to find artists who met our small studio's exacting standards.

In building the business, I had "too much hay on the fork". I used men from other studios at nights, but had to show them exactly what I wanted. The electrification of the work place now permitted (or required) that we work longer hours. My real estate ventures required daily attention. I spent many a night looking after my aged parents. Knowing I was a wreck, my fellow artists insisted that I go fishing or spend more time with my children before I ran off the road. But, I was so worried about the studio when I was away that I could barely relax. Friends and associates saw the toll this was taking, but I gamely plowed ahead until it was too late.

At Hattie's urging, I finally consulted our family doctor. He was a fine doctor, but not a pulmonary specialist, so he missed the consumption that was afflicting my lungs. After a few months of not feeling top dollar with labored breathing, I consulted a lung specialist. He put me under a special camera that we now know as X-rays, immediately identifying the condition: Tuberculosis!

When I returned home to my family that evening, we were a very sad group. 'Consumption", as we knew it, was a killer. We knew friends in our church who had succumbed. With the passing of our fathers, death was very much on our minds. Although the doctors knew that tuberculosis was caused by a pathogen, it was immune to medicinal treatment. The only known cure was to go to a drier climate to "open up" the lungs. One basically had to cure one's self.

Not expecting to live more than a year or two, I turned the management of the studio over to a colleague from the Dickenson's whom I absolutely trusted. Following the advice of the specialist, I took to bed for a complete rest. It took several weeks for me to still my mind from worrying about the business, my family, and myself. After much prayer, I resigned myself to God's grace. He would look after all. If I was to be part of it, so be it. If not, I was in His care.

Brother Nick came out to our place, replacing the windows in one room with screens. This was now my sleeping porch, which I occupied by myself with a stack of blankets. After a while, I settled in to my fate. It was a pretty room, well positioned to catch the early morning light that my painter's eye appreciated. Open to the outside, I listened to the cacophony of bird calls starting as a chirp or two around four in the morning, before building to the crescendo at sunrise. Here was a world outside my window of which I was barely aware. God spoke to me in unexpected ways. After my early awakening, I marked time by the passage of the daily trains of the Grand Rapids and Indiana Railroad. I could even tell which day it was by the different timbre of the railcars of the twice-a-week lumber trains.

The traditional treatment for tuberculosis was to "take the cure" at higher elevations. It was thought that the thinner air was beneficial. My specialist believed these benefits were negligible, perhaps in the range of five percent. The air at our place in suburban Comstock Park was quite good, but there was no escaping the ever-present humidity. I felt like my lungs never "dried out". I was not the only one afflicted with tuberculosis. Many ethnic and religious groups had opened "sanitariums". A popular location for these was in Denver, Colorado, a city large enough to provide the required services in a state blessed with the requisite elements of elevation, sunshine, and low humidity. I am sure I would never have considered taking such a radical step if not for the efforts by some ministers and doctors in the Christian Reformed Church in opening up a sanitarium on the outskirts of Denver.

I was still a young man. It was certainly worthwhile to explore any avenue that increased my chances of continuing a normal productive life. We noted the risks that our families had taken to move from the Netherlands, or how we had moved to New York to further my career. Would this be any different? Hopefully, I could soon return to the good life we had built for ourselves in Western Michigan.

Not long after, we received the application for admittance to the Bethesda Sanitarium in Denver. Hattie carefully filled it out before gathering enough clothes so I could survive (hopefully) on my own. In her state of concern, she did not read the fine print which said not to make the trip until the "patient has been accepted for admittance". I was not on death's door but believed I had little chance of returning, so we were coy about my departure. I confessed to my mother. Sister Minnie had to know, too, since she brought Mother to see me. Our concerns were well-founded, since it was the last time Mother and I would be together. Mother and Minnie were still at our home when I left. Mel drove me to the interurban railway station with Hattie and Helen. After hugging my two older children, admonishing them to look after their mother and the family, I held my beloved Hattie in my arms for what may be the last time. With my eyes glistening, I stoically boarded the interurban with my big trunk, sitting stiffly as I stared straight ahead, my straw hat not moving an inch. I prayed for strength and the mercy of returning to all that I held dear. It had never been harder to submit to the destiny that God had determined. As the trip progressed, I continued to pray. His mercy descended upon me. I knew that things would turn out for the best because His will would be done.

The interurban took me to Muskegon, where I boarded an overnight steamer to Chicago. I splurged on a taxi to the La Salle Street Station where the porters escorted me to a Pullman sleeper car for the trip west. I reflected on how similar this trip seemed to me as the one I took as a seven-year old after we had landed in America. I was scared then, too, but excited to see new places. Perhaps this trip was an extension of that one, continuing further into this country that had been so interesting and good to me. I was supposed to die, but I just did not feel like I would. However, leaving the rolling fecund farms of Illinois and Iowa, and entering the staked prairie of Nebraska, I wondered what I had gotten into. The landscape became increasingly bleak until the sun went down as the rhythm of the swaying car lulled me to sleep. If nothing else, rail travel had certainly improved since my first trip.

The land, if anything, looked worse upon my awakening the next morning. The train crossed a vast desert, punctuated by an occasional cowboy herding scrawny cattle. No one could thrive here. This is where I was supposed to get well? My disposition improved slightly when the conductor pointed out the Rocky Mountains on the horizon. By leaning back in my seat and pressing my head against the glass, I could make out a white smudge on the horizon. This smudge, I learned as we got closer, was snow on the high peaks. I had never seen snowcapped peaks before, so my heart beat a little faster.

Once the train stopped, I stepped from the car, to see an elderly gentleman coming towards me. I thought that he might be from the sanitarium, there to greet me. I introduced myself. He was a bit flustered before replying, "Very nice to meet you, Mr. Veenstra, but I am here it to meet an older crippled lady. I take it you are not her."

I thought it strange that he would be here for her, but not for me as I hailed a cab. The air was certainly thinner as I wrestled my trunk toward the curb. Though surrounded by miles of seemingly nothing, Denver was larger than Grand Rapids. While the city paled in comparison to Chicago, there was plenty of traffic on the surrounding streets as we headed out under the welcoming arch at the station. We left downtown, continuing past blocks of prosperous homes that would not be out of place in Michigan or Illinois. Soon, these were left behind as we continued on a dusty road with other vehicles. I saw, here and there, oases of trees and buildings dotting the vast dry countryside. After a half hour, the taxi pulled into one of these oases that was the Bethesda

Sanitarium. The trees reminded me a lot of those I had planted back home. They were not yet mature, offering meager shade.

At a place catering to the infirm, I expected help with my luggage. Seeing none forthcoming, I left my trunk where the cab dropped it. The driver gladly accepted the fare for the long trip. There was a sign over one of the doors proclaiming "Administration". I made my way towards it. After climbing a small flight of stairs, I tried one leaf and then the other before entering a large room with several desks, each occupied by women studiously reading sheets of paper. The one closest looked up asking, "May I help you?"

"I certainly hope so," I replied. She did not know how much I was counting on that to be true. "I am Harry Veenstra; here to be admitted."

"Mr. Veenstra, I am sorry, but we do not have any record of your coming. Did you receive a letter authorizing your admission?"

"A letter? - why no. I was so weak, my wife filled out the application. Then I came. I did not know that a letter was required. I do know that I have tuberculosis, if that is of any help."

"I am sure that you do. You say that your wife sent in an application? When did she do this?"

Now me: "Let's see, I was in Grand Rapids four days ago, so it would have been two days before that."

"Grand Rapids? As in Grand Rapids, Michigan? I am sorry you came so far and so fast, but you first need approval before admission. Let me see if we have even received your application."

With that, she stood up, turned, and walked towards a door at the rear of the room. The other two women glanced up from their work momentarily with equal looks of pity and disgust before returning to their papers. I stood in a state of confusion and fear. What she said made perfect sense, but it was I who was dying, not she. What is the point of bureaucratic niceties in a situation like this? During this break, I returned to the double doors to see how my trunk was faring. It was still there as I noticed a bus pull up.

Who should step out but the elderly gentleman from the train station, assisting a woman who was visibly crippled. I could have taken the bus, saving the exorbitant cost of the cab ride! My heart sank until I looked past the bus. On the horizon, as far as the eye could see to the left and right was the rampart of the Rocky Mountains. The foreground was the most beautiful hazy blue set off by the stark white of the snow on the high peaks. The words of the Psalmist immediately came to mind, "I lift up my eyes to the hills – where does my help come from?"

Returning inside, I was met by the woman with whom I had spoken. Behind her was a gentleman in a white coat. "Mr. Veenstra, I am Dr. George. Will you please come with me?" We entered a small examination room where he listened to my lungs with the stethoscope.

"Mr. Veenstra, you have come to the right place. Your lungs do not sound all that great. I understand that you know my wife."

"That's right," I replied, "We met her in the Englewood, New Jersey church there a few years back."

"She remembers. She enjoyed her time there."

"As did we. The pastor was an old friend from junior high school."

"Dr. Huizinga. I am in awe of anyone who can manage a congregation and go to medical school at the same time. A stronger man than me, certainly."

After I put my shirt back on, he asked that I wait outside on a bench in the large reception room. I sat there for what seemed like an eternity. It was the day of my wedding anniversary. This was some way to celebrate! Before I hailed the cab, I sent my darling wife a telegram, but it was sure not as good as being there with flowers. Later, Dr. George returned.

"Mr. Veenstra, it is somewhat irregular, but I think we can find room for you. I certainly could not in good conscience send you, or more particularly your lungs, back to Michigan."

"Thank you, thank you very much. I think the trip back would have killed me, if not the TB."

For the first time in about an hour, I felt like I let out my first breath, gulping a deep chest of mile-high air. It felt good, even if my head felt faint. After a brief prayer of thanksgiving, I promised myself I would never miss another anniversary with Hattie.

I was taken to my room. The doctors prescribed several days of bed rest to help me recover from the trip. I slept for most of this time, as I now had a plan to get better, releasing the anxiety of the uncertainty surrounding this drastic change. Fortunately, I had saved enough money that I could afford my treatment while not working for a while. My art studio was still open. Business was not as good without my being there, but it produced a modest income for Hattie and the children. Additionally, every so often, we sold one of the river lots. I made some money, but did not pursue wealth as an ultimate goal. If so, I would have left commercial art, pursuing developing and selling property. However, both businesses balanced out, and I was relieved that we were not destitute. Many of my fellow patients were not so fortunate. The contraction of tuberculosis, especially by the men, financially devastated their families. This stress made getting well doubly difficult.

At first I was restless, without anything to do except "get better." Like my parents on the ship to America, I had no idea what do with myself. Gradually, I eased into the new routine, setting new goals. Before, as a young man, I strove to be the best artist I could be. Now my goal was to get well to return to a family who needed me. This was also an opportunity for spiritual growth. I had plenty of free time to read my "Modern English Translation of the New Testament" while sitting by the small irrigation ditch that ran through the property. Sitting by the bank in the healing sunshine, I felt doubly blessed by the message and the sun's warmth. I was interrupted by no discordant noise except the distinct trill of the meadowlark, a bird new to me in my new locale. At first, the sun was overwhelming and too bright, but after a while, my artist's eye appreciated the sharper detail and high contrasts. I included darker shadows in my own sketches. I did not have any oils or pastels, but saw that when I did, I would employ a palette of bolder colors than I used in Michigan. Not only was the view brighter; it was further. In Michigan, any vista was confined by the canopy of trees, except when at the big lake. Here, you could see sixty miles or more in many directions. I looked at my own life from a longer perspective, giving myself to God's will. I began feeling less sorry, opening myself for Gods' guidance as to what Life would now offer.

The land here is naturally prairie, but over time, people had planted shade trees. The older parts of Denver, a few miles distant, were under a canopy, but it was parched out here on the edges. A ragged line of what I learned were cottonwood trees grew along the irrigation ditch. The staff and patients valiantly siphoned the water from this ditch to encourage a small orchard of fruit trees. Growing fruit here was more difficult than in Michigan where all one had to do was plant the tree to harvest the fruit a few years later.

Adjusting to the rhythms of convalescent life, I knew that this would be a temporary break. The sanitarium had a nine-month time limit. There was so much demand that each bed was needed for new patients in more dire condition. The climate and treatments took effect, diminishing the tubercles in my lungs. The months passed quickly. Dr. George was pleased with my progress but feared a relapse if I returned home, strongly suggesting that I remain in Colorado. This was as shocking a turn of events as the news of when I learned that I had tuberculosis. After months of healing, I was pretty sure I would make it, returning to Michigan to resume my life. Now I knew that God really did have a different plan for me. How would I make a living here? Even with automobiles and electricity, Colorado was far more primitive than when we first moved to Michigan. In Grand Rapids we could choose from over a dozen Christian Reformed Churches; here there was only one. I had met the pastor, Reverend Idzerd Van Dellen, who had his hands full building his young church and conducting weekly Bible study at the sanitarium. His flock was growing; more and more Dutch were moving here from the Midwest. However, there was little manufacturing. I knew that breaking into commercial art, especially at the top, would be impossible. I no longer had surplus capital to take a flyer in land speculation. I would rely on God's guidance.

Hattie and I corresponded frequently. Our letters usually took less than a week to be delivered. We were up to date on each other's lives. I appreciated her heroic efforts in looking after our children and our interests back home. She probably took the news of the move to Colorado better than I did. She was desperate to be reunited, knowing that God would not have created a plan He could not fulfill. Her parents were now both gone. Slowly, through prayer, I worried less envisioning the future planned for us. My brothers would look after our mother.

Preparing to make the trip without me, the family packed up our house. I agonized over not being there to help. I knew all that could go wrong. However, roads and automobiles had improved since my road trip to Wisconsin with my brothers. My greatest relief is that there were now more gas stations along the way. More gas stations meant more motorists. I was sure that there would be plenty of well-meaning strangers to help if they got into a bind. Hattie could not have made the trip without the help of the two oldest children who were now young adults. I was particularly relieved that Mel was with them since he knew more about automobiles than I did.

Since we were now in a strict economy mode, they would camp along the way. Our Studebaker touring car was prepared like a pioneer's covered wagon. On the running board, Mel built a cabinet for groceries with a drop-down counter for food preparation. They bought a large tent with a floor on the recommendation of a friend who traveled frequently. The cots and blankets folded up in a coverall fitted to the rack above the back bumper. They could not store anything in the car, needing the room for five children and their mother! By this time, 1922, there was a network of roads across the country. The most direct route was designated as the "Lincoln Highway". Fortunately, it ran in almost a direct line from Chicago to just north of Denver. This facilitated my family's route finding. The younger children were tasked with spying the distinctive red, white, and blue banding on telephone poles or the concrete pylons marked with the blue "L".

My understanding of the trip was aided by snapshots taken along the way. Hattie and the children started from the Lindemulder Store in late June, no doubt loading up on last minute provisions, allowing Hattie's brothers to look over the car one last time. Hattie boiled and "canned" chickens for the trip. Just like with preserves, if you put the boiled chickens into sterilized jars, they kept safely for up to a month.

Camping grounds were springing up along the route. So many people were taking to the road that towns along the Lincoln Highway mowed a field, drilled a well, and built some toilets so that the migration did not spread across the landscape, relieving itself willy-nilly. The trip reenacted the travels of earlier pioneers, except now the touring car replaced the Conestoga wagon and the trip now took days instead of months. Just like in the covered wagon days, the immigrants gathered around campfires, reviewing their adventures of the day or seeking advice for the next. If they were lucky, someone produced a guitar or harmonica, sharing the American songbook. Many a family enjoyed this camaraderie as way to spend time together, undertaking it voluntarily as a form of recreation. We, as family, used the skills learned on this trip to explore our new home, the Mountain West, by automobile. Out here, the distances were much greater without the transportation infrastructure that we took for granted in the Midwest. There were few trains and certainly no steamers. If you wanted to go anywhere, you had to drive. Moving a big family was cheaper by car, as was carrying our canvas lodging with us.

The first day of their trip was a bit of holiday. Optimism reigned. They got off to a late start at ten-thirty in the morning after saying their goodbyes. Our families did not know if they would see them again. Travel between Michigan and Colorado was a once or twice in a lifetime event, much like when my family moved to the United States from the Netherlands. They drove south to get around Lake Michigan, spending the night in a farmer's yard north of the Indiana state line. The next day was consumed with navigating the traffic of the suburbs of Chicago. All roads went through the center of these many towns, so Mel the driver needed to pay close attention. There were still few traffic signals but many new drivers. With great relief, they camped after that first full day in Chicago Heights, Illinois.

By the next day, the traffic of Chicago would have been in the rear view mirror if our Studebaker had one. It did not, but our next car would. That evening they arrived in Clinton, Iowa, after crossing the Mississippi River. The Lincoln Highway crossed here on one of the first bridges across the river for automobiles and trucks. Mel told me that the cars backed up for a mile before slowly crossing the river. Happy to have made it across, they searched for a campground with room. They celebrated by breaking out a jarred chicken. The terrain of Iowa challenged the Studebaker as it struggled up one hill after another. Our brave pilgrims stopped at the top of longer hills, letting the engine cool before plunging down the other side. Mel was careful that the motor was well fed with oil, conscientiously changing it after the struggle of Iowa.

As the calendar flipped over to July, the Studebaker responded to this thoughtful treatment, carrying the family 251 miles to Council Bluffs, a one-day record. They pushed to get to the city before the thunderheads on the western horizon unleashed their fury. My family was used to summer thundershowers from the big storms that came across Lake Michigan. We loved sitting on the porch in Comstock Park watching these displays of God's majesty as the rain sheeted off the roof. None of those Michigan storms prepared my family for the coming fury, gathering steam unimpeded across the hot American prairie. The clouds towered almost as far the eye could see. Lightning licked the ground under this black seething mass. Mel steered a roadside a motel for shelter rather than pushing on into the maw of these monsters. Hattie agreed, prudence overcoming the effect on the pocketbook, survival being the paramount concern at the moment. The family jammed into one room, watching through the window as the storm hit. Mel kept an eye on how well the side curtains of the Studebaker performed against the onslaught. Hattie and Helen assured the younger girls that all would be well.

So it was in the morning. The day dawned clear if steamy. The floorboards of the car were a little damp but were easily mopped out before Mel cranked the car as Rolf sat at the controls adjusting the spark and throttle as the motor turned over. Loading into the car, they headed down the road. They chose to spend the next night in a motel, too. Perhaps the ground in western Nebraska was still too wet. I knew none of this. Long distance calls were expensive and unreliable. By this time, I had received a letter that they had left on last Thursday, now apprehensively guessing where they were. I waited anxiously but would have been surprised if I knew that they were so close. Even though Nebraska was only one state away, it is a long state. They had many miles to travel to reach me at the foot of the Rocky Mountains. Following the South Fork of the Platte River, they proceeded, camping at night, getting ever closer. Finally, on July 5th, they pulled into Overland Park, Denver's large tourist camp under the cottonwood trees along the South Platte River. Denver wanted tourists to visit the Mile High City, building what some said was the best and largest tourist camp in the nation. Hattie appreciated the convenience of hot and cold water that made laundry possible and food preparation much easier than it had been on the road. My family would call Overland Park home until we could find a permanent place to live. All that the younger girls remembered is the "snow" falling in the summer from the seeding cottonwoods. I now knew why these trees, the tallest in the region, were so named because they littered the ground with seed pods surrounded by white wispy filaments that looked ever so much like cotton. In spite of the ubiquity of these seeds, they could not be spun into cloth. Instead, the seeds piled up on the ground in an untidy mess.

This arboreal outpouring was not the only new natural phenomena to which we would now adapt. I mentioned that the mountains were always on the horizon. This view was always inspirational and a handy reference point when we were finding our way in our new city. I learned that we were not the only pilgrims attracted to the cool of the mountains. Whenever I switched on a light entering a room, a small cloud of moth millers erupted from the surfaces. I came to know that these creatures were harmless, flying about for about a month before continuing on in their life cycle. Hattie did not share my beneficent outlook, waging continual war on this soft cloud blindly darting around the room.

Chapter 15

It was too late on the day they arrived to visit me, but Hattie called the sanitarium. The staff came to my room to tell me that there was a call for me. I could not believe that they had already arrived, so dread filled my heart as I walked to the office. Fear turned to joy when I learned that she was a mere five miles away, coming to see me the following day.

As I floated out of the office, I ran into to a fellow patient. I exclaimed that I would see my wife and my family next day. We continued our conversation in the day room. Unfortunately, it was no longer day, but rather late into the night. The sanitarium had a strict rule that everyone must be in his room by nine o'clock each evening. The nurses performed a bed check, making sure all patients were doing well and resting. Some of the younger patients were tripped up by this rule, but never me. Now, on the day before my discharge, I violated the policy - nowhere to be found when the nurse made her rounds. Since I was to be discharged the next day, I could not be penalized, but never lived down my embarrassment. Several years later, when I served as the secretary on the board of directors of the sanitarium, Dr. George reminded me of my indiscretion. Then, as I did now, I turned as red as if I was a ten-year old caught stealing candy.

My chagrin did not last long when I spied the dusty Studebaker that I knew so well pull into the gate the next morning. It was just as well that only Mel and Hattie came to get me. Hattie and I burst into tears at the relief of not only reuniting, but by the fact that I was still on earth to reunite. Never before had I realized how precious life was. When Mel secured my trunk to the luggage deck on the real bumper, I saw that they would never have made it without him. I asked Hattie what she thought of the place, realizing that her joy of seeing her husband alive had to be tempered by our relocation to the Great American Desert. She commented that it was comfortable because of the lack of humidity, but that "It sure was bright and dry." Like anyone who had never been here before, she was astounded by the rampart of mountains to the west. Here was a natural feature equal in magnificence to Lake Michigan, but so very different.

I said goodbye to my friends before thanking the staff. When I arrived, I was a dead man walking. Now I had a new lease on life. Little did I know that I had not even reached the halfway point of my life. They called these tubercular trips to the West as "taking the cure". I believe I had. I was not completely healthy, continuing with bouts of racking coughs, but thanks to Bethesda, I was on my way.

As we drove toward Overland Park, I sat in the backseat with my bride of the past nineteen years. My goodness, how much had transpired. We laughed at the lines from the Book of Ruth, "Where thou goest, I will go." Little did we know how applicable that verse would be to our lives. If we thought that moving to New Jersey was radical, moving to Colorado was as if to another planet, one much closer to the sun. In New Jersey, we had two children; now we had five. Now I had no job and no prospects, driving to a home in a tent in a tourist park. The refuge of the sanitarium was now past. I now had to return to supporting my family. Fortunately, I had an opportunity to read the Book of Job through, knowing that God would not abandon us. God gave me the opportunity to study his Word while getting well. Now it was my turn to put this blessing into action. I knew that Hattie and I were up to the task. I was grateful and proud of how well she managed without me. Step by step, she assumed tasks that before I had solely done, completing them with aplomb. We had not talked for the last nine months, so we chatted non-stop during the ride with Mel interjecting a detail here and there. After about a half hour, we pulled into Overland Park, where I was hugged by four very happy children. How had they grown so much? The Lindemulders certainly made sure they did not starve while I was away.

I had a surprise for the family. In the interest of making our new home palatable to everyone, I had rented a house in the mountains, which the other patients assured me was the best part of Colorado. They certainly looked beautiful from the plains where the hospital was located, and I was excited to go into them. After being confined for nine months in the sanitarium, I wanted to go somewhere, anywhere. The patients familiar with Colorado described the natural wonders to be seen to the west. I was ready to go and paint. I knew that people would want paintings of the scenery I saw on the horizon.

A few weeks earlier, three other patients and I were considered well enough to leave the sanitarium grounds, so we drove to a small mountain community called appropriately, Evergreen, nestled as it was in a belt of pines. I rented a Ford Model T. Cars were now so common that enough people knew how to drive them to make them available to rent. This was my first opportunity to drive a Ford. A few years back, there were no Fords; now they were everywhere. The first Fords were touring cars, similar to the bathtub on wheels of our Studebaker. Now every other car on the road was a Ford. These small simple vehicles had a reputation for reliability if not comfort. Our rented car took a little adjustment to the spark and throttle on the steering column, but soon we headed towards the small town of Morrison at the foot of the mountains. Our trip was uneventful until we reached Morrison at the mouth of the Bear Creek Canyon. Our car faltered as it headed up the grade. We pulled aside to see if anything was amiss under the hood. We detected nothing, so I suggested that we keep the car in the lower gear. This alleviated the problem. Our driver, like I was from the Midwest, never driving up grades and was unaware that a lower gear was appropriate. The canyon road was so narrow and twisty that several of the blind corners had mirrors so you would not be surprised by the downhill automobiles whizzing down the hill. About an hour after leaving Morrison, we arrived in Evergreen. We were now in the pines that gave the mountains their blue hue from Denver. The air was bracing with a cool breeze. I hoped Hattie and the children would like it as an alternative to hotter plains.

I marveled how well my family worked together as a team without me. Everybody had a role in striking the tent, even four-year old Virginia who gathered the tent stakes. Soon we loaded into the car. It took a bit of rearranging to find room for the new passenger. This was one of the many accommodations everyone made as I was reintegrated back into the family. Mel turned the car west, as we retraced my prior trip, following Morrison Road toward the mountains. In Morrison, we took a brief side trip into Red Rocks Park, with its massive slabs of sandstone uplifted by the larger peaks behind them. In the center of the park were two huge rocks with a large gap between them. One, Ship Rock, was as large as any ship on the ocean, matched in size by the aptly named Creation Rock. Colorado was home to natural marvels larger than anything we ever saw in Michigan.

Mel kept the Studebaker in low gear, slowly negotiating Bear Creek Canyon. After a few stops along the way to cool the overtaxed engine, we reached Evergreen. There, the road turned really steep as we climbed out of the bottom of the canyon toward our cottage. Fortunately, if the road was steep, it was not too long before we pulled up to our new "home". It was a crude place, built strictly for summer use, more of a tent nailed together out of wood than a proper house, but we were so happy to be together that we did not care. Besides, we knew that it was only temporarily for the summer. Ironically, I was now the healthy one in the family. I had acclimated to the altitude, while my strapping boys were out of breath if they performed any strenuous task. Nosebleeds were common during the first weeks as nostrils cracked in the dry air. Our cottage was located on a promontory offering unparalleled views of the Continental Divide, maybe now 15 miles to the west from where we lived. This also meant that we were in the direct path of the winds blowing off the high peaks. One day, after driving into Evergreen to buy groceries, we came back to find rocks on our beds. Helen and the younger children had placed them there to keep the blankets from being blown off. This new location was even better for my battle with tuberculosis. If mile-high Denver was good, our new 7,000 foot elevation location was even better. Here, the air was as crisp as an apple plucked off a tree on a Michigan farm. The scale of our vista was beyond anything we ever saw back home. Every day we observed the Creator at play, waving His hand over the sun, clouds, and peaks. I realized that I would never have experienced such glory if I had not become ill. It is hard to divine the plan that the Lord has for each of us. I was happy for this insight, but even more grateful that I felt stronger with each passing day. All of us adapted to life in the mountains. Some aspects were easy - clothes dried almost as quickly as you put them on the line. Other times were more difficult. The bright sun burned pale skin in under an hour. When a thundershower passed over (which occurred every afternoon for a two-week spell in August), our hovel offered scant protection. Several trees on the promontory bore the effects of lightning strikes. We lived closer to God, which in a sinful world is not always a comfort. A mountain thunderstorm is nature at its most powerful, leaving man very exposed to the power of the Living God.

However, the summer was a holiday. I still could not work, so I spent more time with my children that I ever had before. I rested, getting stronger. Keeping up with the laundry was difficult since we relied on an old long handled pump for our water. Hattie relaxed her strict standards for the appearance of the children. The older boys hiked all over the environs visiting every rock prominence we saw from our porch. The young girls tried to learn the names of the many wildflowers. As August waned and the evenings grew cooler, we realized our summer idyll would not last forever. We needed to enroll the children in school, attend a proper church, and find a house that would not be blown over in the next thunderstorm.

Returning to Denver, we looked at three potential homes, but I was not struck by any of them. We would have to lower our standards after our string of wonderful houses in Michigan. We no longer had our previous means and carpentry here was less advanced than back home. Discouraged, we followed the setting sun back towards the mountains. Driving south on Logan Street, seeing a "for sale" sign, I motioned for Mel to pull over, "Let's look at that one."

He parked the car while I rang the bell. A couple of school teachers showed us through their house. We wanted it, but their price was too high. I countered with an offer that I thought was appropriate, promising an all-cash deal, removing the interference of any bank from the transaction. They asked if we would wait on the porch. After a while, they returned to accept the offer. We had arrived at a very opportune moment. They were on their vacation from school, hoping to go to Europe before returning to the classroom. They could not leave without selling the house; our all-cash offer led to a quick closing so they could leave.

We stayed that night in a Denver hotel, foregoing the trip back to the mountains. The next day I withdrew a sight draft from the bank for the entire amount. Driving back to Evergreen in the afternoon, I held the deed for our new home. At the rear of the house was a large room that the teachers rented as a separate apartment. I directed the carpenter to convert this to a sleeping porch, where I could take advantage of the cool night air. The windows slid out of sight when the room was open, protected from the outside only by screens. With Denver's mild climate, this was a very nice arrangement except during the coldest days of the winter that demanded a little more coal than I liked to burn. The two apartments at the front of house were converted to one dwelling for our large family.

This work required precise scheduling so that we could move in on Labor Day, because school started the following day. The decorator was to finish painting before Mr. Kamp brought our furniture from storage. We arrived at the end of August, spending the night in the second floor apartment with our mountain bedding. The decorator had not finished as promised, but we moved in around his crew. I should have known that furniture would be the sticking point. On the Saturday our furniture was to be delivered, Hattie noticed the Kamp moving van heading out of town toward the mountains on a picnic excursion. One advantage of being part of a small tight community is that we knew where everybody lived and worked. I walked over to the Kamp house to learn from Mrs. Kamp that her husband had forgotten his obligation. I was taken aback. In Grand Rapids this sort of thing did not happen. A man's word was his bond. A tradesman who did not deliver would find himself without customers and little standing in the church. My father, brothers and I built our businesses on this simple principal of doing what we promised. I was disappointed that the decorator did not perform on time, but at least he was trying. Later that Saturday, Kamp finally showed up with our furniture in his van. This would have been fine, except just as he showed up, it began to rain. At first it was just a drizzle, but soon the sky opened up. Usually a thundershower like this lasted under a half hour, but not today. I wondered if I would ever have an uneventful move of our furniture. At least now, I knew where it was even if it was threatened by the weather. Some of our goods were crated for protection. These crates were too large to pass through the doors, needing to be opened outside in the rain. This would have been a complete disaster except for an apparition that immerged from the rain. It was our neighbor Jones, coming over to help carry the furniture to safety inside.

The rain damaged some of the furniture. I decided not to press for damages, because the Kamps were members of the Christian Reformed Church we intended to join. I wanted to enter that community on a good footing. Still, I was confused. Back in Grand Rapids, any trade person, especially one in your church, would do anything they could to satisfy you. In Colorado, it was the opposite. The Dutchmen were the sharpies, but the non-believers were the more ethical businessmen. Our carpenter, who did not attend church, gave us full weight, performing his work conscientiously. Kamp was shoddy and thoughtless. This pattern was reinforced when a couple of other wide-awake Christian Reformed businessmen came by to solicit our business before any concern about our spiritual well-being. I guess that life in the West was still a little wild. I did not consider Grand Rapids to be a very cultured place, but I realized how a thousand little courtesies add up to make a civilization. Colorado may be our new home but it would take some effort to adapt.

Our new home eased our plight. It was in a neighborhood quite similar to where we had grown up, but the houses were newer, many built of brick. Our second floor apartment brought steady income, as did our two parking spaces in our large garage. With the flood of cars now on the streets, people needed a place to park them. We would live in this small home for longer than any other during our married life. We liked the house, but anticipated something much grander, as we had enjoyed before then.

In our new home, I tried to maintain the same schedule that I had at the sanitarium with ample hours for rest. I liked the routine, but without the regimentation of the sanitarium. I got up after Mel and Hattie sent the kids, except for Virginia, off to school. Mel then headed to his own job. This relaxing pace was out of character for me. Before long, my busy fingers were peeling off small flecks of wallpaper in the kitchen. I could not resist the return to my youth as a paperhanger, peeling off more with the palette knife I retrieved from my paint box. In less than an hour, the kitchen was a complete mess, but I kept after it, heating up the kettle to soften up the tough sections (which were most of the wall). I was happy for the distraction, keeping after it for the entire week. This was all well and good, except, as I finished the job, I suffered a small hemorrhage. Though I felt fine, I realized I had a long way to go before being in complete good health. I called Dr. George from the sanitarium for a recommendation of a doctor for my continuing care. This new doctor came to see me a few more times, assuring me everything was under control. I believed him until few weeks later, I had a severe hemorrhagic spasm, hacking up what felt like a quart of blood. I weakly crawled into the bathroom, coughing up my lungs. Poor Virginia looked on aghast at her poor daddy. Hattie ran next door, calling the new doctor, pleading for him to come, which he flatly refused. With this sort of doctor, you can appreciate his minimal billing, but when it comes to your personal health, he left something to be desired. Everyone in Denver knew someone touched by tuberculosis, so Hattie called a physician recommended by our neighbor. He came immediately even though it was now close to midnight. He performed a pneumothorax treatment, collapsing the lung to staunch the bleeding. I felt no better after the treatment, but at least the bleeding and coughing stopped. It is hard to cough when your lung is collapsed. Afterwards, I concertedly took it easy, weathering the storm.

I could not bear the thought of not being here for my children; fervently praying that my life be spared, at least until our baby Virginia was out of her teens. My prayers would be answered. Not only would I see Virginia graduate from high school, but her son do the same. However, that summer I did not feel strong enough to return to church for two months.

It is very hard to bring my active life to a complete halt to get well. This adjustment was as hard as the physical recovery. However, after the incident peeling the wallpaper, I knew I must take it easy to live. Certainly, I read a lot, but even this can be tedious. I felt guilty that I was not carrying my full load for the family. Fortunately, Mel was starting to work, just as I did when I was his age, contributing to the family's coffers. We had saved quite a bit and still received token amounts from the Michigan art studio. Occasionally I sold a lot along the river and money from the land contracts continued to dribble in. We had never been big spenders before, so our savings protected us, but now we had to be very careful.

Within every commercial artist is a fine artist waiting to get out. Any artist feels he can do better without the confines of pleasing a client with one goal - selling more of something. I now had the opportunity to pursue fine painting, experimenting with a heavier build-up of oils on the canvas. As a commercial artist, I concentrated on details, working on illustration board with fine tipped brushes and sharp ink pens. Now I composed based on the aesthetics of the light that I observed. Colorado whetted my appetite. Here the light was bright and bold. I matched it with brighter colors. The landscape here was more primitive than in Michigan. I used a palette knife to give relief to the massive forms of the rocks and mountains I painted. Now driving again, I headed up into the mountains to sketch. I took these sketches back to the studio where I worked them into pleasing compositions. I was still too much a commercial man to be an "en plein air" painter. I like the controlled environment of the studio where I did not worry about wind or dust. Additionally, I had all of my supplies immediately at hand. More paint went onto the canvas. In Michigan, as a young man, I had learned about oils and landscape painting in my art lessons, but here was a chance to practice and improve daily. Now instead of staining my hands with ink, they bore the grime of paint and the scent of turpentine. If Hattie minded, she did not say anything, as long as I confined my materials to my studio on the porch.

At this time, there was great interest in the West. The world was not flooded with the ubiquity of images as it is now, so people wondered what the wonders of the West looked like. Paintings by artists like Albert Bierstadt and Thomas Moran who had made the trek west were held in high esteem. Since there were fewer people out here, there were fewer artists, so I hoped to take advantage of the low supply here and the larger demand back East. My technique with oil paint improved to where I thought I could sell a few paintings.

In the nineteen-twenties, "The Literary Digest" was a popular magazine with a national circulation in the millions. They always featured art work on their cover. I wanted to land my work there, so I gambled on the cost of an express shipment of a completed canvas to New York for their consideration. I remember the day I received a letter from the art director of the magazine, April 25th, 1925, informing me that my painting had been accepted. I was especially relieved since my painting of an imaginary Colorado scene, while pictorial, was in a more modern style than they usually accepted. The letter noted that they had enough illustrations for the entire year, so that the proceeds were long spent by the time my work appeared on the issue for April 10, 1926. I was greatly encouraged by this news, painting now in earnest with an eye on supplementing our income. I sold several other canvases to "Literary Digest". This gave my work credibility leading to orders for other pictures. I sold paintings to calendar houses, railroads, and individuals; but if not for income from Grand Rapids real estate, we would have not fared well.

I did receive several important commissions. In addition to the publicity gained from "Literary Digest", the Denver newspapers covered my work. The Missouri Pacific Railroad hired me to paint their trains negotiating the narrow defile of the Royal Gorge. It was fortunate that the railroads supported my work. Rail was often the only practical way to reach the interior of Colorado and they gave me passes to reach the locales they wanted depicted. It was a great way to explore my new state. Driving the roads with the cars of the time would have tripled the time and doubled the aggravation. With my frail health, I was sensitive to avoiding any additional aggravation.

Chapter 16

Sometime later, I received an unsolicited commission from the Missouri Pacific Railroad to paint the Royal Gorge of the Arkansas River. This magnificent canyon is thousands of feet deep, near where the river emerges from the mountains. The railroad ran right next to the river, representing a major feat of engineering. The railroad operated a passenger train called the "Scenic Limited" through the canyon and wanted me to create a suitable image of it. For once, my commercial art sensibilities augmented my newly acquired fine art skills. At one point the canyon was so narrow that the railroad right-of-way was suspended by steel cables from the side of the cliff. This was called the "Hanging Bridge".

I won this commission after the famed illustrator Maxwell Parish had lost it. I am not sure what the railroad expected from him. He was noted for his dreamy depictions of faraway lands and faraway times. With its dramatic canyons of red-hued sandstone, the Royal Gorge was anything but dreamy. He painted here, turning in some paintings, but they did not meet the executives' needs. The railroad wrote me, so here I was in the Gorge. I would never achieve Parish's fame, but I was happy to pick up this crumb when he did not deliver. He emphasized the poetic qualities of the scene. With my background in commercial art, I knew that the painting had to convey a simple message easily reproducible in color or black and white.

Arrangements had been made for me to drive to a whistle stop west of the Gorge where an early morning train going through the canyon would pick me up. It is quite a thrill to have a huge train stop just for you. The train barely slowed. Two porters jumped off, grabbing my equipment, hurriedly helping me up the steps. I knew that railroads ran on tight schedules, but I thought this alacrity was exceptional.

A heavy-set gentleman in tweed suit and a tight collar sat down next to me. After a few introductory remarks, he inquired after my business.

"Mr. Feenstra, it is very nice to make your acquaintance. It is not every day that I am ordered to pick up passengers at unscheduled stops. How is it, if I may be so bold, that you warrant such consideration?"

"It's Veenstra, with a V. I would have thought that your headquarters would have informed you that they commissioned me to paint a picture of the Scenic Limited crossing the Hanging Bridge."

"No, they tell me nothing - only to make an unscheduled stop at Parkdale and pick up a passenger without a ticket."

"Well, I am sorry if I inconvenienced you. I thought railroads are in the business of picking up and dropping off passengers," I replied as evenly as I could, unsure of where this conversation might be going.

"Oh, indeed we are," he continued, "I would be happy about it, if I was given enough time to do it. I am responsible to make sure this train rolls into Pueblo on time, which would be no problem if we made no stops, let alone yours. The "brass' have been giving me the works. Today they added an extra car; adding at least ten minutes, and then I got the wire to pick you up. I am sorry to lay this all out for you; I just wanted to know what was all so important about one passenger turning my train into a jitney service."

Having some experience with dealing with railroad executives, I shared his pain. They acted as if the Creator had extended his power to them, and that they were given dominion over the rest of us. I guess ordering the coming and goings of mighty locomotives goes to a man's head. When we arrived at the stop near the Hanging Bridge, with the porters' help, I departed the train even more quickly than I had boarded it. After all this commotion, the whistle echoed down the canyon until out of earshot. I stood alone with just the sound of the river and wind through the few trees clinging to craggy walls of the canyon.

"Well, I hope he likes the painting," I thought to myself, setting up my easel and positioning my umbrella for shade. I worked for the rest of day, quite pleased with what I captured. There was still a half-hour before my train to leave the canyon was scheduled to arrive, so I scrambled down along the river to get a closer look at the Hanging Bridge. There I discovered it was actually supported by concrete piers standing in the water. The locomotives pulling the trains were now so massive that they would have pulled the bridge from the canyon wall without the added support. When the tourists stepped off the trains, they were positioned close to the train so that the myth behind this marvel of engineering was not exposed.

I again encountered the section chief from the morning on the train that picked me up. He still perceived me still as a threat to the orderly operation of his railroad, making sure that the porters were as motivated as he. I certainly had no reason to complain about the speed of service when riding the "Katy Line".

Locked in deadly competition, I cannot believe that railroad executives talked much to each other. But for some reason, I gained a reputation as a railroad artist. Maybe they used the same art houses in Chicago for their pre-press work and saw my work there. In any case, I was next engaged by the Santa Fe Railroad. They did not want me to merely paint their trains, but commissioned me to paint some of the great landmarks in the territory they served. They were opening a new office in Oklahoma City to serve the burgeoning oil traffic. For it, they asked that I paint a large canvas depicting Longs Peak, at over 14,000 feet in elevation, the eastern most point of the Continental Divide.

Close to the plains, it dominates the northwestern skyline viewed from Denver. I jumped at the chance to paint a major canvas with minimal commercial intent. I would not have to put any bridges or locomotives in the foreground. Longs Peak is so massive, it dominates the immediate country around it. I chose Nymph Lake as my vantage point. I liked how the composition proceeded from the dreamy soft edge of the mossy lake toward the jagged ridge buttressing the peak in the background. The large canvas gave me room to expand on this vista. One of the challenges of painting in the West is that the land is so vast that it is hard to capture. Large canvases are required, but they are expensive to execute, because of the time needed to include every observed detail. Now that I had a client willing to foot the bill, I planned my route for conquering the mountain with the same painstaking attention to detail as an alpinist.

Hattie and I rented a house for a week at Bear Lake in Rocky National Park. From there, it was short hike up to Nymph Lake where I prepared my sketches. You must believe me that I was still not a full strength when my long-suffering wife had to lug my supplies up the steep grade to the lake. We both had trouble sleeping at the high altitude; around 10,000 feet above sea level. I reassured myself that this was probably the best air ever for my tuberculosis. If that were the case, maybe no air at all would be the healthiest. This was a disease where I died a lot to get better a little. However, the following morning I felt as grand as ever brewing a cup of coffee, cooking bacon and eggs over our wood stove. If there is anything that tastes better than this simple breakfast in the cool Rocky Mountain air, I have yet to try it. Life out here was rawer, more intense, and more immediate than it was in Michigan. Of course, it was also harder. In my condition, I did not always welcome the struggle. The sunlight breaking over the ridge was like a curtain lifting on the scene. I could not wait to get started. In four days, I had prepared enough sketches that I was ready to draw a formal compositional study. I knew enough from my days as a commercial artist to get approval before proceeding, sending this off to the Santa Fe offices in Chicago. Soon after, I received a telegram authorizing me to proceed with the larger canvas.

This work was very gratifying, but wearing on both my health and finances. I painted standing, holding my arm up grasping my brushes. This led to a bout of rheumatism. Once again, I must pace myself. Fewer canvases meant less income, so I considered alternatives. In order to feel better, I took advantage of the Radium Hot Springs in Idaho Springs, a gold camp an hour above Denver in the mountains. Hattie and I boarded the narrow-gauge Colorado and Southern railroad's two-car train wending its way through Clear Creek Canyon. At the springs, we rented a small cabin, signing up for the complete regimen of 19 baths. The water was very soothing, but I never got over walking into the narrow mine shaft leading to the tubs. The sulphurous vapors in the dim shadowy light were not a bad image of hell.

To make ends meet, I started selling real estate. I doubt if there is any business like real estate for meeting a broad cross section of humanity. Never was this truer than in the case of Jane Lewis. I personally sold a small house to Mrs. Lewis where the purchase price included a horse and saddle, an automobile, and the lease of a mountain cabin. I did not know Mrs. Lewis, but she had an honest face (maybe I should say a "horse face", because she was certainly a horse trader.) She spoke of her cottage as having a bathroom. We envisioned spending a month in the mountains where the girls could ride our new horse. Shortly after closing on the deal, I took the family up to Allen's Park to our new summer home. Wait, did I say summer home? What we found was a filthy shack with doors swinging wide open. Cows from a nearby ranch had wandered in leaving behind what my children referred to as "postal cards". In this, the cows were prolific "correspondents". The promised bathroom was a privy a short distance from the "cottage". The privy was not well named, because you could see into it and it was completely open to sky. I relished communing with nature, but this was all too much. Pity the person who answered the call of nature on a rainy day.

After inspecting this so called real estate, I took delivery of the car with some trepidation. As it pulled up, my fears were alleviated, since it appeared to be a very smart Pontiac. I took my new vehicle out for a ride, relishing its performance until shifting into third gear. The car bucked like an unbroken bronco. I am not sure what made me feel worse, being saddled with this piece of junk or being such a fool. Having no need of a second car, I advertised the Pontiac for sale. A young man came by, liked the car, and even more, its price. We headed out for a test drive. I had warned him about the shimmy, but he claimed that he could fix it. We drove all the way to downtown, before turning left towards the mountains over the Colfax Street viaduct. The further we drove, the more nervous I became. I do not believe in miracle cures, especially when it came to automobiles, and did want this young man to drive away without experiencing the nauseating bucking sensation. Finally the Pontiac gyrated with more abandon than ever. I was not happy about losing the sale, but happier not foisting this wreck off on this unsuspecting young man. Well, bless the young; he took the car, believing he could fix the problem.

Mrs. Lewis' mischief did not end there. A few weeks later, the young man pulled up to my curb. I was about to explain that he bought the car "as is". I made no warranty about its mechanical condition.

"No, Mr. Veenstra, that's not it," he explained. "There is still an unpaid loan on this car with the Colorado National Bank."

"Go see Mrs. Lewis who sold me the car. If she does not make good on the loan, I will pay it off and then visit the Lewis with the District Attorney on the investigation of fraud."

"Thank you Mr. Veenstra. I thought you were a stand-up guy."

This pleased me very much, since I did not want a young person to think all of his future transactions would be crooked.

Apparently, this was enough. I did not hear from him or Mrs. Lewis again. That did not mean I was done with her. I still had to collect the horse. Growing up, I had seen the whole gamut of horseflesh, so I expected the worse. Mrs. Lewis directed me to a ranch south of Denver, telling me to take my pick of any of the horses there. I asked an elder in our church who came from a ranching family to accompany me to pick out the most promising mount. At the ranch, one of the hands directed us to the corral to take our pick. The elder and I climbed up to the top rail, watching the horses mill about. After a few minutes, he pointed to one that we should take. The hands roped the mare, slipping a halter over her head. Without a stock truck, we drove back toward Denver slowly as the elder held the halter through the passenger window. There was certainly a lot less traffic back then. The horse, skeptical of this mode of transport, tossed her head wildly. The elder used language that I am sure he never used sitting in the church's consistory. I could barely blame him. His arm was bruised from slamming into the edges of the car window frame by the unruly animal. However strong his language, he did not take the Lord's name in vain; I had to give him credit for that. After a harrowing hour, we arrived at his ranch. Not having any way to transport the horse to the mountains, I left the horse with him for a while. I could not find a buyer, finally selling the mare to the elder for the cost of boarding her and fifteen dollars.

The saddle I never did get. The woman who perpetrated all this was the perfect picture of honesty, innocence, and virtue. I am sure she was pleased with how she got the best of a "crooked" real estate agent.

Chapter 17

Hattie and I loaded the younger kids - Rolf, Alta, and Virginia into our trusty Star with the intention of exploring the mountains to the southwest of Denver. I had finally bought a new car. The Studebaker had served us well, carrying the family like prairie schooner across the vastness of Nebraska to our new home out West, but its motor was worn out from my forays into the mountains painting or surveying mountain properties. The Star was a worthy competitor to the Ford Model T. I appreciated the extra power of its sturdy six cylinder Continental engine. I knew that we would put it to the test in the mountains.

We rigged the car for cross-country travel, unsure of where we would be spending our nights or what accommodations we might find. We carried bedding, some folding cots for the children, food, and cooking utensils. This new car was a closed sedan, sheltering us better from the elements than the open "touring" style of the Studebaker. The drawback is that it was smaller, so that the kids, though still small, were squished in back. Rolf often rode with Hattie and me in the front, leaving the backseat to the girls. We strapped a spare tire and inner tubes to the rear bumper, with the family's impromptu kitchen on the right running board. We carried a small stove, but liked to cook over a campfire, preferring the smell of crackling pine to the hiss of the gasoline burner.

At the end of our first day, we arrived in Buena Vista, a town appropriately named if there ever was one. Arrayed before us was the mighty Sawatch Range, the backbone of the state. Both the Star and I were happy not to cross them. Instead, we followed the Arkansas River south towards New Mexico. We found a small tourist cabin, no more than a log cabin, but the glorious sunset and gurgling river compensated for the primitive conditions.

The next morning we headed south. Cresting a small rise, we entered another large mountain valley, this time the San Luis. Here, barely one hundred miles from Denver, the Hispanic influence was more pronounced. Many of the signs on the buildings were in

Spanish, catering to the local inhabitants. We motored down the valley in the shadow of the Sangre de Cristo Range, named by the conquistadores for the "Blood of Christ" when sunset bathed the range in a rosy glow. I promised to return to paint these dramatic jagged peaks. Before long, we were in Alamosa, named for the cottonwoods growing in profusion along the banks of the Rio Grande River. Here a small colony of fellow Dutchmen had immigrated, building a small Christian Reformed Church that we attended on Sunday. Eager for contact from the outside, they received us graciously. We stayed in town the following Monday, the Fourth of July, joining these families at a picnic under the cottonwoods. We knew some of them from their previous visits to Denver or from their daughters moving to Denver to find work and husbands. Most of these families were farmers who took advantage of the abundant sunshine and water to grow hardy crops during the abbreviated season. Hattie and I felt quite at home since it was like being back in Friesland, only here there were mountains instead of steeples on the horizon. The hardscrabble existence was centered on the country church, the same as in the Netherlands. I rarely reflected on my early life in the old country much anymore. Life in the West was focused on the future, not the past.

The next day, our travels became more adventurous. We drove off the one Colorado road map we possessed. From now on, we made our way by dead reckoning, carefully reading road signs hopefully pointing to the next town. The quality of the roads diminished. We began the day negotiating flooded sections where the late spring run-off overwhelmed the capacity of the primitive bridges and culverts of the braided streams feeding the Rio Grande River. After a harrowing morning, we left the valley floor, climbing the grade over Cumbres Pass. Along the way we saw a "Galloping Goose" of the Denver & Rio Grande Western's Railroad rolling along the narrow gauge rail bed that our road followed over the pass. This was a truck adapted to drive on rails. A Buick motor freight truck in the front was attached to a conventional railcar at the rear. This ungainly creature was mounted on rails, moving along quite smartly once it developed a head of steam…err, gasoline. It looked like a freight truck on steel wheels with a cow catcher. Why it was painted silver, I will never know. The kids cheered to see such a preposterous device. Designed as a cost saving measure, this vehicle was less expensive to operate than even a two-car train. Towns like Chama, New Mexico, where we were heading, depended on rail service for mail and perishables. These ungainly contraptions were a lifeline until the roads were paved in the coming decades.

To my eye, there was not much difference between New Mexico and the older version further south. Here, Anglos were the minority. No one in Chama spoke English except for Mr. Garcia, the proprietor of the local general merchandise store. I was hoping that he might be interested in the property we had listed in his town. He was probably the only one who could afford it. If I could sell him this house, showplace of the village, the commission would pay for our trip. George R. Becker, a cattleman had inherited it from his wife's father. She was Hispanic, and I am sure Mr. Garcia wanted to see the property returned to what he deemed as the rightful Hispanic ownership. Mr. Becker had reached a tough end; driving back from Denver on a business trip, he pushed his luck crossing Cumbres Pass in an early winter storm, becoming stuck before freezing to death. The spread was now owned by Denver investors. There was a ready market for the ranch, but the large house was too far from any metropolitan area. One of the investors gave me the keys to place, so we moved in. It was spacious enough, but the lack of furniture made for a different kind of accommodation. The kids enjoyed the sound of their voices echoing off the walls. This amused me for, oh, all of about two minutes. We had only a flashlight for illumination, but in early July, the sun rises early and goes down late. We made sure we prepared dinner during daylight on the two nights we stayed there. Hattie and I tried fishing in the Chama River, a renowned trout stream, but landed only one fish, hardly enough to feed the five of us. Mr.

Garcia attributed the poor fishing to the murky water due to the late run-off from the Rockies when he came by to inspect the residence. I could tell that he wanted it, but was not of the means of Mr. Becker. Knowing that there would be few buyers in Northern New Mexico, he made a low offer the following morning. Having accomplished what I had come for, I folded the contract into my pocket, setting out for the rest of trip.

From Chama, it is not too far to the state capital of Santa Fe, a city named by the earlier Spanish friars for the Holy Faith of Saint Francis of Assisi. New Mexico grew increasingly foreign as we drove towards the capital. Passing ancient Indian pueblos, we crested a ridge, descending into the city. Consisting almost entirely of adobe buildings, Santa Fe seemed little changed from its seventeenth century origin as a provincial capital except for the automobiles now ringing the central plaza. In contrast to the tall buildings of downtown Denver, here everything was low-rise. Many of the streets were not paved. Our children loved the buildings made of mud and the Indians selling jewelry in the shade of the loggia of the Palace of the Governors to one side of the Plaza. Back in the Netherlands, many buildings date back to the seventeenth century, when the country was the trading master of Europe. I had never seen equally ancient buildings in America until we came to New Mexico. The Palace of the Governors dates back to before the Pilgrims landed on Plymouth Rock. The Indian pueblos are even older. While I enjoyed the charm of these old structures, none were particularly grand except for maybe the cathedral.

We were most impressed by Orchard Camp, our New Mexico home for the next few days while exploring the colonial city. It was the last word in such camps. It claimed a hundred shade trees and spaces for over as many cars. There were reading rooms with free stationery for regaling the folks back in Denver and Grand Rapids with tales of our exotic adventure. The commodious washroom offered ample hot and cold water and sanitary toilets. In the nineteen-twenties, motels with individual baths were not yet available. Tourists flocked to these "camps" where you either rented a cabin or pitched a tent. After the primitive conditions of Chama, we reveled in the luxury, happy to wash off the grime from the road.

In school in Holland, we were taught of the oppression by Spain during the sixteenth century before the Netherlands won its independence. We now experienced the Spanish culture directly. Even if I did not agree with the tenets of their Catholic faith, especially the near deification of Mary, I appreciated that it was as a strong as mine. We loved hearing the carillon in the cathedral peeling forth at the beginning and end of the day, reminding one and all of the centrality of God in this enchanted community. When the great bells silenced after the sun went down, a couple of songsters gathered around the campfire with a guitar and banjo. In the romance of the moment, I thought that they were fellow travelers like us, but thinking back, they must have worked for the camp to augment our experience. Whatever their motivation, their easy-going patter and singing made for a delightful evening under the New Mexico stars.

Conditions became much more primitive when we headed west from Santa Fe on Route 66 into Indian Country. The Christian Reformed Church had established missions bringing Christ's salvation to the members of the Navaho people, or as they call themselves, "Diné". Named after an oasis in the Bible, The Rehoboth Mission is outside of Gallup. There, after brief introductions, we were assigned rooms in the Mission House, quarters to unmarried members of the mission. This was tough duty in the Lord's service. We were in the high desert; sere and windswept, with nary a shade tree in sight. The landscape was not softened by any vegetation above the waist. Instead, the horizon was punctuated by soaring rock cathedrals. The Navajo were resistant to the gospel. Each convert was hard won.

If ever there was an environment antithetical to all that a Dutchman thought was beautiful, this was it. The mission staff was worn to the bone. Everyone kept their emotions to themselves. If not exactly welcoming, they were not very forthcoming, even if eager for word from the "outside". Though they could ill afford much hospitality, they were eager that visitors share their experience with the churches upon which they depended. I certainly gained an appreciation for their work. This experience would have a profound effect on the fourteen-year old Rolf, who many years later would return as the lead pastor. Throughout his life he was never one to shrink from a challenge, spiritual or otherwise. I came to appreciate how the unusual landscape could erode one's moral fiber.

In the afternoon, we attended a service in the chapel conducted by Rev. Calvin Hayenga, who came from the mission in Zuni, where he was stationed. He invited us to visit him there. He was more relaxed that the folks at Rehoboth. We agreed, but I warily eyed the mud splattered across his Model T. The following day, we headed for Zuni. The weather was good. The roads that had splattered Hayenga's car were sufficiently dry for us to arrive without too much trouble. Once we turned off of Route 66 in Gallup, the roads became gravel, but the rain and light traffic assured that they were passable. By early afternoon, we arrived. Zuni is even more remote than Rehoboth, so the missionaries there were glad to see us. That evening after putting the kids to bed, we retired with the staff to the large living room of the Indian trader in the area. Piñon pine logs blazed in the fireplace and Mr. Vander Wagen, who owned the trading post in the area, passed out small glasses of peach brandy he had made himself. As the evening progressed, the small glasses added up. Making our way back to our beds, we discovered we were all a little looped. I was embarrassed to be so foolish, but chalked it up to the extraordinary locale. Everything was different in New Mexico, especially in this remote corner.

We paid for our sins the next morning. The children were up early, needing to be fed, when all their parents wanted was another hour of sleep. After feeding the children and ourselves, we packed up, saying goodbye to Rev. Hayenga. I commented that evening was not particularly "Christian" in character. He concurred, explaining it was an isolated event, but reflecting the need for release from the constant pressure under which they labored. He explained the Indians had been fighting to protect their gods and culture for over five-hundred years, becoming quite resistant to the message of the missionaries. This would eventually be overcome, but not until the church brought needed services like medicine and education to the native peoples. I appreciated his work. Upon returning home, I sent him a check for seventy-five dollars for a pet project he wanted to undertake. A commission check for that amount had arrived in the mail at home while we were in New Mexico and I thought that Rev. Hayenga could put it to better use than I.

We headed towards Holbrook. Rev. Hayenga drove ahead of us for a mile or so, guiding us on two wagon ruts across the otherwise unmarked desert. He then sent us on our way with a breezy, "Just follow the tracks." This was easy to do, except when we came to a fork, guessing which way would correctly lead across the imponderable waste. There were no bridges or culverts, so every so often, our car bogged down in mud. Everyone got out to push except for me, the only driver on this trip. When I gave the car the gas, everybody at the rear, including Hattie was splattered with mud from the spinning tires. I might have found this slightly amusing if I was not so terrified of becoming completely stuck in the middle of nowhere. How far was it back to that Indian and his flock of sheep? Would he speak English? Did he have a horse to go get help?

About five miles past Zuni, we came up behind another car stuck in the mud in an arroyo. I got out to investigate, disturbingly finding a corpse behind the wheel. I was about to walk back to our car when the skinny arm dangling over the door stirred and the eye of an old weather-beaten Indian opened, balefully staring at me. Stuck, he was waiting until someone came along to help him, and here we were. I asked him a couple of questions to which his only reply was, "No, Push!" We all got behind his rattletrap, Hattie being excused this time, shoving his car across the arroyo. We thought he would return the favor, helping us cross, but his dust cloud disappeared off in the distance. Hattie was especially angry, since she was again relegated to the rear bumper. We finally made it across. We probably would not have been stuck if his car had not been there since our momentum would have carried us across.

At last we were back to the highway, crossing the Petrified Forest to Holbrook, where we rented a cabin in a cottage camp. The next morning we continued west, blithely unaware of the further trials awaiting us. We were a little ways out of town when the right rear tire blew out. This main highway was still only a gravel road. Earlier in the day, a road grader had preceded us, exposing a good-sized stone with a razor-sharp edge that sliced our sidewall wide open. The spare that I bought in Denver was now ruined beyond repair. I mounted our spare and we drove on to the spur that leads to the South Rim of the Grand Canyon. About half-way there, the spare gave way. The main highway had been bad, but this road was awful. The sides of the road were littered with husks of many discarded tires, shredded by the rocks in the road.

Punctures were a fact of life in early motoring. However, things were much better now in the twenties than they had been earlier in the century when my brothers and I drove to Wisconsin. I pulled out the patch kit, jacked up the car setting about making the repair. I put a small boot patch in the casing where the rock had entered, patched the inner tube, before pumping up the tire. With a flat, pumping up the tire was worse than changing it. Men at the beginning of the century developed massive upper arms from all of the tire pumping. I was now forty-seven years old, so I was not overly-developed, just overly sore.

I had hoped to buy new tires at the Grand Canyon, but there were none to be found. Perhaps the truck bringing them had too many blowouts to make it. Any appreciation I might have for the scenery was affected by the nagging thought of the trip back to

Williams without a spare tire on the very marginal road, not to mention poisoning from alkaline water.

After a few days my stomach quieted and we could no longer delay our return, starting down the road with great trepidation towards Williams, Arizona, sixty long miles away. We had not gone far when the repaired tire gave out again. I flagged down a man to take me back to the canyon to repair the tire. I hired an Indian to drive me back to my waiting family. After another episode of burning biceps, our luck and tire the held all the way to Williams.

We rented cabins at a place called Mountain Springs. Later that evening we happily learned that the cabin was steam heated, because in the mountainous desert, temperatures, even in the middle of summer plunged into the forties at night, even after a blisteringly hot day. That evening in the public bath house, I met two men just arrived from California across the Mojave Desert. Judging from their appearance, they had a pretty rough go of it. I had intended to continue further west, but after our trouble with the tires and hearing their tales of heat and single track roads across the sand, I decided that Williams should be the extent of our trip.

We attended church in Williams, grateful for a "down day" in our relentless travels. Monday, we got up at four in the morning, our usual starting time. With the early start, we arrived in Gallup, a good day's travel. The new tire that I bought in Williams held the rest of the way home. Now that we drove east, the roads improved imperceptibly, day by day. The next day took us to Cortez, back in our home state of Colorado. Denver, however, was nearly four hundred miles and several mountain ranges away. Between Cortez and Durango are the Indian ruins at Mesa Verde, now a national park. I was impressed by the size of the ancient villages. I was not aware that the first Americans had haunted these precincts for so long. The children enjoyed following the footsteps of the ancients, imagining what it was like to live in a house where you climbed a ladder to reach your tiny dark room. Their kivas, subterranean chambers for religious activities, were different than my idea of a church, but the ranger told us that tobacco probably figured as prominently as it did in the Dutch churches of my youth. With that thought, I turned, looking out from the top of the mesa, seeing maybe as far as one-hundred miles into New Mexico, knowing, that, indeed, I had come long way in life.

Chapter 18

We were happy to be in the little town of Durango, Colorado. Whistles from the steam engines on the narrow gauge railroad echoed off the surrounding canyon walls. More importantly, we were above the heat of the desert floor. We rented a tourist court cabin sheltered by majestic ponderosa pines. Our children loved the vanilla smell released by scratching the bark. Since we did not have far to go the next day, we allowed the sunlight to seep a little deeper into the canyon before we departed up the Las Animas River Valley. We easily outpaced the morning train paralleling our route. We kept climbing to the mountain town of Silverton. We stopped for a picnic before continuing our journey over the "Million Dollar Highway", so named for either its cost or the views.

This was the most dramatic road I have ever driven. Hattie sat next to me nervously exclaiming, "Oh Harry!" around each bend. We were soon among the highest peaks in the nation on little more than a narrow goat path paved with a scrim of asphalt. Fortunately, we were on the inside of the highway, next to the mountain. To the left, on the outside of the downhill lane, the cliff plunged thousands of feet. I was only too happy to drive this section of road slowly. Our automobile happily obliged wheezing over Red Mountain Pass. After the pass, the way down to Montrose through Ouray was anticlimactic except for the thrilling mountain vistas encountered at every hairpin curve. It was hard for me to sightsee while keeping my line of sight focused on the center of my lane.

We continued down tributaries of the Colorado River until reaching the river itself at Grand Junction. This country was like Michigan with country lanes threading through miles of fruit orchards. Except that in Michigan, there were no sandstone mesas on the horizon. Also, the humidity was lower and the sun was brighter than in the Midwest. Coming to the river, we followed it up to the vacation town of Glenwood Springs, where we rented a room that was so horrible that we drove on the next day, a Sunday, to find a new place. This was the first time that we had driven on a Sunday. Our travels took us up an old railroad grade that was smooth and wide, one of the best roads of the entire trip.

We thought it was tops until we reached the tunnel through which a train used to travel. This was the Carlton Tunnel, boring for over two and one-half miles under the Continental Divide. It was unlit, so the dim head lights of our Star did not penetrate very far into the gloom. There is nothing quite as lonely as being in the center of the earth with a mile of rock separating you from daylight in each direction. The tunnel also served as a conduit bringing precious snow run-off through the mountains from the western side to the drier east. A large metal pipe was constructed on one side of the tunnel to convey these flows. Leaking in various places, it contributed to the overall dankness.

This was not the worst of it. As a former railroad tunnel, it was quite narrow, especially after the addition of the water pipe. Only one-way traffic was permitted, with the different directions alternating hourly. When we arrived, we were in a hurry, misreading the correct time for our east-bound entry. As we bravely soldiered on through the gloom, I had plenty of time to recall the sign, mentally decipher its meaning, and understand my error. There was no turning back. The motorists on the east side were none too happy to see us exiting like moles blinking in the bright sun. Fortunately, they had not entered the tunnel, seeing our headlights far off in the dark. We were treated to some pretty rough language that I am sure would have been worse if I had not had a lady and children in the car. Subsequently, I learned that previous vehicles had met in the tunnel, resulting in fighting and bloodshed. If the people on the east side had insisted on coming though, I would have been forced to back up almost the entire way, not an easy task with my headlights aimed the wrong way.

The lesson was overwhelming. This is the confusion that results from driving on the Lord's Day. Driving down to the Arkansas River Valley, I thanked God for his lesson and that my family was safe. I appreciated why my friends back in their homes in Denver thought I was crazy for embarking on a trip beyond the bounds of then-known civilization. I figured if I put the big things in God's care I could push the boundaries on the little things. After all, I have the Creator of the Universe in my corner.

We were now in familiar mountains. After spending the night in Leadville, not far from the Mount of the Holy Cross, we returned back to Denver over familiar Kenosha Pass. We had been gone for nearly a month. Little could we imagine the fascinating country that was on the doorstep of our new Rocky Mountain home. We encountered different and ancient cultures, daily chipping away at our ignorance as we traveled further across the high desert. We discovered that there were now tourist camps scattered across the country that catered to the needs of travelers like us. These varied in quality, but they were all generally acceptable. Some, like the Orchard Camp in Santa Fe, were downright enjoyable. And we saw two marvels - the majesty of the Grand Canyon and the mysterious ancient villages of Mesa Verde, built right into the sides of cliffs. Our children gathered experiences that stayed with them for life. Hattie also recalled pushing the car through the mud. "But honey," I reminded her, "Without following Rev. Hayenga's suggested route, we would never have met that almost dead Indian."

"You're right Harry. He is the one acquaintance from our trip whom I will remember forever. My only wish is that the next time I meet him, he will be sleeping on the road, not in his car, and we will not stop!"

At the end of the nineteen twenties, we were unaware of the economic precipice on the horizon. I sold an oil painting here and there. With this and the money coming in from the Michigan real estate, we made ends meet. Michigan was doing better than Colorado. Michigan built cars. People wanted the new cars that were faster, safer, and more reliable. I had built a small nest egg, so I started looking for a better return than I realized from our savings account. I knew little about stocks and bonds, so I looked for a property I could sub-divide. There was no property in the city in my price range, so I investigated in the mountains. We had spent a fair amount of time in the mountains southwest of Denver along Turkey Creek. Here are many lovely valleys punctuated by dramatic granite outcrops. Now that cars were more reliable, people from Denver were building cabins to beat the summer heat on the plains. As I had in Grand Rapids on the river, I thought that I might cater to this market. I finally found the right piece of property between the towns of Bailey and Conifer, but I could not get the owner to agree to terms. This only whetted my appetite. A few weeks later, I saw an ad for a property that seemed to be right what I was looking for. After I responded, two men came to see me the next day. They had developed a resort for negroes on Coal Creek and were hoping for more capital or to sell it outright. This property was in steeper mountains, but it was larger than the other property on which I had made an offer. I assured them that I was interested. In those days, real estate sales were segregated. If Negroes (as African Americans were referred to in those days) wanted to buy property, they had to look in specific areas. These men realized that there was no resort area for Negroes and sought to remedy this deficiency in the market. I did not care if a man's skin was black, as long as his money was green, so I drove up the canyon to size up the property. Once there, I saw that I could not scrape together enough money to finish the project.

This did not finish their interest in me. Not long after, the two men called me back with a different proposal. They claimed to be entrepreneurs like me looking for safe places to invest. They, too, did not trust the stock market, thinking that stocks were horribly "over-priced". Both were conservatively dressed, spoke well, and were not overly friendly. When they came to see me, they brought several boxes of chocolate covered candy which I sampled. It was delicious. They explained that the candy was made from prickly pear cactus infused with honey covered in chocolate. They outlined a very profitable enterprise, since the cactus could be harvested for free in desert. Having just been in the desert, I knew that the Indians and other residents of New Mexico and Arizona would not take kindly to strangers with machetes chopping through their backyards. As a Dutchman, I always had cocoa in the house. Knowing that it was not cheap, I declined their offer.

They were still not done with me yet. A month later, two different men called on me. One was deeply tanned, claiming to have just returned from the "Sierra Madre Mountains of Mehico". While there, he found the gold vein he had been searching for over the past eight years. They now needed the "twenty investors" who would share in this, "The greatest gold strike of the twentieth century." They persuaded me to meet them at their bank downtown where they pulled out deeds, ore samples, and assays from a safe deposit box, no doubt to augment the sense of extreme value. Again, I demurred from writing a check.

Quite some time later, I was walking down Seventeenth Street, the heart of Denver's financial district, and what should I see, but all of my visitors together, animatedly talking. I should have known that they had marked me for a sucker, passing my name between them, hoping I would take one of their baits. Many people fell for schemes such as this. It was a time of loose and easy money, and speculation was rampant. The value of assets skyrocketed. If you were not making money, you were thought a fool. This left me with a sense of unease. I had always believed that you must create value to make money. This logic now was turned on its head. Many people fell prey to "get rich quick" schemes. I knew that real estate had softened. Other assets may as well. I was happy that my money was still in the bank, safely earning its infinitesimal interest.

Once again, I confronted what to do with our savings. Having had poor luck with finding a real estate deal, I considered stocks and bonds. I made an appointment with Boettcher and Company, the most respected and established brokerage in the Denver. I was assigned to one of their brokers, outlining that I only wanted to invest in the strongest and most conservative securities.

"Mr. Veenstra, I think you will find these Continental Oil Company shares are just for you. This company was just listed for the public ownership. You will get in on the ground floor. They have proven reserves. If they liquidate, the value of the reserves is worth more than the stock. You have seen their filling stations throughout Colorado?"

Indeed I had, so I bought at $95 a share.

"Mr. Veenstra, take these shares, put them in an safety deposit box and forget about them."

I should have followed his advice, but I ignored it when they plunged to $33 per share, where I sold. I had bought a few weeks before the Great Crash of 1929. I was not ruined but was certainly hurt. Since I did not have a particularly robust income, "money in the bank" contributed to my peace of mind. Everywhere around me things went from bad to worse. More businesses failed or dramatically slowed. More men on my block were in my position of being under-employed. Those who participated in the tremendous stock run-up were especially hard hit, and yes, several of them did take their lives leaping from the downtown towers built to house their offices in the tidal wave of speculation. During this period, I avoided Seventeenth Street, so as not be assaulted from above by despondent traders.

Far more worrying was when the Denver bank where we kept our savings closed its doors, taking our money with them. We netted practically nothing out of the final settlement. Back then, these accounts were not insured, so many savers, like us, lost everything.

This was not the end of our woes. I lost the key to my safety deposit box, placing some stock certificates in the care of a young broker. When his firm faced a liquidity crisis, he pledged my shares, along with those of his firm, as collateral for a loan to tide them over. I do not have to tell you what happened. They went bankrupt; my shares were lost along with theirs. I dropped into their office before their bankruptcy became common knowledge. With tears in his eyes, the young man promised that he would pay me back personally. My lawyer's office was nearby. I hurried over to see if anything could be done before my shares were irretrievably lost. "No," was the extent of our conversation.

I refused to take these reverses lying down, pursuing any angle to recoup my losses, but nothing could be done in the teeth of the roaring bear market. I subscribed to an expensive New York investment service that reviewed my portfolio, sending me weekly letters and the occasional wire when prompt action (usually to sell at a loss) was advisable.

I even engaged a man who taught classes in investment management at the University of Denver. He was deemed a genius - so successful at managing a hypothetical portfolio that he quit his job to set up his own fund. His play investments were hypothetical money makers, but in the real world, he too was devoured by the bear. My savings were part of the snack.

You may ask yourself why did I not get out of the market sooner? It comes down to two reasons. First, my income depended on the dividends that stocks paid. In a nice, normal market, this would have tided my family over nicely. Second, at each plateau in the market's inexorable dive, we were sure it had hit the bottom.

Here's an example. I had bought the safest investment I could think of - bonds issued by the Baltimore and Ohio Railroad. These guilt-edged securities paid a low rate of interest, but should have been as reliable as anything in the market. The railroad ran into financial problems, and the redemption price of these securities shrunk to a 60 percent discount. This did not bother me, because I still redeemed the interest from my coupons. But then the railroad defaulted, suspending payment of the interest. I had no choice but to sell. If I had held on, eventually I would have been paid back, but I needed the income.

Finally came the day when I wearily came home from downtown, saying to Hattie, "Well, that's it; it's all gone." Our savings from a lifetime of work, the profits from the land sales, the money she had inherited: all evaporated. We had some equity left in the house, but against it we held a mortgage. In reality, I felt a sense of relief, for the last year and a half I had been treading water, fighting to protect our net worth. Now that I had hit bottom all I could do was look up.

It was hard to realize that this was part of God's will. Up until now, I thought that He rewarded me for being faithful, being clever, and obeying His commandments. He showed that it could just as easily be taken away. All that remained was His love and how we shared it with those around us. He let me know that I was nowhere near as smart as I thought. This was a reminder, as was my physical breakdown, of who was really in charge of my life. Hard lessons are not easily learned. At first, I only begged for mercy, uncertain of how I would provide for my family. After time, I realized that He would provide, as he always had; all we had to do is believe. My prayers were answered. My despair and self-pity gave way to thanksgiving. I realized that only through this trial would my faith be forged on the anvil of adversity. Without this opportunity, I would never have realized the redemptive power of our Lord Jesus Christ to help us escape from the bonds of this world. If I leaped from a window, I would fly straight up.

The Lord gave me a great helpmate in this work. Never once did Hattie reproach me for my purblind investment decisions or complain. She only gave me comfort and support. She was not unaware of the course of events, and I tried not to worry her needlessly, but our predicament must have come as quite a shock. I could always depend on her when the chips were down. She reminded me that we were comparatively young. The Lord had blessed me with restored health and we could only courageously go on depending on His help and guidance for the future. To which I say "Amen".

Chapter 19

These were the steps that lead to my climb up the shoulders of the Mount of the Holy Cross in the dawn of this July morning. The walk has been a microcosm of my life and all that I have learned: try your best, keep going, and trust in the destination. You can never anticipate all the twists and turns that life will take. Your trust in Jesus is the only guide you will need. I thought I would die and I didn't. I went broke and it really did not matter. I was rich in spirit and love. Money looks pretty tawdry in comparison. Even on this hike, the day is brightening.

To paint this picture, we traveled to the tiny town of Redstone that is really no more than a collection of mines perched on a mountain side. Redstone is over a hundred miles west of Denver, with the Continental Divide in between. To get there, Hattie and I took the Missouri Pacific Railroad, the "Katy Line", from Denver to Pueblo. We traveled one hundred miles south along the plains before entering the mountains toward our destination. Departing from Pueblo, we spent the day climbing through beautiful scenery to Leadville, a small metropolis in a broad valley very high in the mountains. The air off the Sawatch Range was bracing, but my breathing was labored during the twenty-minute stop-over while the tender was refreshed with coal and water. We climbed over Tennessee Pass before descending into Redstone. Once there, we stepped on to the wooden platform of the gingerbread station before making our way to the town's only hotel. After checking in, we walked to the post office to meet the Postmaster. I had contacted him earlier to be my guide to the mountain.

He took us into his office behind the counter. There, on the walls were photographs of him as a much younger man dressed in fringed buckskin standing in front of a string of mules loaded with what I learned was photographic equipment. Just after the postmaster had arrived in Redstone, the famous photographer W.H. Jackson retained him as a guide to take him to the sacred mountain. I was proud to follow in this tradition. However, in the twentieth century I did not sport the beards and long rifles of the Jackson party. Neither did I need the elaborate equipment. In his day, Jackson used "wet plates" where the photo emulsion had to be applied to glass plates in the field. Knowing how difficult it was to do this in the lab from my own earlier days, I was duly impressed at the lengths Jackson underwent in taking his pictures. Jackson had photographed the Mount of the Holy Cross in 1873, so our guide was now advanced in years, but I had trouble keeping up with him. Of course, he was not the one recovering from consumption. Because of the constant cool temperature of his mountain town, he wore long woolen underwear year round, adding a second pair in the winter.

As we said goodbye for the evening, he said he would be at the hotel at four o'clock the following morning with horses to take us to the point where we could view the mountain with plenty of time to prepare my studies. I arranged for the hotel to prepare an early breakfast. After eating it, I waited in the lobby with my easel, paint box and umbrella. My guide came in, crest fallen and profusely apologetic, since the promised horses could not be rounded up. How you could find horses in the pre-dawn dark was beyond me in the first place. I felt fine, pretty sure I could make it on foot. Secretly, I breathed a sigh of relief, not wanting to ride a horse in the dark anyway. Previously sketching near Estes Park, Colorado, I had seen other tenderfeet return from horseback rides, gingerly dismount, moaning as they massaged sore thighs.

After what must have been two hours, I felt like I was not sure if I could go any further. As I rested on my walking stick, my guide exhorted me that we were almost there. I set forth again, soon coming to an outcrop. There, across a small valley, I saw the most ethereal sight of my life, the Mount of the Holy Cross, illuminated by the rising sun.

I was momentarily breathless, not just from the hike. I stared in silence for over a minute. My guide, having no doubt witnessed this reaction from others, kept his silence. I knew that this was merely a physical phenomenon; snow on rocks, but after what I had been through during the past two years, it struck me very profoundly. I thanked my Savior for being alive to experience this glory; His glory, rededicating myself to His plan for me. If I was not to be rich or live in Grand Rapids, so be it. I committed my life to whatever new the Creator willed for me. Financially, I was broke, but spiritually, my bank account was full. My life would go on, with as many triumphs and scrapes as before. But now I had learned the lesson that I was put on earth to learn - that nothing in this life prepares you for this life or the life to come other than faith in the redeeming message of Jesus Christ. It is only through him that we receive the transcendent power to live life fully and forever escape he bonds of death. I thanked Him for my life and His sharing his grace with me.

I set up my easel and started working on my studies. I may have paint under my fingernails, but my heart was still in the heavens. I knew that soon we would have to pack up and walk down the mountain. Already at noon, we could see the inevitable thunderheads building over the distant peaks. My life would go on with its triumphs and tribulations. But I knew that whatever came my way, I would be prepared with my savior with me every step of the way. From this point forward, every step of my life would be towards spending the rest of my days in his glory. I am so grateful that he opened the path for me. It is also there for you. If there is anything to be learned from this simple tale, it is that life is not worth living without Christ by your side. With all the changes I have encountered, it is only constancy on which I have relied. Take up our savior's challenge. You won't be disappointed. I sure wasn't.

Scott Van Genderen

Additional print and Kindle copies of "Life Before Heaven" are available from Amazon.com

To see photographs of Harry and Hattie and their family and more examples of Harry's art, visit the "Life Before Heaven" page on Facebook.com.

Scott Van Genderen

Author's Note

Harry remained rich in spirit for the rest of has days, of which he was blessed with many. After the climb to the Mount of the Holy Cross, he felt well enough to return to Michigan to continue his career in commercial art. Much later, at the age of 92, he sat down to compose his reminiscences for the benefit of his family. He was a bit chagrined and overwhelmed when the enterprise resulted in over 200 typewritten pages. But, when you lived as long he did, a lot happens. I was impressed by his story, not only because of the adventures that he recounts, but how he steadfastly organized his life around an abiding faith in his Lord and Savior. For your interest, I dramatized his life. If this is a work of fiction, it is one that is firmly based in reality. The account is certainly more true than not.

This story would not have come about without the efforts of several family members over the years. First, Harry had to live his life, and then graciously share it with us. He was a good journal keeper, so his prodigious memory was backed up by his diaries. His oldest daughter, Helen produced a clean, typewritten manuscript in the days before electric typewriters, word processors, and copiers.

More recently, my wife Heidi photographed me in Cadaques, Spain. Our daughter, Nora, provided the graphic design of the cover using Harry's artwork.

Without their efforts, this book would not be in your hands. Their help was instrumental, but the errors are mine alone.

Scott VanGenderen   Washington, D.C

Made in the USA
Charleston, SC
26 March 2015